"If you want to wed communication theory with practice in ways that promote authenticity, foster community and serve the needs of others, then this book will challenge you. If you want to respond faithfully to postmodern messages in ways that demonstrate your commitment to biblical truths and respect for others, then this book will serve you and those around you well. In engaging and accessible ways, Muehlhoff and Lews help readers to think Christianly about communication by illuminating complex communication theories and concepts from biblical perspectives. This book is a reminder that Scripture treats words, and our use of them, very seriously."

ROBERT H. WOODS JR., Spring Arbor University

D0250382

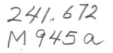

CHRISTIAN WORLDVIEW ✛ INTEGRATION SERIES

Authentic COMMUNICATION

Christian Speech

Engaging Culture

TIM MUEHLHOFF
AND TODD V. LEWIS

IVP Academic

An imprint of InterVarsity Press
Downers Grove, Illinois

InterVarsity Press
P.O. Box 1400, Downers Grove, IL 60515-1426
World Wide Web: www.ivpress.com
E-mail: email@ivpress.com

InterVarsity Press® is the book-publishing division of InterVarsity Christian Fellowship/USA®, a movement of students and faculty active on campus at hundreds of universities, colleges and schools of nursing in the United States of America, and a member movement of the International Fellowship of Evangelical Students. For information about local and regional activities, write Public Relations Dept., InterVarsity Christian Fellowship/USA, 6400 Schroeder Rd., P.O. Box 7895, Madison, WI 53707-7895, or visit the IVCF website at <www.intervarsity.org>.

All Scripture quotations, unless otherwise indicated, are taken from the Holy Bible, New International Version®. NIV®. *Copyright © 1973, 1978, 1984 by International Bible Society. Used by permission of Zondervan Publishing House. All rights reserved.*

Design: Cindy Kiple

ISBN 978-0-8308-2815-9

Printed in the United States of America ∞

Library of Congress Cataloging-in-Publication Data

Muehlhoff, Tim, 1961-
  Authentic communication: Christian speech engaging culture/Tim Muehlhoff, Todd Lewis.
    p. cm.—(Christian worldview integration series)
    Includes bibliographical references and indexes.
    ISBN 978-0-8308-2815-9 (pbk.: alk. paper)
    1. Communication—Religious aspects—Christianity. 2. Christianity and culture.   I. Lewis, Todd Vernon, 1949- II. Title.
    BV4597.53.C64M84 2009
    241'.672—dc22

                                                                                2009042062

P	20	19	18	17	16	15	14	13	12	11	10	9	8	7	6	5	4	3	2	1
Y	27	26	25	24	23	22	21	20	19	18	17	16	15	14	13	12	11	10		

CONTENTS

SERIES PREFACE

A CALL TO INTEGRATION AND THE
CHRISTIAN WORLDVIEW INTEGRATION SERIES

Life's short and we're all busy. If you're a college student, you're *really* busy. There's your part-time job (which seems full time), your social life (hopefully) and church. On top of that you're expected to go to class, do some reading, take tests and write papers. Now, while you are minding your own business, you hear about something called "integration," trying to relate your major with your Christianity. Several questions may come to mind: What is integration, anyway? Is it just a fad? Why should I care about it? And even if I do care about it, I don't have a clue as to how to go about doing it. How do I do this? These are good questions, and in this introduction we're going to address them in order. We are passionate about helping you learn about and become good at integrating your Christian convictions with the issues and ideas in your college major or your career.

WHAT IS INTEGRATION?

The word *integrate* means "to form or blend into a whole," "to unite." We humans naturally seek to find the unity that is behind diversity, and in fact coherence is an important mark of rationality. There are two kinds of integration: conceptual and personal. In conceptual integration, *our theological beliefs, especially those derived from careful study of the Bible, are blended and unified with important, reasonable ideas from our profession or college major into a coherent, intellectually satisfying Christian worldview.* As Augustine wisely advised, "We must show our Scriptures not to be in conflict with whatever [our critics] can demonstrate about the nature of things from reliable sources."[1] In personal integration we seek to live a unified life, a life in which we are the same in public as we are in private, a life in which the various aspects of our personality are consistent with each other and conducive to a life of human flourishing as a disciple of Jesus.

The two kinds of integration are deeply intertwined. All things being equal, the more authentic we are, the more integrity we have, the more we should be able to do conceptual integration with fidelity to Jesus and Scripture, and with intellectual honesty. All things being equal, the more conceptual integration we accomplish, the more coherent will be our set of beliefs and the more confidence we will have in the truth of our Christian worldview. In fact, conceptual integration is so important that it is worth thinking some more about why it matters.

SEVEN REASONS WHY INTEGRATION MATTERS

1. *The Bible's teachings are true.* The first justification for integration is pretty obvious but often overlooked. *Christians hold that, when properly interpreted, the teachings of Holy Scripture are true.* This means two things. If the Bible teaches something relevant to an issue in an academic field, the Bible's view on that topic is true and thus provides an incredibly rich resource for doing work in that academic field. It would be irresponsible to set aside an important source of relevant truth in thinking through issues in our field of study or vocation. Further, if it looks like a claim in our field tends to make a biblical claim false, this tension needs to be resolved. Maybe our interpretation of Scripture is mistaken, maybe the Bible is not even talking about the issue, maybe the claim in our field is false. Whatever the case, the Christian's commitment to the truth of Scripture makes integration inevitable.

Adolfo Lopez-Otero, a Stanford engineering professor and a self-described secular humanist, offers advice to thinking Christians who

---

[1]Augustine *De genesi ad litteram* 1.21, cited in Ernan McMullin, "How Should Cosmology Relate to Theology?" in *The Sciences and Theology in the Twentieth Century*, ed. Arthur R. Peacocke (Notre Dame, Ind.: University of Notre Dame Press, 1981), p. 20.

want to have an impact on the world: "When a Christian professor approaches a non-believing faculty member . . . they can expect to face a polite but condescending person [with a belief that they possess] superior metaphysics who can't understand how such an intelligent person [as yourself] still believes in things which have been discredited eons ago."[2] He goes on to say that "[Christian professors] cannot afford to give excuses . . . if they are honest about wanting to open spiritual and truthful dialogue with their non-believing colleagues—that is the price they must pay for having declared themselves Christians."[3] While Lopez-Otero's remarks are directed to Christian professors, his point applies to all thinking Christians: If we claim that our Christian views are true, we need to back that up by interacting with the various ideas that come from different academic disciplines. In short, we must integrate Christianity and our major or vocation.

2. *Our vocation and the holistic character of discipleship demand integration.* As disciples grow, they learn to see, feel, think, desire, believe and behave the way Jesus does in a manner fitting to the kingdom of God and their own station in life. With God's help we seek to live as Jesus would if he were a philosophy professor at Biola University married to Hope and father of Ashley and Allison, or as a political philosopher at Baylor University married to Frankie.

Two important implications flow from the nature of discipleship. For one thing the lordship of Christ is holistic. The religious life is not a special compartment in an otherwise secular life. Rather, the religious life is an entire way of life. To live Christianly is to allow Jesus Christ to be the Lord of every aspect of our life. There is no room for a secular-sacred separation in the life of Jesus' followers. Jesus Christ should be every bit as much at home in our thinking and behavior when we are developing our views in our area of study or work as he is when we are in a small group fellowship.

Further, as disciples of Jesus we do not merely have a job. We have a vocation as a Christian teacher. A job is a means for supporting our-

---

[2]Adolfo Lopez-Otero, "Be Humble, but Daring," *The Real Issue* 16 (September-October 1997): 10.
[3]Ibid., p. 11.

selves and those for whom we are responsible. For the Christian a vocation (from the Latin *vocare*, which means "to call") is an overall calling from God. Harry Blamires correctly draws a distinction between a general and a special vocation:

> The general vocation of all Christians—indeed of all men and women—
> is the same. We are called to live as children of God, obeying his will in
> all things. But obedience to God's will must inevitably take many dif-
> ferent forms. The wife's mode of obedience is not the same as the nun's;
> the farmer's is not the same as the priest's. By "special vocation," there-
> fore, we designate God's call to a [person] to serve him in a particular
> sphere of activity.4

As Christians seek to discover and become excellent in their special vocation, they must ask: How would Jesus approach the task of being a history teacher, a chemist, an athletic director, a mathematician? It is not always easy to answer this question, but the vocational demands of discipleship require that we give it our best shot.

Whatever we do, however, it is important that we restore to our culture an image of Jesus Christ as an intelligent, competent person who spoke authoritatively on whatever subject he addressed. The disciples of Jesus agreed with Paul when he said that all the wisdom of the Greeks and Jews was ultimately wrapped up in Jesus himself (Col 2:2-3). For them, Jesus was not merely a Savior from sin; he was the wisest, most intelligent, most attractive person they had ever seen.

In the early centuries of Christianity the church presented Jesus to unbelievers precisely because he was wiser, more virtuous, more intelligent and more attractive in his character than Aristotle, Plato, Moses or anyone else. It has been a part of the church's self-understanding to locate the spiritual life in a broader quest for the good life, that is, a life of wisdom, knowledge, beauty and goodness. So understood, the spiritual life and discipleship to Jesus were seen as the very best way to achieve a life of truth, beauty and goodness. Moreover, the life of discipleship was depicted as the wisest, most reasonable form of life available so that a life of unbelief was taken to be foolish

---

4Harry Blamires, *A God Who Acts* (Ann Arbor, Mich.: Servant Books, 1957), p. 67.

and absurd. *Our schools need to recapture and propagate this broader understanding of following Christ if they are to be thoroughly Christian in their approach to education.*

3. *Biblical teaching about the role of the mind in the Christian life and the value of extrabiblical knowledge requires integration.* The Scriptures are clear that God wants us to be like him in every facet of our lives, and he desires commitment from our total being, including our intellectual life. We are told that we change spiritually by having the categories of our minds renewed (Rom 12:1-2), that we are to include an intellectual love for God in our devotion (Mt 22:37-38), and that we are to be prepared to give others a reasonable answer to questions others ask us about why we believe what we believe (1 Pet 3:15). As the great eighteenth-century Christian thinker and spiritual master William Law put it, "Unreasonable and absurd ways of life . . . are truly an offense to God."[5] Learning and developing convictions about the teachings of Scripture are absolutely central to these mandates. However, many of Jesus' followers have failed to see that an aggressive pursuit of knowledge in areas outside the Bible is also relevant to these directives.

God has revealed himself and various truths on a number of topics outside the Bible. As Christians have known throughout our history, common sense, logic and mathematics, along with the arts, humanities, sciences and other areas of study, contain important truths relevant to life in general and to the development of a careful, life-related Christian worldview.

In 1756 John Wesley delivered an address to a gathering of clergy on how to carry out the pastoral ministry with joy and skill. In it Wesley catalogued a number of things familiar to most contemporary believers—the cultivation of a disposition to glorify God and save souls, a knowledge of Scripture, and similar notions. However, at the front of his list Wesley focused on something seldom expressly valued by most pastoral search committees: "Ought not a Minister to have, First, a good understanding, a clear apprehension, a sound judgment, and a

---

[5]William Law, *A Serious Call to a Devout and Holy Life* (1728; reprint, Grand Rapids: Eerdmans, 1966), p. 2.

capacity of reasoning with some closeness?"[6]

Time and again throughout the address Wesley unpacked this remark by admonishing ministers to know what would sound truly odd and almost pagan to the average congregant of today: logic, metaphysics, natural theology, geometry and the ideas of important figures in the history of philosophy. For Wesley study in these areas (especially philosophy and geometry) helped train the mind to think precisely, a habit of incredible value, he asserted, when it comes to thinking as a Christian about theological themes or scriptural texts. According to Wesley the study of extrabiblical information and the writings of unbelievers was of critical value for growth and maturity. As he put it elsewhere, "To imagine none can teach you but those who are themselves saved from sin is a very great and dangerous mistake. Give not place to it for a moment."[7]

Wesley's remarks were not unusual in his time. A century earlier the great Reformed pastor Richard Baxter was faced with lukewarmness in the church and unbelief outside the church. In 1667 he wrote a book to meet this need, and in it he used philosophy, logic and general items of knowledge outside Scripture to argue for the existence of the soul and the life to come. The fact that Baxter turned to philosophy and extrabiblical knowledge instead of small groups or praise hymns is worth pondering. In fact, it is safe to say that throughout much of church history, Scripture and right reason directed at extrabiblical truth were used by disciples of Jesus and prized as twin allies.

In valuing extrabiblical knowledge our brothers and sisters in church history were merely following common sense and Scripture itself. Repeatedly, Scripture acknowledges the wisdom of cultures outside Israel; for example, Egypt (Acts 7:22; cf. Ex 7:11), the Edomites (Jer 49:7), the Phoenicians (Zech 9:2) and many others. The remarkable achievements produced by human wisdom are acknowledged in Job 28:1-11. The wisdom of Solomon is compared to the wisdom of the "people of the east" and Egypt in order to show that Solomon's wisdom surpassed that of

---

[6]John Wesley, "An Address to the Clergy," in *The Works of John Wesley*, 3rd ed. (Grand Rapids: Baker, 1979), p. 481.

[7]John Wesley, *A Plain Account of Christian Perfection* (London: Epworth Press, 1952), p. 87.

people with a longstanding, well-deserved reputation for wisdom (1 Kings 4:29-34). Paul approvingly quotes pagan philosophers (Acts 17:28), and Jude does the same thing with the noncanonical book *The Assumption of Moses* (Jude 9). The book of Proverbs is filled with examples in which knowledge, even moral and spiritual knowledge, can be gained from studying things (ants, for example) in the natural world. Jesus taught that we should know we are to love our enemies, not on the basis of an Old Testament text but from careful reflection on how the sun and rain behave (Mt 5:44-45).

In valuing extrabiblical knowledge our brothers and sisters in church history were also living out scriptural teaching about the value of general revelation. We must never forget that God is the God of creation and general revelation just as he is the God of Scripture and special revelation.

Christians should do everything they can to gain and teach important and relevant knowledge in their areas of expertise. *At the level appropriate to our station in life, Christians are called to be Christian intellectuals, at home in the world of ideas.*

4. *Neglect of integration results in a costly division between secular and sacred.* While few would actually put it in these terms, faith is now understood as a blind act of will, a sort of decision to believe something that is either independent of reason or makes up for the paltry lack of evidence for what one is trying to believe. By contrast, the Bible presents faith as a power or skill to act in accordance with the nature of the kingdom of God, a trust in what we have reason to believe is true. Understood in this way, we see that faith is built on reason and knowledge. We should have good reasons for thinking that Christianity is true before we completely dedicate ourselves to it. We should have solid evidence that our understanding of a biblical passage is correct before we go on to apply it. We bring knowledge claims from Scripture and theology to the task of integration; we do not employ mere beliefs or faith postulates.

Unfortunately, our contemporary understanding of faith and reason treats them as polar opposites. A few years ago I (J. P.) went to New York to conduct a series of evangelistic messages for a church. The series was in a high school gym and several believers and unbelievers came each night. The first evening I gave arguments for the existence of God from science and philosophy. Before closing in prayer, I entertained several questions from the audience. One woman (who was a Christian) complained about my talk, charging that if I "proved" the existence of God, I would leave no room for faith. I responded by saying that if she were right, then we should pray that currently available evidence for God would evaporate and be refuted so there would be even more room for faith! Obviously, her view of faith utterly detached it from reason.

If faith and reason are deeply connected, then students and teachers need to explore their entire intellectual life in light of the Word of God. But if faith and reason are polar opposites, then the subject matter of our study or teaching is largely irrelevant to growth in discipleship. Because of this view of faith and reason, there has emerged a secular-sacred separation in our understanding of the Christian life with the result that Christian teaching and practice are privatized. The withdrawal of the corporate body of Christ from the public sphere of ideas is mirrored by our understanding of what is required to produce an individual disciple. Religion is viewed as personal, private and a matter of how we feel about things. Often, Bible classes and paracurricular Christian activities are not taken as academically serious aspects of the Christian school, nor are they integrated into the content of "secular" areas of teaching.

There is no time like the present to recapture the integrative task. Given the abandonment of monotheism, the ground is weakened for believing in the unity of truth. This is one reason why our *uni*versities are turning in to *multi*versities.[8] The fragmentation of secular education at all levels and its inability to define its purpose or gather together a coherent curriculum are symptoms of what happens when monotheism, especially Christian monotheism, is set aside. At this critical hour the Christian educator has something increasingly rare and distinctive to offer, and integration is at the heart of who we are as Christian educators.

---

[8]See Julie Reuben, *The Making of the Modern University* (Chicago: University of Chicago Press, 1996).

5. *The nature of spiritual warfare necessitates integration.* Today, spiritual warfare is widely misunderstood. Briefly, spiritual warfare is a conflict among persons—disembodied malevolent persons (demons and the devil), human beings, angels and God himself. So far, so good. But what is often overlooked is that this conflict among persons in two camps crucially involves a clash of ideas. Why? The conflict is about control, and persons control others by getting them to accept certain beliefs and emotions as correct, good and proper. This is precisely how the devil primarily works to destroy human beings and thwart God's work in history, namely, by influencing the idea structures in culture. That is why Paul makes the war of ideas central to spiritual conflict:

> For though we live in the world, we do not wage war as the world does. The weapons we fight with are not the weapons of the world. On the contrary, they have divine power to demolish strongholds. We demolish arguments and every pretension that sets itself up against the knowledge of God, and we take captive every thought to make it obedient to Christ. (2 Cor 10:3-5 NIV)

Spiritual warfare is largely, though not entirely, a war of ideas, and we fight bad, false ideas with better ones. That means that truth, reason, argumentation and so forth, from both Scripture and general revelation, are central weapons in the fight. Since the centers of education are the centers for dealing with ideas, they become the main location for spiritual warfare. Solid, intelligent integration, then, is part of our mandate to engage in spiritual conflict.

6. *Spiritual formation calls for integration.* It is crucial that we reflect a bit on the relationship between integration and spiritual/devotional life. To begin with, there is a widespread hunger throughout our culture for genuine, life-transforming spirituality. This is as it should be. People are weary of those who claim to believe certain things when they do not see those beliefs having an impact on the lives of the heralds. Among other things, integration is a spiritual activity—we may even call it a spiritual discipline—but not merely in the sense that often comes to mind in this context. Often, Christian teachers express the spiritual aspect of integration in terms of doxology: Christian integra-

tors hold to and teach the same beliefs about their subject matter that non-Christians accept but go on to add praise to God for the subject matter. Thus, Christian biologists simply assert the views widely accepted in the discipline but make sure that class closes with a word of praise to God for the beauty and complexity of the living world.

The doxological approach is good as far as it goes; unfortunately, it doesn't go far enough in capturing the spiritual dimension of integration. We draw closer to the core of this dimension when we think about the role of beliefs in the process of spiritual transformation. Beliefs are the rails on which our lives run. We almost always act according to what we really believe. It doesn't matter much what we say we believe or what we want others to think we believe. When the rubber meets the road, we act out our actual beliefs most of the time. That is why behavior is such a good indicator of our beliefs. The centrality of beliefs for spiritual progress is a clear implication of Old Testament teaching on wisdom and New Testament teaching about the role of a renewed mind in transformation. Thus, *integration has as its spiritual aim the intellectual goal of structuring the mind so we can see things as they really are and strengthening the belief structure that ought to inform the individual and corporate life of discipleship to Jesus.*

Integration can also help unbelievers accept certain beliefs crucial to the Christian journey and aid believers in maintaining and developing convictions about those beliefs. This aspect of integration becomes clear when we reflect on the notion of a plausibility structure. Individuals will never be able to change their lives if they cannot even entertain the beliefs needed to bring about that change. By "entertain a belief" we mean to consider the *possibility* that the belief *might* be true. If someone is hateful and mean to a fellow employee, that person will have to change what he or she believes about that coworker before treating the coworker differently. But if a person cannot even entertain the thought that the coworker is a good person worthy of kindness, the hateful person will not change.

A person's plausibility structure is the set of ideas the person either is or is not willing to entertain as possibly true. For example, few people would come to a lecture defending a flat earth, because this idea is just not part of our common plausibility structure. Most people today simply cannot even entertain the idea. Moreover, a person's plausibility structure is largely (though not exclusively) a function of beliefs already held. Applied to accepting or maintaining Christian belief, J. Gresham Machen got it right when he said:

> God usually exerts that power in connection with certain prior conditions of the human mind, and it should be ours to create, so far as we can, with the help of God, those favorable conditions for the reception of the gospel. False ideas are the greatest obstacles to the reception of the gospel. We may preach with all the fervor of a reformer and yet succeed only in winning a straggler here and there, if we permit the whole collective thought of the nation or of the world to be controlled by ideas which, by the resistless force of logic, prevent Christianity from being regarded as anything more than a harmless delusion.[9]

If a culture reaches the point where Christian claims are not even part of its plausibility structure, fewer and fewer people will be able to entertain the possibility that they might be true. Whatever stragglers do come to faith in such a context would do so on the basis of felt needs alone, and the genuineness of such conversions would be questionable, to say the least. And believers will not make much progress in the spiritual life because they will not have the depth of conviction or the integrated noetic structure necessary for such progress. This is why integration is so crucial to spirituality. It can create a plausibility structure in a person's mind, "favorable conditions," as Machen put it, so Christian ideas can be entertained by that person. As Christians, our goal is *to make Christian ideas relevant to our subject matter appear to be true, beautiful, good and reasonable to increase the ranking of Christian ideas in the culture's plausibility structure.*

7. *Integration is crucial to the current worldview struggle and the contemporary crisis of knowledge.* Luther once said that if we defend Christ at all points except those at which he is currently being attacked, then we have not really defended Christ. The Christian must keep in mind the

---

[9]J. Gresham Machen, address delivered on September 20, 1912, at the opening of the 101st session of Princeton Theological Seminary, reprinted in *What Is Christianity?* (Grand Rapids: Eerdmans, 1951), p. 162.

tensions between Christian claims and competing worldviews currently dominating the culture. Such vigilance yields an integrative mandate for contemporary Christians that the Christian Worldview Integration Series (CWIS) will keep in mind. There is a very important cultural fact that each volume in the series must face: *There simply is no established, widely recognized body of ethical or religious knowledge now operative in the institutions of knowledge in our culture.* Indeed, ethical and religious claims are frequently placed into what Francis Schaeffer called the "upper story," and they are judged to have little or no epistemic authority, especially compared to the authority given to science to define the limits of knowledge and reality in those same institutions. This raises pressing questions: *Is Christianity a knowledge tradition or merely a faith tradition, a perspective which, while true, cannot be known to be true and must be embraced on the basis of some epistemic state weaker than knowledge? Is there nonempirical knowledge in my field? Is there evidence of nonphysical, immaterial reality (e.g., linguistic meanings are arguable, nonphysical, spiritual entities) in my field? Do the ideas of Christianity do any serious intellectual work in my field such that those who fail to take them into consideration simply will not be able to understand adequately the realities involved in my field?*

There are at least two reasons why these may well be the crucial questions for Christians to keep in mind as they do their work in their disciplines. For one thing, Christianity claims to be a knowledge tradition, and it places knowledge at the center of proclamation and discipleship. The Old and New Testaments, including the teachings of Jesus, claim not merely that Christianity is true but that a variety of its moral and religious assertions can be known to be true.

Second, knowledge is the basis of responsible action in society. Dentists, not lawyers, have the authority to place their hands in our mouths because they have the relevant knowledge—not merely true beliefs—on the basis of which they may act responsibly. If Christians do little to deflect the view that theological and ethical assertions are merely parts of a tradition, ways of seeing, a source for adding a "theological perspective" to an otherwise unperturbed secular topic and so forth that fall short of conveying knowledge, then they inadvertently contribute to the marginalization of Christianity precisely because they fail to rebut the contemporary tendency to rob it of the very thing that gives it the authority necessary to prevent that marginalization, namely, its legitimate claim to give us moral and religious knowledge. Both in and out of the church Jesus has been lost as an intellectual authority, and Christian intellectuals should carry out their academic vocation in light of this fact.

We agree with those who see a three-way worldview struggle in academic and popular culture among ethical monotheism (especially Christian theism), postmodernism and scientific naturalism. As Christian intellectuals seek to promote Christianity as a knowledge tradition in their academic disciplines, they should keep in mind the impact of their work on this triumvirate. Space considerations forbid us to say much about postmodernism here. We recognize it is a variegated tunic with many nuances. But to the degree that postmodernism denies the objectivity of reality, truth, value and reason (in its epistemic if not psychological sense), to the degree that it rejects dichotomous thinking about real-unreal, true-false, rational-irrational and right-wrong, to the degree that it believes intentionality creates the objects of consciousness, to that degree it should be resisted by Christian intellectuals, and the CWIS will take this stance toward postmodernism.

Scientific naturalism also comes in many varieties, but very roughly a major form of it is the view that the spatiotemporal cosmos containing physical objects studied by the hard sciences is all there is and that the hard sciences are either the only source of knowledge or else vastly superior in proffering epistemically justified beliefs compared to nonscientific fields. In connection with scientific naturalism some have argued that the rise of modern science has contributed to the loss of intellectual authority in those fields like ethics and religion that supposedly are not subject to the types of testing and experimentation employed in science.

Extreme forms of postmodernism and scientific naturalism agree that there is no nonempirical knowledge, especially no knowledge of immaterial reality, no theological or ethical knowledge. *The authors of the CWIS seek to undermine this claim and the concomitant privatization and noncognitive treatment of religious/ethical faith and belief.* Thus, there will be three integrative tasks of central importance for each volume in the series.

HOW DO WE ENGAGE IN INTEGRATION? THREE INTEGRATIVE TASKS

As noted earlier, the word *integration* means "to form or blend into a whole," "to unite." One of the goals of integration is to maintain or increase both the conceptual relevance of and epistemological justification for Christian theism. To repeat Augustine's advice, "We must show our Scriptures not to be in conflict with whatever [our critics] can demonstrate about the nature of things from reliable sources."[10] We may distinguish three different aspects of the justificatory side of integration: direct defense, polemics and Christian explanation.

1. *Direct defense.* In direct defense we engage in integration with the primary intent of enhancing or maintaining directly the rational justification of Christian theism or some proposition taken to be explicit within or entailed by it, especially those aspects of a Christian worldview relevant to our own discipline. Specific attention should be given to topics that are intrinsically important to mere Christianity or currently under fire in our field. Hereafter, we will simply refer to these issues as "Christian theism." We do so for brevity's sake. Christian theism should be taken to include specific views about a particular area of study that we believe to be relevant to the integrative task, for example, that cognitive behavioral therapy is an important tool for applying the biblical mandate to be "transformed by the renewing of your mind" (Rom 12:2).

There are two basic forms of direct defense, one negative and one positive.[11] The less controversial of the two is a negative direct defense where we attempt to remove defeaters to Christian theism. If we have a justified belief regarding some proposition P, a defeater is something that weakens or removes that justification. Defeaters come in two types.[12] A rebutting defeater gives justification for believing not-P, in

---

[10]Augustine *De genesi ad litteram* 1.21.
[11]See Ronald Nash, *Faith and Reason* (Grand Rapids: Zondervan, 1988), pp. 14-18.
[12]For a useful discussion of various types of defeaters, see John Pollock, *Contemporary Theories of*

this case, that Christian theism is false. For example, attempts to show that the biblical concept of the family is dysfunctional and false, or that homosexuality is causally necessitated by genes or brain states and that therefore it is not a proper object for moral appraisal are cases of rebutting defeaters. An undercutting defeater does not give justification for believing not-P but rather seeks to remove or weaken justification for believing P in the first place. Critiques of the arguments for God's existence are examples of undercutting defeaters. When defeaters are raised against Christian theism, a negative defense seeks either to rebut or undercut those defeaters.

By contrast, a positive direct defense is an attempt to build a positive case for Christian theism. Arguments for the existence of God, objective morality, the existence of the soul, the value and nature of virtue ethics, and the possibility and knowability of miracles are examples. This task for integration is not accepted by all Christian intellectuals. For example, various species of what may be loosely called Reformed epistemology run the gamut from seeing a modest role for a positive direct defense to an outright rejection of this type of activity in certain areas; for example, justifying belief in God and the authority of Holy Scripture. *The CWIS will seek to engage in both negative and positive direct defense.*

2. *Polemics.* In polemics we seek to criticize views that rival Christian theism in one way or another. Critiques of scientific naturalism, physicalism, pantheism, behaviorist models of educational goals, authorless approaches to texts and Marxist theories of economics are all examples of polemics.

3. *Theistic explanation.* Suppose we have a set of items that stand in need of explanation and we offer some overall explanation as an adequate or even best explanation of those items. In such a case our overall explanation explains each of the items in question, and this fact itself provides some degree of confirmation for our overall explanation. For example, if a certain intrinsic genre statement explains the various data of a biblical text, then this fact offers some confirmation

---

Knowledge (Totowa, N.J.: Rowman & Littlefield, 1986), pp. 36-39; Ralph Baergen, *Contemporary Epistemology* (Fort Worth: Harcourt Brace, 1995), pp. 119-24.

for the belief that the statement is the correct interpretation of that text. Christian theists ought to be about the business of exploring the world in light of their worldview and, more specifically, of using their theistic beliefs as explanations of various desiderata in their disciplines. Put differently, we should seek to solve intellectual problems and shed light on areas of puzzlement by using the explanatory power of our worldview.

For example, for those who accept the existence of natural moral law, the irreducibly mental nature of consciousness, natural human rights or the fact that human flourishing follows from certain biblically mandated ethical and religious practices, the truth of Christian theism provides a good explanation of these phenomena. And this fact can provide some degree of confirmation for Christian theism. *The CWIS seeks to show the explanatory power of Christian ideas in various disciplines.*

WHAT MODELS ARE AVAILABLE FOR CLASSIFYING INTEGRATIVE PROBLEMS?

When problem areas surface, there is a need for Christians to think hard about the issue in light of the need for strengthening the rational authority of Christian theism and placing it squarely within the plausibility structure of contemporary culture. We will use the term *theology* to stand for any Christian idea that seems to be a part of a Christian worldview derived primarily from special revelation. When we address problems like these, there will emerge a number of different ways that theology can interact with an issue in a discipline outside theology. Here are some of the different ways that such interaction can take place. These represent different strategies for handling a particular difficulty in integration. These strategies will be employed where appropriate on a case-by-case basis by the authors in the series.

1. *The two-realms view.* Propositions, theories or methodologies in theology and another discipline may involve two distinct, nonoverlapping areas of investigation. For example, debates about angels or the extent of the atonement have little to do with organic chemistry. Similarly, it is of little interest to theology whether a methane molecule has three or four hydrogen atoms in it.

2. *The complementarity view*. Propositions, theories or methodologies in theology and another discipline may involve two different, complementary, noninteracting approaches to the same reality. Sociological aspects of church growth and certain psychological aspects of conversion may be sociological or psychological descriptions of certain phenomena that are complementary to a theological description of church growth or conversion.

3. *The direct-interaction view*. Propositions, theories or methodologies in theology and another discipline may directly interact in such a way that either one area of study offers rational support for the other or one area of study raises rational difficulties for the other. For example, certain theological teachings about the existence of the soul raise rational problems for philosophical or scientific claims that deny the existence of the soul. The general theory of evolution raises various difficulties for certain ways of understanding the book of Genesis. Some have argued that the big bang theory tends to support the theological proposition that the universe had a beginning.

4. *The presuppositions view*. Theology may support the presuppositions of another discipline and vice versa. Some have argued that many of the presuppositions of science (for example, the existence of truth; the rational, orderly nature of reality; the adequacy of our sensory and cognitive faculties as tools suited for knowing the external world) make sense and are easy to justify given Christian theism, but are odd and without ultimate justification in a naturalistic worldview. Similarly, some have argued that philosophical critiques of epistemological skepticism and defenses of the existence of a real, theory-independent world and a correspondence theory of truth offer justification for some of the presuppositions of theology.

5. *The practical application view*. Theology may fill out and add details to general principles in another discipline and vice versa, and theology may help us practically apply principles in another discipline and vice versa. For example, theology teaches that fathers should not provoke their children to anger, and psychology can add important details about what this means by offering information about family systems, the nature and causes of anger, and so forth. Psychology can devise

various tests for assessing whether a person is or is not mature, and theology can offer a normative definition to psychology as to what a mature person is.

The Gospel of John begins with these words: "In the beginning was the Word, and the Word was with God, and the Word was God. He was with God in the beginning." And this Word, according to John, "became flesh and made his dwelling among us." Thus, for Christians our faith is founded on God's communication to us in the person of Jesus Christ, the incarnate Word. What's more, Christians believe that God provided to his followers a written Word of God, the Bible. It serves, among other things, as a means by which God communicates his love for us as well as what he expects of us as human beings and followers of Christ. So, the nature of communication and what it means to be human are central to the Christian message. In this book, *Authentic Communication,* the authors provide an introduction to the study of communication that takes seriously Christian theology and anthropology as aspects of a knowledge tradition that can provide us with real insights that can illuminate the discipline of communication studies.

We hope you can see why we are excited about this book. Even though you're busy and the many demands on your time tug at you from different directions, we don't think you can afford not to read this book. So wrestle, ponder, pray, compare ideas with Scripture, talk about the pages to follow with others and enjoy.

A FINAL CHALLENGE

In 2001 atheist philosopher Quentin Smith published a remarkably insightful article of crucial relevance to the task of integration. For over fifty years, Smith notes, the academic community has become increasingly secularized and atheistic even though there have been a fair number of Christian teachers involved in that community. How could this be? Smith's answer amounts to the claim that Christians compartmentalized their faith, kept it tucked away in a private compartment of their lives and did not integrate their Christian ideas with their work. Said Smith:

This is not to say that none of the scholars in their various academic fields were realist theists [theists who took their religious beliefs to be true] in their "private lives"; but realist theists, for the most part excluded their theism from their publications and teaching, in large part because theism . . . was mainly considered to have such a low epistemic status that it did not meet the standards of an "academically respectable" position to hold.[13]

Smith goes on to claim that while Christians have recaptured considerable ground in the field of philosophy, "theists in other fields tend to compartmentalize their theistic beliefs from their scholarly work; they rarely assume and never argue for theism in their scholarly work."[14]

This has got to stop. We offer this book to you with the prayer that it will help you rise to the occasion and recapture lost territory in your field of study for the cause of Christ.

Francis J. Beckwith
J. P. Moreland
Series Editors

---

[13]Quentin Smith, "The Metaphysics of Naturalism," *Philo* 4, no. 2 (2001): 1.
[14]Ibid., p. 3. The same observation about advances in philosophy has been noted by Mark A. Noll in *The Scandal of the Evangelical Mind* (Grand Rapids: Eerdmans, 1994), pp. 235-38.

ACKNOWLEDGMENTS

I (Tim) would like to thank my students at UNC-Chapel Hill and Biola University for being patient as I developed and refined my thoughts on communication. Special thanks to Megan Frost for her research help. I am indebted to my friend and mentor Julia Wood who gave me the confidence, skills and encouragement to think for myself. Deep appreciation and love goes to my wife, Noreen, whose selfless sacrifices make a life of teaching and scholarship a reality. J. P. Moreland, thank you for recognizing the value of communication and making us a part of this project.

I (Todd) would like to dedicate this book to my wife, Ginny, my two grown sons, Jon and Ric, their wives, Angie and Jeri, and our growing family, which currently includes two grandsons, Harrison and Jackson. Most of the ideas and applications in my chapters come from my treasure trove of experiences over my more than thirty-five years of teaching at Biola University. There must be thousands of students who have taken my general education and major courses over those years, and virtually all of them have made some significant contribution to my academic and spiritual growth. I have been made all the richer for my experiences with them, and I hope that my shared and applied thoughts in this book help new generations of learners as well.

Tim and Todd would both like to thank two individuals. Jim Hoover, as our editor, thank you for your patience, guidance, insight and encouragement. You made a daunting process go much easier, and we appreciate it. Em Griffin, thank you for taking time to read an early draft of our work and offer key suggestions and positive feedback.

INTRODUCTION

In the movie *Cast Away*, Chuck Noland (played by Tom Hanks) is a FedEx troubleshooter who finds himself in trouble when his Pacific-bound jet violently crashes in a tropical storm. As the only survivor he is stranded on a deserted island which will be his home for the next four years. To survive he learns to build a fire, chart weather patterns, spear fish and even perform minor surgery. As months turn into years Noland realizes that his greatest threat is not a lack of nutrition or protection from the elements, but his utter aloneness. The daily communication he had with coworkers, family and lover is gone. He yearns to be acknowledged by another. His desperation leads him to form a relationship with the movie's most unlikely character, Wilson. Wilson is a volleyball that washes up from the crash. With a bloody palm print as a crude face, Wilson becomes a lifeline of communication. Every decision—thoughts of suicide, dangers of escaping into the Pacific waters, rationing of food—is discussed in detail with Wilson.

In his four years of seclusion, Hank's character comes to appreciate what most of us seldom think about: the necessity of communication. Communication is, for most of us, a routine part of everyday life that we take for granted. After all, we've been communicating our entire lives, haven't we? One of the goals of *Authentic Communication* is to help students studying communication at the university level challenge and undo the naturalness of communication. As students and professors who have dedicated ourselves to exploring the field of communication, we need to challenge our propensity to take communication for granted.

However, communication majors aren't the only ones who should be interested in communication. Christians, inside and outside the university, need to reclaim a deep appreciation for human communication. A central claim of this volume is that *through the study and practice of communication we accomplish crucial aspects in the life of a believer.*

When reading the Scriptures we immediately encounter challenging commands and expectations that are given to all believers. Paul informs us that in the Christian community "if one part suffers" then all should share in his or her pain (1 Cor 12:26). If a dispute arises between us and another believer, we are asked to "[speak] the truth in love" and deal with conflict and anger before the setting of the sun (Eph 4:15, 25-26). Husbands are asked to love and sacrifice for their wife (Eph 5:25) just as Christ loved and sacrificed himself for the church. In return, a wife is asked to "respect" her husband (Eph 5:33) with the same reverence reserved for Christ. All believers are called to be harmonious, sympathetic, brotherly, compassionate and humble in spirit (1 Pet 3:8). Remarkably, God has entrusted his gospel to human communicators and asked that it be taken to all people groups (Mt 28:19-20).

As followers of Christ, how are we to accomplish these daunting commands?

Part of the answer will be a constant reliance on the Holy Spirit, prayer and a deep understanding of the Scriptures. However, it will also require that each of us become students of communication. What unifies each of these biblical commands is that communication skills are necessary to fulfill them.

The command to share in the suffering of others entails our empathizing with each other. Communication scholars define empathy as the ability to project into a person's point of view in an attempt to experience his or her thoughts, feelings and perspective. Empathy is a foundational communication skill. Paul's call to resolve conflict requires that believers understand two important communication concepts: communication spirals and the power of words. A positive spiral is a pattern of communication in which positive, confirming messages are reinforced and reciprocated between individuals. If we want a person we are experiencing conflict with to listen to *our* version of the disagreement, then we must listen to his or hers. The idea of communication spirals is not new. In a letter to the church in Galatia Paul tells us that what we "sow" we will most certainly "reap" (Gal 6:7).

Those seeking to resolve interpersonal conflict must also understand the power of words. The writers of the book of Proverbs describe "reckless words" as a piercing sword (Prov 12:18). Readers are advised to drop a "matter before a dispute breaks out" because "starting a quarrel is like breaching a dam" (Prov 17:14). If we are to resolve conflict, we must understand the distinction drawn by the Scriptures between a productive dialogue and a quarrel.

Paul's command for husbands and wives to love and respect each other requires a broad array of communication skills. In a poll sponsored by the National Communication Association, readers were asked to list the main reasons for divorce in America. Above finances, sexual problems, interference from family members and previous relationships, individuals stated that communication problems are the number one reason marriages fail. If Christian marriages are to be distinct in a culture of divorce and we are to fulfill our calling to love and respect each other, then we must communicate in ways that bring honor to Christ and health to our marriages. The call to communicate God's story to a diverse world requires a careful consideration of the fundamentals of persuasion and person-centered communication.

Each of these communication concepts—empathy, conflict management, communication spirals, words and symbols, interpersonal communication, persuasion, and person-centered communication—will be discussed in *Authentic Communication*. We know that in many cases our handling of each of these communication concepts, while substantive, just touches the surface. Indeed, entire books have been written about each of the concepts of this volume. While our book is written primarily to students majoring in communication, our goal is help every follower of Christ understand how his or her faith is expanded, challenged and put into action by a clear understanding of communication.

HOW THE BOOK IS ORGANIZED

In the first section of this book we discuss key components of communication. In chapter one we define communication and discuss how we can improve our communication competence. It is surprising that communication scholars still struggle to develop a definition of communication that respects its deep complexity. Chapter two explores the role our perceptions play in how as communicators we view ourselves and others. The narratives individuals create to explain themselves and the world are deeply influenced by our uniquely diverse perceptions, which in turn are influenced by culture, media and what we are conditioned to perceive. Chapter three explains that we express our ideas, feelings and philosophies through words or symbols. The writers of Proverbs gives the ultimate compliment to words when they boldly state that our speech has the power to dispense either life or death (Prov 18:21). Section one concludes with an introduction to the study of persuasion and rhetorical theory (chap. 4). The apostle Paul informs the church at Corinth that anyone who has come to "fear the Lord" should now seek to "persuade men" (2 Cor 5:11). A Christian's ability to persuade those outside the Christian community will be helped by an understanding of the principles of persuasion.

Section two takes these communication concepts and applies them to key issues, opportunities and questions facing a Christian communicator. Christ calls his followers to love and forgive each other as he loves and forgives us, so how do we address the inevitable interpersonal conflicts that threaten our unity (chaps. 5-6)? How can we utilize rhetorical theories in helping us winsomely present the Christian worldview in a communication environment dominated by blogs, text messages, Facebook, MySpace and YouTube (chap. 7)? As Christian communicators in a discipline progressively influenced by postmodern theorists, how do we present an alternative view of truth, morality, knowledge and spirituality (chaps. 8-10)? In recent years communication scholars have become increasingly concerned with how individuals approach and talk about our differences. What do we do as Christian communicators when encountering people who not only disagree with us but are hostile (chap. 11)? Finally, how can today's Christian communicator engage in social justice and speak for those in society who have been abandoned and silenced (chap. 12)?

Each of the issues raised in *Authentic Communication* will be addressed by appealing to leading communication scholars such as Julia T. Wood, John Durham Peters, Walter Fisher, Brant Burleson, Em Griffin, Dwight Conquergood, Kenneth Burke, Ron Arnett, Quentin Schultze and Stephen Littlejohn, along with Christian thinkers, statesmen and theologians such as J. P. Moreland, C. S. Lewis, Duane Litfin, William Lane Craig, G. K. Chesterton, D. A. Carson, John Woodbridge, Timothy Keller, Michael Green, Craig Hazen, Charles Malik and William Wilberforce. In each of the chapters we seek to explore how the Scriptures illustrate, challenge and broaden our understanding of communication. However, integration is often a two-way street—communication theory and concepts also help us understand the Scriptures.

One of the ancient writers of the book of Proverbs states that "a word aptly spoken" can be compared to "apples of gold in settings of silver" (Prov 25:11). Just as a metalsmith carefully studies how precious metals like silver and gold can be brought together to form fine jewelry, so we ought to study the wonderful complexity and mystery of human communication. What took Chuck Noland four years to learn on a deserted island, we can discover by exploring how communication theorists and the Scriptures approach what we do every day—communicate.

PART ONE

Understanding the Components of Communication

THE POWER OF
HUMAN COMMUNICATION

What is your reaction as you read these startling facts?

- People who lack strong relationships have two or three times the risk of early death, regardless of whether they smoke, drink alcoholic beverages or exercise regularly.

- Terminal cancer strikes socially isolated people more often than those who have close personal relationships.

- Divorced, separated and widowed people are five to ten times more likely to need mental hospitalization than their married counterparts.

- Social isolation is a major risk factor contributing to coronary disease, comparable to physiological factors such as diet, cigarette smoking, obesity and lack of physical exercise.[1]

For students of communication these facts confirm the belief that "personal communication is essential to our well being."[2] Communication scholar and theologian Reuel Howe was so fascinated by the power of communication to foster human connection that he titled his now classic book *The Miracle of Dialogue*. He writes:

> Dialogue is to love, what blood is to the body. When the flow of blood stops, the body dies. When dialogue stops, love dies and resentment and

---

[1]Taken from Ronald Adler, Lawrence Rosenfeld and Russell Proctor, *Interplay: The Process of Interpersonal Communication*, 10th ed. (New York: Oxford University Press, 2007), pp. 3-4.
[2]Ibid.

hate are born. But dialogue can restore a dead relationship. Indeed this is the miracle of dialogue: it can bring a relationship into being, and it can bring into being once again a relationship that had died.[3]

The writers of the book of Proverbs support Howe's assessment and state that our communication has the potential to "nourish" those around us (Prov 10:21). Yet Proverbs also warns of what communication scholars identify as the *dark side* of communication, which includes verbal abuse, sarcasm, hate speech, diatribe, humiliation and ridicule.[4] As you read this volume keep in mind that all communication is a two-edged sword—it can deeply affirm or disconfirm. The writers of Proverbs acknowledge both the promise and dark side of communication when they write that "through the blessing of the upright a city is exalted, but by the mouth of the wicked it is destroyed" (Prov 11:11).

Since communication plays a vital role in our individual and collective lives, it is crucial that we carefully define it.

DEFINITION OF COMMUNICATION

Definitions are extremely important to communication scholars and theorists. How we define something facilitates how we conceptualize and approach it. Defining communication has proven to be surprisingly difficult. In 1970, after researching communication journals, textbooks and articles, Frank Dance identified over one hundred definitions of communication and concluded that scholars are trying to "make the concept of communication do too much work for us."[5] The Oxford Dictionary offers a dense twelve hundred word definition of communication that covers not only human communication but communication between animals and among machines. For the sake of this volume we will define communication as "a systemic process in which individuals interact with and through symbols to create and interpret meanings."[6] Each part of this definition warrants careful consideration.

---

[3]Reuel Howe, *The Miracle of Dialogue* (New York: Seabury Press, 1963), p. 3
[4]For further study see Brian Spitzberg and William Cupach, eds., *The Dark Side of Interpersonal Communication* (Hillsdale, N.J.: Lawrence Erlbaum, 1994).
[5]Frank Dance, "The Concept of Communication," *Journal of Communication* 20 (1970): 210.
[6]Julia Wood, *Communication Theories in Action*, 3rd ed. (Belmont, Calif.: Wadsworth, 2004), p. 9.

Communication is systemic. When we communicate with another person, our communication takes place within multiple systems. Factors such as time, situation, culture, gender, location and personal histories all interact to influence communication. For example, college students often notice that they act and communicate differently when they go home to visit their parents. While at school they are independent and assertive, yet at home they regularly defer to the wishes of their parents. "We have to recognize that all parts of a system interact; each part affects all others. In other words, elements of communication systems are interdependent; each element is tied to all other elements."[7]

The systemic nature of communication helps us understand, in part, why many New Testament listeners considered the gospel to be foolishness (1 Cor 1:18, 23). In a Roman system it made no sense to worship a crucified criminal. How could individuals revere as a god a man who had been judged a criminal and subjected to a humiliating and barbaric form of execution? When the Romans began using crucifixion as a form of execution, it had clear limits. The individual being crucified must be a foreigner or slave convicted of murder, rebellion, or armed robbery. The idea of a Roman being crucified was unthinkable. The Roman statesman Cicero described crucifixion as *crudelissimum taterrimumque supplicium* (a most cruel and disgusting punishment).[8] Cicero reflects a Roman system of culture and value: "To bind a Roman citizen is a crime, to flog him is an abomination, to kill him is almost an act of murder: to crucify him is—what? There is no fitting word that can possibly describe such a horrible deed."[9] Followers of Christ would also face similar resistance from Jews of the day who believed that anyone crucified was under God's curse (Deut 21:22-23).

Yet, in the Christian system, Christ's crucifixion is "the power of God and the wisdom of God" (1 Cor 1:24). When presenting the gospel the early church soon realized that the culture, location and personal histories of their audience created a communication system that would present

---

[7]Julia Wood, *Everyday Encounters: Interpersonal Communication*, 5th ed. (Belmont, Calif.: Wadsworth, 2007), p. 24.
[8]Cicero, quoted in John Stott, *The Cross of Christ* (Downers Grove, Ill.: InterVarsity Press, 1986), p. 1.
[9]Ibid., p. 24.

significant challenges to the proclamation of the gospel.

Because all communication occurs within systems, the presence of *noise* must be considered. Noise within a system is anything that distorts or interferes with our communication. Typically communication scholars identify four types of noise: physical, physiological, psychological and semantic. *Physical noise* refers to elements within our environment such as background noise, extreme temperatures, poor lighting and crowds. *Physiological noise* includes hunger, fatigue, illness and other physiological factors that influence how we interpret messages. In a classic study participants were not allowed to eat (physiological noise) for fourteen hours and then placed in a room that was dimly lit (physical noise). Participants were told to record images being shown on a screen when in fact no images were being projected. As hunger increased individuals recorded seeing food-related images.[10] *Psychological noise* includes thoughts and feelings we have that affect our communication and our interpretation of others' communication. Psychological noise is evident in the following exchange: "A Baptist said of an Episcopalian, 'I cannot hear you because of what I expect you to say.'"[11] *Semantic noise* occurs when the very words we use are not understood in the same way by other people. Though the word *niggardly* means "stingy" or "miserly," a white staff member of the mayor of Washington, D.C., was forced to resign for using the word when black residents interpreted it as a racial slur.

When reading through the Gospels it is notable how Jesus takes into consideration the presence of noise. When he observes that the crowds following him are hungry and tired (physiological noise) he has them sit and gives them food (Lk 9:13). When he encounters the Samaritan woman at the well he acknowledges her feelings of shame (psychological noise) at having multiple husbands (Jn 4:18). When speaking with Nicodemus semantic noise surfaces over the phrase "born again" (Jn 3:3) prompting Jesus to clarify that he is speaking of

---

[10]David C. McClelland and John W. Atkinson, "The Projective Expression of Needs: The Effect of Different Intensities of the Hunger Drive on Perception," *Journal of Psychology* 25 (1948): 205-22.

[11]Howe, *Miracle of Dialogue*, p. 14.

a spiritual birth, not a physical rebirth.

Communication is a process. Communication is always in motion. What happened before your conversation with a person will influence your current interaction, and what happens during the conversation will influence future conversations. Every conversation must take into account what Bakhtin called the "already spokens" of human dialogue. He explains: "Every utterance must be regarded primarily as a response to preceding utterances. . . . Each utterance refutes, affirms, supplements, and relies on the others, presupposes them to be known, and somehow takes them into account."[12]

The process of communication is evident every time I (Tim) talk with a friend who lives in Detroit. We first met as communication majors our sophomore year at Eastern Michigan University. Since then, we have spent hundreds of hours talking about sports, work, theology, parenting, politics and so on. Sometimes he calls me and simply says, "This stinks" and hangs up. Because of all of our "already spokens," he doesn't need to say more. The phrase *this stinks* means that our favorite professional hockey team—the Detroit Red Wings—have lost. If he calls and says, "This *really* stinks," then we have lost to our most hated rival—the Colorado Avalanche. Our ability to speak in shorthand is based on all the *already spokens* that have taken place between us.

Bakhtin notes another key aspect of the process of communication: "The word in living conversation is directly, blatantly, oriented toward a future answer-word; it provokes an answer, anticipates it and structures itself in the answer's direction."[13] When my friend from Detroit calls we usually banter about sports and then move on to more serious topics like family and careers. When we talk about work, I know that we'll eventually talk about how these difficult financial times forced him to leave his dream job to work at a boring job to pay bills and provide for his family. In talking about our careers I try to be sensitive to his difficult situation and be as supportive as possible. Each of my re-

---

[12]M. M. Bakhtin, *Speech Genres and other Late Essays*, ed. C. Emerson and M. Holquist, trans. V. McGee (Austin: University of Texas Press, 1986), p. 91.

[13]M. M. Bakhtin, *The Dialogic Imagination: Four Essays by M. M. Bakhtin*, ed. M. Holquist and Vadim Liapunov, trans. Vadim Liapunov and Kenneth Bostrom (Austin: University of Texas Press, 1981), p. 220.

sponses is given in response to his trying situation and the daily stress it produces.

This interaction also illustrates that the process of communication is not limited to the mere transference of ideas or information. Communication is "not something that is either accomplished or not, depending upon whether a message was accurately received, but rather a certain sort of opportunity or possibility realized, an experience of self and other, however good or bad."[14]

Use of symbols. There is no way for a person to have direct access to another person's thoughts, emotions, ideas or perspective. We must rely on symbols to express our views, ideas and perspectives. To understand the nature of symbols it is useful to consider the difference between signs and symbols. Signs have a natural relationship to the object they represent. When a mountain lion crouches, it is a sign he or she is ready to pounce. Dark clouds are a sign that rain is likely. The cries of a baby are a signal that he or she is most likely hungry, tired or upset. Each of these signs (crouching lion, dark clouds, crying baby) is directly connected to what it signifies and requires little effort on our part to interpret them.

The same cannot be said about symbols. Symbols have no natural relationship to what they represent. For example, what does it mean when someone gives you a thumbs-up gesture? If you were a gladiator in ancient Rome and the thumbs-up was given by the emperor it meant you were to *kill* your opponent (a concealed thumb granted mercy). During World War II it took a positive spin when pilots would give the thumbs-up to signal to a crew that all systems were working. Today, in Iran and Greece the thumbs-up sign is equivalent to flipping someone off.[15] Unlike signs, symbols are inherently arbitrary, abstract and ambiguous. Because the signal to kill an opponent is arbitrary, the emperor could have signaled death through any motion he desired (fist in the air, open hand, standing up). Symbols are abstract in that they

---

[14]Gregory J. Shepherd, "Communication as Transcendence," in *Communication as . . . : Perspectives on Theory,* ed. Gregory J. Shepherd, Jeffery St. John and Ted Striphas (Thousand Oaks, Calif.: Sage, 2006), pp. 23-24.

[15]Jeanna Bryner, "From Kennedy to Clinton: Why Everyone is Thumbs-up," LiveScience.com, May 22, 2008 <www.livescience.com/health/080522-thumbs-up.html>.

merely stand for ideas, people, objects or situations. There are degrees of abstractness. For instance, the word *table* (since it has a physical referent) is less abstract than words like *justice, courage, patriotism* or *love*. Symbols are ambiguous because their meanings are often unclear and dependent on context. Even symbols that have concrete referents are often interpreted differently. Jacques Ellul writes:

> Even the simplest word—*bread*, for instance—involves all sorts of connotations. In a mysterious way, it calls up many images which form a dazzling rainbow, a multitude of echoes. When the word bread is pronounced, I cannot help but think of the millions of people who have none. I cannot avoid the image of a certain baker friend of mine, and of the time during the Nazi occupation when bread was so scarce and of such poor quality. The communion service comes to me: the breaking of bread at the Last Supper and the image of Jesus, both present and future.[16]

The arbitrary, abstract and ambiguous nature of symbols adds both to the mystery and frustration of symbol-dependent communication. As Ellul concluded, "All language is more or less a riddle to be figured out."[17] The riddle of language is slowly unraveled by first establishing definitions and then creating a common meaning between communicators.

Meanings. This last element, shared meanings, is at the heart of our definition of communication. When I speak with another person, I convey my thoughts through symbols that must be interpreted. The listener works to understand what my symbols stand for or represent. In turn, I seek to discern how my symbols are being interpreted. In short, communication is a reciprocal process of meaning making. If a simple word like *bread* can bring up a multitude of connotations, then imagine the effort that will be needed when a couple having marital problems discusses symbols such as *commitment, trust, fidelity* or *respect*. Ellul notes that the ambiguity of language forces individuals to be creative in

---

[16]Jacques Ellul, "Seeing and Hearing: Prolegomena," in *The Reach of Dialogue: Confirmation, Voice, and Community*, ed. Rob Anderson, Kenneth Cissna and Ronald Arnett (Cresskill, N.J.: Hampton Press, 1994), p. 121.
[17]Ibid., p. 123.

their explanation of symbols and the creation of meaning: "He does not understand, and I see that. So I speak again, weaving another piece of cloth, but this time with a different design. I come up with what I think will reach him and be perceived by him. The uncertainty of meaning and the ambiguity of language inspire creativity."[18]

The fostering of meaning between communicators is further complicated by the recognition that all communication involves two levels of meaning. The *content level* expresses the literal or denotative meaning of the words being spoken. The *relationship level* expresses the amount of liking, responsiveness and power that exists between two people. If we tell our teenage son to be home by midnight or he's grounded, the content level is that he must be home by the specified time. The relationship level is that we, the parents, have the power to place restraints on him that are not negotiable.

Both levels of communication are crucial to the communication process and present their own difficulties. Using symbols to establish the content level of communication requires, suggests Ted Striphas, that we view communication as a type of translation.

> I want you to imagine translation as something that occurs not only between people who seem to speak different languages but, perhaps more important, as a process that takes place constantly—and necessarily—between those who appear to share a common language as well.[19]

In today's diverse culture the content level of communication cannot be assumed merely because we use a seemingly common vocabulary of symbols. All of us need to become adept translators of the symbols we use on a daily basis.

Philosopher J. P. Moreland and educator Klaus Issler illustrate the need for translation when describing the ambiguity surrounding a symbol relevant to all of us—happiness. Most parents would say that they want their children to be happy (content level). Yet how do we define happiness? In today's culture happiness is "identified with a feeling

---

[18]Ibid., p. 122.
[19]Ted Striphas, "Communication as Translation" in *Communication as . . . : Perspectives on Theory*, ed. Gregory Shepherd, Jeffrey St. John and Ted Striphas (Thousand Oaks, Calif.: Sage, 2006), p. 233.

and, more specifically, a feeling very close to pleasure."[20] Thus the goal of many parents is to arrange life so that their children can experience a continuous pleasurable feeling, be it playing Halo, having the most up-to-date cell phone or getting placed in honors math. The difficulty with such a modern definition is that happiness is dependent on external circumstances. In contrast, many scholars appeal to a definition in line with Aristotle that suggests happiness "is a life well lived, a life of virtue and character, a life that manifests wisdom, kindness, and goodness."[21]

The relationship level of communication is established by how we relate to or acknowledge others. The Jewish mystic and philosopher Martin Buber identified three broad ways we relate to others. In an *I-It relationship* we do not even acknowledge or recognize the humanity of a person. When individuals walk out of a coffee shop and ignore the pleas of a homeless person asking for spare change, an I-It relationship is possibly established. *I-You* relationships are formed when we acknowledge the humanity of people, but only engage them on a surface level. The people who serve us lunch at the cafeteria, garbage collectors, casual work associates, mail carriers or bus drivers can easily be placed into this category. We foster an *I-Thou* relationship with a person when we view him or her as being unique and irreplaceable. In these rare relationships we look past the social role of a person and embrace and open ourselves to his or her humanity.

The relationship level of communication presents an interesting challenge to Christian communicators. Each person we come in contact with carries with him- or herself the *imago Dei*—the image of God. The word "image *(tselem)* means an object similar to something else and often representative of it."[22] Of all the creatures God created we carry a unique likeness to God and represent him as his image bearers. In light of this theological truth I-It relationships must not be tolerated by Christians. In God's perspective every image bearer, though flawed

---

[20]J. P. Moreland and Klaus Issler, *The Lost Virtue of Happiness: Discovering the Disciplines of the Good Life* (Colorado Springs: NavPress, 2006), p. 16.
[21]Ibid., p. 25.
[22]Wayne Grudem, *Systematic Theology* (Grand Rapids: Zondervan, 1994), p. 442.

by sin, is unique and deeply loved. As Eugene Peterson states, "There are no dittos among souls."[23]

COMMUNICATION COMPETENCE

Simply defining communication will not make us more effective communicators. Scholars use the term *communication competence* to identify individuals whose communication is both effective and appropriate. *Effectiveness* involves the ability to construct, present and achieve communication goals in a given context. It is one thing to recognize that a friend or family member needs comfort, and another altogether to craft and present a message that accomplishes the goal of providing "aid and security during times of stress that leads a person to feel he or she is cared for by others."[24]

The effectiveness component of communication competence was vividly demonstrated by Microsoft founder Bill Gates while speaking at a technology conference. Gates was arguing that mosquito-transmitted malaria was a deadly problem for children in Africa resulting in thousands of deaths a day. To get his point across, Gates opened a jar of mosquitoes and let them loose on the crowd. An uneasiness rapidly moved through the audience as people swatted away potentially malaria-ridden mosquitoes. Gates stood silent and watched the reaction. He then assured them the mosquitoes were harmless. A collective sigh of relief arose and his point was made.

Communication competence also includes a focus on *appropriateness*, which entails adapting our communication goals and style to a particular context. Situational factors such as timing, cultural and social setting, the person with whom we are speaking, and existing communication norms must all be considered. How we relate to a coworker during a coffee break may not be appropriate or professional when in the office with customers present. Many couples show different expressions of affection when in private and public contexts. Balancing the

---

[23]Eugene Peterson, *Subversive Spirituality* (Grand Rapids: Eerdmans, 1997), p. 188.
[24]Brant Burleson, "Comforting Messages: Significance, Approaches, and Effects," in *Communication of Social Support: Messages, Interactions, Relationships, and Community*, ed. Brant Burleson, Terrance Albrecht and Irwin Sarason (Thousand Oaks, Calif.: Sage, 1994), p. 3.

effectiveness and appropriateness of communication can be tricky. While many people gave Bill Gates high marks for dramatically making his point, they felt his letting mosquitoes loose on an unsuspecting crowd was inappropriate for that setting.

Focusing on the appropriateness of communication helps make sense of seemingly contradictory advice found in the book of Proverbs concerning how to respond to a person acting foolishly:

> Do not answer a fool according to his folly,
> or you will be like him yourself.
> Answer a fool according to his folly,
> or he will be wise in his own eyes. (Prov 26:4-5)

These ancient writers are quick to point out that there is no standard script for handling a person spouting wild opinions rooted in folly. In the first scenario, a communicator should avoid getting drawn into a foolish argument in which an on-looking crowd will judge both participants as fools. In a different context it may be wise to grant the person his or her premise and then show how the argument being advanced contradicts itself. For example, in today's cynical age many hold to a form of skepticism that questions whether we can know anything. It may be wise to grant the skeptic's assertion and then ask how he or she *knows* we cannot know anything.

Old Testament scholar David Hubbard summarizes the book of Proverbs' focus on context and the appropriateness of communication: "Judging how the fool will respond, what he needs, and how the audience will react is part and parcel of applied wisdom. Both proverbs are valid, each in its own setting."[25] As Christians interested in presenting a Christian worldview, the effectiveness and appropriateness of our communication must be equally pursued.

Conclusion

In writing a history of human communication, John Durham Peters states that communication is "central to reflections on democracy, love,

---

[25]David A. Hubbard, *Proverbs*, The Communicator's Commentary 15 (Dallas: Word, 1989), p. 399.

and our changing times." Peters argues for a deep appreciation of communication by noting that some "of the chief dilemmas of our age, both public and personal, turn on communication or communication gone sour."[26]

Our understanding of what can keep communication from going sour deepens when we consider in chapter two the role perception plays in how we view and communicate with others.

[26]John Durham Peters, *Speaking into the Air: The History of the Idea of Communication* (Chicago: University of Chicago Press, 1999), p. 1.

PERSPECTIVE TAKING

ENGAGING THE VIEWS OF OTHERS

Kevin Roose's friends thought he'd lost his mind.

After his junior year at Brown University in Providence, a school proud of its liberal positions, he transferred to what many consider the *most* conservative school in America—Liberty University. Liberty was founded in 1971 by Jerry Falwell with the intent to teach creationism, the Bible as the Word of God and the complete rejection of socialism. Roose said he did it to round out his education by immersing himself with people whose perspectives were diametrically opposed to his. During the semester he wrote for the school newspaper, joined student groups, sang in Falwell's church choir and even went on an evangelistic trip to Daytona Beach to share a faith he didn't profess. In order to fit in he had to give up smoking, drinking and, hardest of all, swearing. To help with his language he studied a book he picked up at a Christian bookstore: *30 Days to Taming Your Tongue.*

Kevin admitted that his view of Liberty was fairly negative and he imagined students there as belonging to a cloistered, frightened community who hated liberals and sewed Hillary Clinton voodoo dolls. Yet the people he met surprised him. Yes, he encountered radicals whose beliefs angered him; yet most of the people he encountered he described as "rigorously normal." They were students who worried about their future, scoring dates in Bible classes, Facebook devotees and, behind closed doors, fans of hip-hop and R-rated movies. When his semester was finished, Liberty students were shocked to learn of his identity and read about themselves in *The Unlikely Disciple: A Sinner's Semester at America's Holiest University.*

What Roose and Liberty students engaged in that semester is what communication theorists call *perspective taking.* When we meet people, we try to make sense of them by asking key questions: Who is this person? Why is she or he acting this way? What kind of person is this? Are my perceptions of this person accurate? The difficulty is that we have no direct access to another person's thoughts or feelings. Communication historian John Durham Peters explains our predicament:

> Our sensations and feelings are, physiologically speaking, uniquely our own. My nerve endings terminate in my own brain, not yours. No central exchange exists where I can patch my sensory inputs into yours, nor is there any sort of "wireless" contact through which to transmit my immediate experience of the world to you.[1]

That's the frustrating part of communication, isn't it? When I (Tim) talk to my teenage son on a cell phone or check in with my wife while at work or interact with a student during office hours, I really can't know *exactly* what he or she is thinking. I can only infer what a person is thinking by judging the words he or she uses, nonverbal cues and responses to my clarifying questions. This is the same frustration acutely experienced by Liberty students as they interacted with an undercover Brown student turned author. As Liberty students and faculty answered Roose's questions, they had no access to his thoughts or experience.

The only being other than us who has *direct* access to our thoughts, feelings and experiences is God. The psalmist states that God perceives our thoughts from "afar" and before we utter a word God knows it "completely" (Ps 139:2-4). As human communicators we have no such advantage. The only way we can transmit our identities and our experience of the world is through the verbal and nonverbal symbols described in chapter one. "A word is (or can be) a revelation from one interior to

---

[1]John Durham Peters, *Speaking into the Air: A History of the Idea of Communication* (Chicago: University of Chicago Press, 1999), p. 4.

another. What is inside me can get inside you—the word does it."[2] We view the world in a unique manner and are dependent on imperfect symbols to communicate our experience and perception to others. In this chapter we consider the role perception plays in communication. Specifically, we consider the relationship between perception and narratives, influences on our perception, common mistakes in perception, and how we can improve perception by engaging in perspective taking with others.

PERCEPTION AND NARRATIVES

As we observe the world around us, we often create uniquely different interpretations of what is there and what it means. Communication scholars note that our perceptions of others are organized and communicated in the form of a narrative. Walter Fisher argues that the fundamental characteristic of humans is that we are *homo narrans* or storytellers. The idea that we are by nature storytellers "holds that symbols are created and communicated ultimately as stories meant to give order to human experience."[3] Fisher defines narration as "symbolic actions—words and/or deeds—that have sequence and meaning for those who live, create, and interpret them."[4] To impose order in our lives we transform our experience into stories or narratives that includes sequences of action, plot and characters. When telling friends about our day on campus, we tend not to merely tell them about discrete events. Rather, we put these events in a sequence that loosely resembles a plot. Individuals, like characters, take on good or bad qualities and are often developed in great detail. The highlight of our day is perhaps saved for last like the climax of a story.

This pull toward stories and narrative is powerful. When Randy Pausch, a computer-science professor at Carnegie Mellon was asked to be the speaker at "The Last Lecture" series, he accepted even though he had less than a year to live. Before agreeing to speak Pausch

---

[2]Eugene Peterson, *Subversive Spirituality* (Grand Rapids: Eerdmans, 1997), p. 28.
[3]Walter Fisher, *Human Communication as Narration: Toward a Philosophy of Reason, Value, and Action* (Columbia: University of South Carolina Press, 1987), p. 63.
[4]Ibid., p. 58.

had been diagnosed with pancreatic cancer as evidenced by eleven tumors in his liver. Once he accepted the invitation he was dumbfounded as to how to present a lifetime of learning into one final lecture. He finally settled on presenting his life in narrative form. "If I was able to tell my story with the passion I felt, my lecture might help others find a path to fulfilling their own dreams."[5] Pausch's lecture was filled with stories from his life that gave shape to his ideas and pedagogy.[6] Narrative, concludes cultural studies scholar and ethnographer Dwight Conquergood, is a "search for meaning" that "privileges experience, process, action, and peril."[7] For Conquergood, narratives are not merely a vehicle for explaining what we believe, but a key tool in how we come to believe.

Seeking to organize our often chaotic world into a narrative that has sequence and meaning tells us much about the God who created us and the meaning he has injected into our existence. Eschewing a postmodern rejection of transcendent meaning and value, Christians hold to the belief that God is purposefully directing the individual narratives of his followers. Even the difficulties of life serve a higher purpose and add to the maturity of a believer (Rom 8:28; Jas 1:2-5). Our yearning for meaning points us toward the ultimate source of meaning. "Every time someone tells a story and tells it well and truly, the gospel is served. Out of the chaos of incident and accident, story making words bring light, coherence and connection, meaning and value. If there is a story, then maybe, just maybe, there is (must be!) a Storyteller."[8]

INFLUENCES ON PERCEPTION

Our perception of the world and the stories we tell are powerfully influenced by a multitude of factors. The following factors, while not exhaustive, play a significant role how we organize our perceptions and the narratives we create.

Culture. While there are many definitions of culture, we find it useful

---

[5] Randy Pausch, *The Last Lecture* (New York: Hyperion, 2008), p. 10.
[6] On July 25, 2008, Randy Pausch lost his battle with cancer.
[7] Dwight Conquergood, "Storied Worlds and the Work of Teaching," *Communication Education* 42 (1993): 337.
[8] Peterson, *Subversive Spirituality*, p. 187.

to view culture as "a community of meaning and a shared body of local knowledge."[9] The institutions, structures, customs and practices of a culture work to mirror and support this shared body of meaning and knowledge. Specifically, institutions, customs and cultural practices perceive "certain social groups, values, expectations, meanings, and patterns of behavior as natural and good and others as unnatural, bad, or wrong."[10] For example, while Americans perceive assertive communication and straight talk as signs of a confident communicator, Japanese value indirectness in achieving communication goals.[11] Within each culture there are *cocultures* that individuals choose to identify with, support and unify around a common narrative that advances a particular perception of race, religion, ethnicity, ethics, sexual orientation and so forth.

Communication scholars W. Barnett Pearce and Stephen W. Littlejohn give a powerful example of the role culture and cocultures play in shaping perception. Kavosh Dehpanah was born on a small farm 150 miles east of Tehran. Kavosh works long hours to provide for a family that consist of both of his grandmothers, one of his grandfathers, two brothers and sisters, and two cousins. Like 95 percent of the population of Iran, Kavosh and his family are Shiite Muslims. They pray five times a day to Allah and follow, without question, the teachings of the local imam or holy man. The teachings of imam carry the same authority as Allah. The imam regularly tells Kavosh and others in his coculture that a great war is being waged between all Islamic nations and the great Western devil—America. If America is not stopped, Islam and the holy teachings of the Qur'an will be destroyed. The ultimate form of worship to Allah is to die in defeating the enemies of Islam. With this perspective in mind, Kavosh accepts an invitation to join a terrorist cell. In a secluded camp he learns to handle explosives and is soon ready for a mission. He is sent to southern Europe where he and fellow comrades hijack a plane of fifty-three terrified passengers. The plane is quickly

---

[9]Alberto Gonzales, Marsha Houston, and Victoria Chen, eds., introduction to *Our Voices: Essays in Culture, Ethnicity, and Communication* (Los Angeles: Roxbury, 2004), p. 5.

[10]Julia Wood, *Gendered Lives: Culture, Gender, and Communication*, 8th ed. (Belmont, Calif.: Thompson/Wadsworth, 2007), p. 30.

[11]Peter Hall, "Structuring Symbolic Interaction: Communication and Power," *Communication Yearbook* 4 (1980): 50.

surrounded by an assault team. Propelled by the desire to be a martyr for Allah and the Iranian value of *aberu* (saving face), there is no thought of surrender. They set off explosive devices and everyone on board dies. Within our Western culture, we would most likely perceive Kavosh as a terrorist. Yet within Kavosh's coculture he is viewed as a triumphant warrior of God.[12]

Social position. Not everyone born into a particular culture perceives that culture in the same way. Standpoint theorists argue that a person's social location within culture and the particular groups he or she is born into powerfully shape how he or she thinks about others, themselves and the social world. The social, material and symbolic circumstances of particular groups influence and guide group member's perceptions of all facets of life.[13] For example, a student raised in a white, middle-class location may not receive much encouragement to develop friendships with lower-class African American classmates. Consequently, this student is unlikely to interact in any depth with African American classmates. Within certain locations the African American student is not just viewed as being different in regard to race or class, but the difference is widened to include a sense of what is and is not valuable.

The roots of standpoint theory are linked to the observations of nineteenth-century German philosopher Georg F. W. Hegel, who noted that the institution of slavery is perceived differently based on social location. The slave owner or master perceives slavery only as it relates to his self-interests. He has no need to be aware of the slave's perspective, needs or desires other than how those influence production. The slave, however, needs to be aware of not only his or her own needs, but also must be keenly attuned to the needs and perspective of the master. Hegel's conclusion was that, where power relationships exist, there is never one single perspective of society. Ironically, while the

---

[12]This story is not meant to suggest that all members of an Iranian culture support terrorism. Rather, it shows the power Kavosh's coculture has in shaping his perception of God, honor, violence and America. To read the entire story, see W. Barnett Pearce and Stephen W. Littlejohn, *Moral Conflict: When Social Worlds Collide* (Thousand Oaks, Calif.: Sage, 1997), pp. 120-22.

[13]Unless there is a political consciousness of a person's own location and that of the dominant group, there can be no standpoint.

perspectives of those in lower-class locations tend to be ignored or devalued, they may actually have a more comprehensive perspective of society than those in power.

We perceive what is named. In any given day we are bombarded with a staggering amount of data and stimuli. A key part of perception is deciding what we will attend to. We often attend to stimuli that are intense (something that is loud, large or unusual) or repetitive (people or situations we come in regular contact with). We also tend to perceive stimuli that have labels or names. Julia Wood notes that naming "is perhaps the fundamental symbolic act" and is crucial in that "naming evokes notice and confers importance; conversely, not naming obscures awareness and significance."[14] Prior to the 1970s the term *sexual harassment* did not exist to name unwelcome verbal or nonverbal behavior of a sexual nature in which professional advancement or success is dependent on sexual responsiveness. Before this term came into our legal and cultural vocabulary many women in the workforce believed that lewd remarks, sexual banter, pinups on the walls, unwelcome physical touch or demeaning sexual jokes were simply "boys being boys" in the workplace. Only when these actions were named and recognized by the courts did men and women more readily perceive the reality and occurrence of sexual harassment.

We perceive what we are primed to perceive. Social psychologists Susan Fiske and Shelley Taylor explain that the phenomenon of priming "describes the effects of a prior context on the interpretation of new information."[15] If we read an article on the prevalence of germs in public eateries, then we are primed to notice the cleanliness of the next restaurant we visit. The effects of priming on perception are evident in a study where the primed group, in this instance a group of men who watch a pornographic movie, are then in an unrelated context interviewed by a female involved with the study. The majority of male participants interprets her actions as highly sexual and later can remember

---

[14]Julia Wood, "Gender and Moral Voice: Moving from Woman's Nature to Standpoint Epistemology," *Women's Studies in Communication* 15 (1992): 3.
[15]Susan T. Fiske and Shelley E. Taylor, *Social Cognition* (New York: McGraw-Hill, 1991), p. 258.

only her physical features. According to priming studies, the reason why the men perceived her actions as sexual is because "recently and frequently activated ideas come to mind more easily then ideas that have not been activated."[16]

In another study subjects were primed for hostility by watching the actions of volatile individuals, such as rock star Alice Cooper and Indiana basketball coach Bobby Knight. In a second, unrelated context these same participants are asked to listen to a speaker and describe his style. The participants perceive the speaker as hostile and competitive even though the speaker was instructed beforehand to be noncombative.

Church historian John Woodbridge, in his assessment of the church's propensity to use culture-war rhetoric, argues that we may be priming ourselves to view mere critique of Christian principles as personal attack and those who simply disagree with us as hostile adversaries. "Culture-war rhetoric leads us to distort other's positions, to see enmity in place of mere disagreement."[17] By adopting the rhetoric of war Christians may prime themselves to perceive others as "friend or foe" and approach complex issues with an either-or mindset.

Media, technology and perception. In our media-saturated and technology-driven culture, perception is greatly influenced by the content of media and the technologies that are designed to make life more efficient. Sociologist Barry Glassner argues that our perception of danger has been deeply influenced by the media's disproportionate fascination with rare but sensational dangers such as homicide and road rage. Researchers from Emory University analyzed the coverage of health dangers in popular magazines and newspapers, and discovered that the eleventh-ranked cause of death in America, homicide, received the same amount of coverage as the leading cause of death, heart disease. Between 1990 and 1998 as the murder rate was declining by 20 percent nationally, "the number of murder stories on network newscasts increased by 600 percent (*not* counting stories about O. J. Simpson)."[18]

---

[16]Ibid., p. 257.

[17]John D. Woodbridge, "Culture War Casualties: How Warfare Rhetoric Is Hurting the Work of the Church," *Christianity Today*, March 6, 1995, p. 22.

[18]Barry Glassner, *The Culture of Fear: Why Americans Are Afraid of the Wrong Things* (New York: Basic Books, 1999), p. xxi.

The same is true with our perception of road rage. In a 1998 story in the *Los Angeles Times* the writer declared that road rage had become an "exploding phenomenon across the country" and was particularly evident in the Pacific Northwest.

> Only after wading through twenty-two paragraphs of alarming first-person accounts and warnings from authorities did the reader learn that a grand total of five drivers and passengers had died in road rage incidents in the region over the previous five years. An average of one death a year constitutes a plague?[19]

The media are powerful force in shaping how we view ourselves, others and the world we inhabit.

What role do the technologies we utilize on a daily basis play in perception? Nicholas Carr asks a provocative question: "Is Google making us stupid?" Utilizing the thoughts of Marshall McLuhan, Carr observes that the Internet is changing how we perceive complex arguments found in lengthy books or articles. The "Net seems to be chipping away my capacity for concentration and contemplation. My mind now expects to take in information the way the Net distributes it: in a swiftly moving stream of particles."[20] Carr cites a five-year study from University College London analyzing computer logs recording how readers interact with online journal articles, e-books and other written information on two popular research sites. Researchers noted that individuals would hop from source to source typically reading only one or two pages of an article and seldom return to a previously skimmed article. The study concludes:

> It is clear that users are not reading online in the traditional sense; indeed there are signs that new forms of "reading" are emerging as users "power browse" horizontally through titles, contents pages and abstracts for quick wins. It almost seems that they go online to avoid reading in the traditional sense.[21]

Carr's fears are worth considering. Is it possible that the Internet is

---

[19]Ibid., p. 4.
[20]Nicholas Carr, "Is Google Making Us Stupid? What the Internet Is Doing to Our Brains," *Atlantic*, July-August, 2008, p. 57.
[21]Ibid., p. 58.

changing how we perceive and our desire to engage Plato's *Republic*, Tolstoy's *War and Peace* or a lengthy article in the *New Yorker?* For Christians, Carr's observations are particularly salient. Is the alarming rate of Bible illiteracy growing among evangelicals due to a perception that the contents of the Scriptures are too complex and not easily skimmed for information? Why struggle through Paul's epistle to the Romans, when *The Daily Bread* gives us a verse, commentary and suggested prayer in one short page?

Because our perception of the world has been influenced by many factors, the narratives we create to explain the world and our experience are unique and often vastly different than narratives created by those around us. Communication scholars call the ability to understand the viewpoint of another as *perspective taking*. Before we explore this important skill it will be useful to first examine common errors we make in perceiving others.

ERRORS IN PERCEPTION

As soon as we observe the behaviors of another person, we engage in what psychologists call attribution—assigning meaning to the actions of a person. One of the most common errors in perception and attribution is what scholars label the *fundamental attribution error*, which occurs when we automatically attribute internal reasons rather than situational factors to explain why someone did something. Our roommate tells us that he or she did poorly on a test. We immediately conclude that the roommate is lazy and lacks the personal discipline to study rather than considering how starting a new job earlier in the week may have affected his or her studying. Individuals who have prejudiced views of particular groups easily fall into this perceptual error. If a person of a particular ethnic background is out of work, an individual may quickly judge that person to be lazy rather than considering the current state of the job market.

In perceiving the actions of others it is crucial that we are aware of this fundamental error in perception. Making sense of the behavior of another person must always take into account relevant situational factors. Consider John's account of Jesus encountering a Samaritan woman who comes to draw water at Jacob's well at the sixth hour (Jn 4). Starting from daybreak the sixth hour would put her at the well during the intense heat of the noonday sun. Why not wait until a cooler time, when she could draw water with other women? If we automatically assume internal reasons—she's antisocial—we slip into this fundamental error. When Jesus acknowledges that she has had five previous husbands and is currently living with a sixth man, a key situational factor is revealed. In light of existing cultural mores, to show up at the well in the cool of the day would put her in contact with other women who would most likely shun her.

In contrast to the fundamental attribution error, a mistake we make when perceiving ourselves and the reasons for our own behaviors, is the *self-serving bias*. This error happens when we are quick to give credit to ourselves for good things that happen but blame the situation when bad things occur. When I do well on a test I attribute it to discipline and acuity, yet when I receive a low grade it is due to an unfairly worded exam. This bias easily leads to an unrealistic assessment or perception of personal intellect or competence. With these errors in mind let's move to a key skill in understanding the perspective of another.

PERSPECTIVE TAKING

Claudia Hale and Jesse Delia, communication researchers specializing in the study of perception, describe perspective taking as "the capacity to assume and maintain another's point of view" and is, according to them, the "basic social cognitive process in communication."[22] Perspective taking is a process "in which inferences are made about situations and others and inferences about other's inferences."[23] Since we can never fully take on the perspective of another, perspective taking will always be an interpretive process—that is, it will necessarily be filtered through our own minds. Central to perspective taking is an attempt to distance ourselves from our views long enough to explore and understand the views of another.

---

[22]Claudia L. Hale and Jesse G. Delia, "Cognitive Complexity and Social Perspective-Taking," *Communication Monographs* 43 (1976): 195.
[23]Ibid., p. 197.

In part, the aim of perspective taking is to create thick, complex descriptions of others and understand how they view the world. The idea of *thick descriptions*—multilayered accounts of others—comes from Princeton anthropologist Clifford Geertz, who observed that "man is an animal suspended in webs of significance that he himself has spun."[24] Each person we encounter, and the groups he or she belongs to, has created a complex view of the world evidenced by daily practices and rituals and expressed through narrative. Central to Geertz's way of thinking is a desire to understand the behavior of others through their personal motives and systems of meaning. For Geertz thin descriptions of culture, traditions, social codes or individuals lack detail and depth. Thin descriptions summarize events, narratives or actions and approach the complex actions of others solely from the perspective, assumptions, and values of the one attempting to engage in perspective taking. In short, thin descriptions "give superficial, partial, and sparse accounts. They use few words to describe complex, meaningful events."[25]

As followers of Christ in the academy, we know the pain caused by thin descriptions of faith. In his classic work *Why I Am Not a Christian*, noted atheist philosopher Bertrand Russell gives a thin description of why people believe in God. "Religion is based, I think, primarily and mainly upon fear. It is part the terror of the unknown and partly, as I have said, the wish to feel that you have a kind of elder brother who will stand by you in all your troubles and disputes. Fear is the basis of the whole thing."[26] For intelligent men and women of faith in the academy such a thin description is hurtful. In light of this pain, Christian communicators must avoid thin descriptions of those who challenge our worldview. If we expect others to offer thick descriptions of the intellectual and emotional reasons why we are people of faith, then we must offer thick descriptions of the complex reasons people reject our faith or choose another faith tradition.

In contrast, Geertz states that a thick description goes below the

---

[24]Clifford Geertz, "Thick Descriptions: Toward an Interpretive Theory of Culture," in *The Interpretation of Cultures* (New York: Basic Books, 1973), p. 5.
[25]Norman K. Denzin, *Interpretive Interactionism*, 2nd ed. (Thousand Oaks, Calif.: Sage, 2001), p. 103.
[26]Bertrand Russell, *Why I Am Not a Christian* (New York: Simon & Schuster, 1957), p. 22.

surface to give as rich and multilayered an account of another person as possible. Thick descriptions "present detail, context, emotion, and the web of social relationships that join persons to one another. . . . In thick descriptions the voices, feelings, actions, and meanings of interacting are heard, made visible."[27] The book of Proverbs acknowledges the complexity of human motives and states that the "purposes of a man's heart are deep waters, but a man of understanding draws them out" (Prov 20:5). Old Testament scholar William McKane writes that this proverb suggests that understanding another person is like dropping a bucket into a person's heart, where opinion and intellectual judgments are made, and then drawing it back out.[28]

A powerful example of perspective taking comes from the work of performance-theory scholar Anna Deavere Smith and her attempt to engage the perspectives of participants and victims of the Crown Heights riots of 1991. In the summer of 1991 racial tensions exploded in the Brooklyn neighborhood of Crown Heights when a black child was killed by a car in Rebbe Menachem Schneerson's motorcade. A small contingent of African Americans deemed it murder and retaliated by killing a Jewish student. It was into this racial tension Smith entered, armed with a pocket tape recorder and a desire to listen.

To scholars like Smith, how we come to understand someone is just as important as what we discover about that individual. In order to write thick descriptions of members of the Crown Heights community, Smith engaged the participants directly, allowing them access to her as she herself sought access to them. By this approach Smith avoided what Antonio Gramsci calls the "intellectual's error" that consists in "believing that one can know without understanding and even more without feeling."[29]

Over the course of a month Smith interviewed over two hundred members of the community and presented twenty of those viewpoints in a one-woman show called "Fires in the Mirror." She then invited the

---

[27]Geertz, "Thick Descriptions," p. 100.

[28]William McKane, *Proverbs* (London: SCM Press, 1970), p. 536.

[29]Antonio Gramsci, *Selections from the Prison Notebooks*, trans. Quintin Hoare and Geoffery Smith (New York: International Publishers, 1971), p. 418.

Crown Heights community to attend the show to see themselves per-
formed. During postplay discussions with the audience Smith witnessed the effect of her performance. Some blacks felt she was too harsh
on their community. Some Jewish people felt she had not gone far
enough. These perceptions aside, almost everyone in the audience felt
affirmed, not because a verdict of "right" was reached but simply because she had entered into and honored their perspective through richly
thick descriptions.

Notice that Smith's form of perspective taking was not merely a cognitive exercise. To engage the perspectives of Crown Heights' residents,
she walked their streets and placed herself in the midst of the devasta-
tion caused by the riots. Scholars like Smith point out that this partici-
patory approach to perspective taking is far from unique to Smith. In
fact, long before Smith did her work, it was described by abolitionist
Frederick Douglass in his classic work *Narrative of the Life of Frederick
Douglass*. Douglass describes how moved he was by hearing the passionate songs of slaves traveling to the slave owner's house to receive an
allowance. Douglass concluded that the "mere hearing of those songs"
did more to convince him of the horrific nature of slavery than the
"reading of whole volumes of philosophy on the subject" ever did.[30]
Douglass argued that we could not experience the ills of slavery while
sitting in a reading chair. An individual must place him- or herself in
the "deep pine woods" and "analyze the sounds that shall pass through
the chambers of the soul."[31]

As Christian communicators there is much to be learned about the
type of perspective taking described in this chapter and advocated by
Smith. Our bookstores are filled with books about postmodernism,
competing religions, New Age philosophy and so on. While this information is valuable as a type of introduction, key questions must be
asked: Do we know any of these individuals on a personal level? Are we
relating to a person or someone's analysis of him or her? Are our descriptions of those outside our community thin or thick?

---

[30]Frederick Douglass, *Narrative of the Life of Frederick Douglass* (1845; reprint, New York: Dover
   Publications, 1995), p. 36.
[31]Ibid.

Christians are often surprisingly hesitant to engage in perspective taking with those outside our community. To engage in perspective taking and offer thick descriptions of those who disagree with or reject the Christian worldview is often met with a hostile response from within the Christian community. Such a response is what guest editor Philip Yancey encountered when *Christianity Today* ran articles on Mahatma Gandhi. Readers encountered a thick description of Gandhi that included his taking up at great personal cost the cause of India's untouchables and, ironically, his decision to abandon his wife to pursue rigid, often extreme spiritual disciplines. Yancey wrote that he was shocked by the angry tone of many responses. "So, it's Gandhi on the cover this month," wrote one reader. "Who will it be next month, Ayatollah?"[32]

Resistance to perspective taking seems to be rooted in mistakenly equating perspective taking with condoning the views of another. Members of the Harvard negation project offer a valuable clarification: "Understanding their point of view is not the same as agreeing with it. It is true that a better understanding of their thinking may lead you to revise your own views about the merits of a situation. But that is not a *cost* of understanding their point of view, it is a *benefit*."[33] Perspective taking allows us to understand the systems of meaning created by individuals, craft person-centered responses to specific concerns and *clarify our own thinking*. After spending a semester at Liberty University Kevin Roose said he is rethinking his relationship to God and faith. Upon returning to Brown University he now prays occasionally, has started reading the Gospel of John and is considering attending church. His semester of perspective taking wasn't just about him getting to know Liberty students but was a time to understand his own thoughts and perspective toward religion.

---

[32]Philip Yancey, *Open Windows* (New York: Thomas Nelson, 1985), p. 182. Yancey offers his rationale for selecting Gandhi: "I do not write about Gandhi because he had the answers for our planet. To the contrary, I write merely because he asked the questions most eloquently. We may reject his answers, surely, but can we do so before first considering his questions?" (p. 182).

[33]Roger Fisher and William Ury, *Getting to Yes: Negotiating Agreement Without Giving In* (New York: Penguin Books, 1991), p. 24.

Merely engaging in perspective taking does not ensure that we accurately understand the experiences, thoughts or emotions of another. All of us have experienced being misunderstood or misreading the views of another. Central to perspective taking is the ability to check our perceptions.

PERCEPTION CHECKING

Communication scholars Ronald Adler, Lawrence Rosenfeld and Russell Proctor suggest that perception checking has three distinct parts: (1) a description of the behavior noticed, (2) two possible interpretations of the behavior, (3) a request for clarification about how to interpret the behavior.[34] Suppose you perceive that the reason a friend isn't returning your text messages is that she is angry at you (an attribution). You can check your perception by saying: "I've sent you a couple of messages, and you've not responded yet [description of behavior]. I'm not sure if you've been too busy to respond [first interpretation] or if you are angry at me [second interpretation]. Are we okay? [request for clarification]." Instead of assuming that your perception of another person's behavior is correct, perception checking allows the other person the opportunity to explain his or her actions. Perception checking is inherently a collaborative process that accomplishes multiple communication goals. "Besides leading to more accurate perceptions, it signals an attitude of respect and concern for the other person, saying, in effect, 'I know I'm not qualified to judge you without some help.'"[35]

When checking our perceptions with others, it is important to keep in mind that individuals may not always fully understand why they behave in particular ways. As mentioned earlier in this chapter, when Proverbs compares the purposes of the human heart to deep waters (Prov 20:5), it is suggesting that our motives may not always be obvious to others or ourselves. Perception checking is perhaps one way that our motives can surface and be more readily understood by both parties.

---

[34]Ronald Adler, Lawrence Rosenfeld, and Russell Proctor, *Interplay: The Process of Interpersonal Communication*, 10th ed. (New York: Oxford University Press, 2007), p. 104.
[35]Ibid.

CONCLUSION

Perception and the process of perspective taking have been creatively described by philosopher and political organizer Maria Lugones as "world-traveling." Lugones writes that deciding to love her estranged mother required "that I see with her eyes, that I go into my mother's world . . . that I witness her own sense of herself from within her world."[36] For Christians, "world traveling" has clear biblical precedent. Could it not be argued that in part the incarnation was God engaging in perspective taking? The writer of Hebrews states that we have a high priest who is not immune to our feelings and thoughts, but who traveled into our world and observed it through our own eyes (Heb 4:15).

While our perceptions of the world may differ greatly, we all seek to use words to convey our perceptions to others. Chapter three explores the power, limits and mystery of words.

---

[36]Maria Lugones, "Playfulness, World-Traveling, and Loving Perception" in *The Woman That I Am: The Literature of Culture of Contemporary Women of Color*, ed. S. Madison (New York: St. Martin's Press, 1994), p. 627.

WORDS! WORDS! WORDS!
WE CAN ONLY IMAGINE

Words! Words! Words!
Like harmless bullets
Fired at my brain.
Long words! Lost words . . .
Words are everywhere.
People spit them out
All the time
And most of the time
They are wasted.

NORMAN C. HABEL, "ONE WORD"

It is most interesting that God uses the concept of *logos* or *Word* to describe his essence as well as the root component to establish a relationship with human beings. The nature of the Greek word *logos* suggests more than merely a "referent or symbol." To the Greek mind *logos* meant reason, creative control, perhaps even revelation of new truth.[1] Not by accident or coincidence, the apostle John inspirationally begins his Gospel by explaining that "in the beginning was the Word, and the Word was with God, and the Word was God" (Jn 1:1). If we are to find the right words to be used at the right times, we probably need to re-

---

[1]Charles C. Ryrie, "Explanatory Reference Point to John 1:1," *The Ryrie Study Bible* (Chicago: Moody Press, 1986), p. 1452.

think our theology of words because the ultimate Word came to live among us and use our basic unit of communication to help us understand more about God and his love for us. How this theology of words resonates with our God can only be imagined, but the process compels us to try to actualize the imagined universe.

Tim reminds us that in part the incarnation was God engaged in perspective taking. I (Todd) explore the notion in this chapter that perspective taking and our ability to accurately and fairly perceive others as well as God and his Son, Jesus Christ, require a sensitivity to the understanding and use of the basic element of oral communication: words.

WORDS MAKE US TRULY HUMAN: A BIBLICAL PERSPECTIVE

Author, language columnist and critic Richard Lederer underscores this biblical notion of "word as beginning" when he says,

> The boundary between human and animal—between the most primitive savage and the highest ape—is the language line. The birth of language is the dawn of humanity; *in our beginning was the word*. We have always been endowed with language because before we had words, we were not human beings. [Words] tell us that we must never take for granted the miracle of language.[2]

Throughout human history, this unique ability to create referent points or symbols made cultural advances possible. Words were the symbols that evolved to symbolize not only empirically verifiable objects but also ideas, feelings and philosophies. This use of symbolic communication facilitated the specialization and cooperation of joint labor tasks. But, as Charles Larson reminds us, "Like the opening of Pandora's box, the use of visual and verbal symbols to communicate also allowed humans to engage in less-constructive behaviors such as lying, teasing, breaking promises, scolding, demeaning, and propagandizing."[3] I might add one other negative quality as well: arrogance.

---

[2]Richard Lederer, *The Miracle of Language* (New York: Pocket Books, 1991), p. 3 (italics added).

[3]Charles U. Larson, *Persuasion: Reception and Responsibility*, 12th ed. (Boston: Cengage Learning, 2010), p. 117.

From the earliest descriptions of human endeavors, the Bible focuses on language and word usage as inherently powerful. The tower of Babel narrative in Genesis 11 establishes a time when all humans spoke and understood the same language. The story indicates that this linguistic unity contributed to political power, building projects and ultimately that previously mentioned word *arrogance*. God certainly wasn't threatened by Babel's builders; he knew no tower could reach him. But there is underlying pride in the linguistic unity that was disrupted when God confused the language and scattered the people over all the earth. The building project came to an abrupt halt. Theologian Charles Ryrie has a fascinating aside on this incident that also shows the power of words as well as cultural perceptions. He says that there is a Hebrew verb closely linked to *Babel* that means "to confuse," but the Babylonians (and their descendants the Iraqis) prefer to use the meaning of the word *Babel* more acceptable to them: "gate of God."[4]

Since the tower of Babel we have spent eons attempting to communicate through our variety of words what we mean and what we intend, and the entire field of communication has evolved into "a study of miscommunication" at times. We take the perspective in this book that choosing appropriate communication requires not only sensitivity to context, timing and civility but also awareness of basic word choices. The Bible certainly has had much to say about words and how we use them to communicate with others. Take, for example, some of these references found in Proverbs:

> With his mouth the godless destroys his neighbor,
> but through knowledge the righteous escape. (Prov 11:9)

> The words of the wicked lie in wait for blood,
> but the speech of the upright rescues them. (Prov 12:6)

> Reckless words pierce like a sword,
> but the tongue of the wise brings healing. (Prov 12:18)

---

[4]Charles C. Ryrie, "Explanatory Reference to Genesis 11:9," *The Ryrie Study Bible* (Chicago: Moody Press, 1986), p. 21.

I think frequently of the times I hear myself (or someone else) say, "Hey, just kidding!" after some scathing or tacky remark that clearly hurts the person it's directed to. We think that trying to cover our true intent by placing it in the realm of "teasing" makes the utterance benign, but it doesn't. Eventually we learn that the old childhood saying "Sticks and stones can break my bones, but words (names) can never hurt me" is certainly not true. I would hope that a growing relationship with my God would show a definite change in the way I use words, hopefully to experience the "rescue" that the author of Proverbs describes. I think we all need to be rescued from ourselves most often—and it will take time and godly help to make the adjustments.

For many years I had a plaque with a paraphrase of Proverbs 10:19 on a wall in my school office. Reading this verse each new day helped me keep my attempts to communicate with basic words in perspective:

> Don't talk so much. You keep putting your foot in your mouth. Be sensible and turn off the flow.[5]

I wish I could say that I actively practiced this wise advice, but I find that I have to keep reminding myself of its truth and practicality when I am sitting in a department chairs' meeting with my fellow colleagues at Biola University. I tend to have comments full of words on virtually every subject, but, truth be told, not every word I utter adds to the relational perspective essential to carry out the university's business. I'm learning to "be sensible and turn off the flow," but it is a long, slow process.

James, the half-brother of Jesus and early leader of the fledgling Jerusalem Christian church, wrote a scathing reminder of the power for good and evil that words can have. Using the linguistic device of symbolic objectification or metaphor, James refers to the human tongue as the source of our decision-making ability to use words for good or evil:

---

[5]*The Way: An Illustrated Version of the Living Bible* (Wheaton, Ill.: Tyndale House Publishers, 1971), p. 537.

The tongue is a small part of the body, but it makes great boasts. Consider what a great forest is set on fire by a small spark. The tongue also is a fire, a world of evil among the parts of the body. It corrupts the whole person, sets the whole course of his life on fire, and is itself set on fire by hell. (Jas 3:5-6)

James was not suggesting that to prevent evil the devout should never say another word. Many monastic hermits of the Middle Ages misapplied these verses and had their tongues cut out so that they could not say words, thus preventing sin, or so they thought. Since words begin with a thought, the foolish action of cutting out a person's tongue won't solve any problem and leaves him or her with a maimed ability to communicate. James does suggest that the "tongue" can best be understood in a metaphorical sense as "fire." Now fire has the capacity to warm, to heat, to bake or to facilitate existence; fire also has the power to consume, destroy and reduce to ash objects as diverse as homes or fellow human beings. For James the point of linking the use of language and words by means of the tongue is to seek discipline and sensitivity through process, not removal or nonuse. His advice is universal and never without contemporary application. Politicians are continually having to apologize for embarrassing comments, apparently made in secret or "off the record," only to discover a live microphone has picked it up, and within minutes the sound bite is on the Internet and replayed on television talk shows. During the 2008 presidential campaign, political activist Jesse Jackson was caught by his recorded words of trash-talking soon-to-be President Barack Obama. The political career of Rod Blagojevich came to an abrupt end, not with merely a vote of the Illinois State Legislature but with recorded obscenities and plans to sell Obama's Senate seat to the highest bidder. Words are lethal weapons, seldom set for stun and frequently aimed in our own direction.

WORDS AS SYMBOLS AND MEANING

James' use of *tongue* as a symbol echoes the study of language and communication pioneered by philosopher and linguist Suzanne K. Langer. She says that "symbols are not proxy of their objects, but are vehicles for the conception of objects."[6] These symbols with a common meaning (e.g., the color red for stop, the skull and crossbones for poison, etc.) are called *concepts*. Langer describes three aspects of meanings in words: *signification, denotation* and *connotation*. Signification is usually a sign that accompanies the thing being considered (e.g., the triangle on the bottom of recyclable plastic containers). Denotation refers to the dictionary definition or most common understanding of a word. Connotation consists of your emotional or experiential understanding of a word. The denotation of the word *danger* from the *American Heritage Dictionary* is "exposure or vulnerability to harm or loss." The connotation of the word *danger* for someone like me living in Southern California would be an earthquake alert I might hear on the radio or television, compelling me to duck and cover.

For Christians, we may make the assumption that if someone *signifies, denotes* and by our own *connotations* uses words and symbols that seem to be identified with us that they are indeed the same as we are. This would not be a wise or prudent assumption. Cults or sects may use the same words as Christians yet mean something completely different. The Unification Church, founded in the 1950s by Sun Myung Moon and established in the United States in the mid-1970s, has frequently asked to be considered another Protestant denomination, but the implied doctrine that Moon is the "Lord of the Second Advent" and the reincarnation of Jesus Christ puts the sect at odds with historical Christian doctrine and theology.[7] For example, the 1970s popular praise chorus "Father, I Adore You," sung in most Christian churches today, is also sung at many Unification Church gatherings. But one of the titles given to Moon is "True Father" or "True Parent," so the connotation of this song for "Moonies" does not link "Father" with God but with Sun Myung Moon as the "True Parent."[8] Perhaps a more contemporary example might be the "spiritual" language used by Oprah Winfrey. Visit Oprah's website (www.oprah.com) and read the "spirituality"

---

[6]Suzanne K. Langer, *Philosophy in a New Key* (New York: New American Library, 1951), p. 60.
[7]See Frederick Sontag, *Sun Myung Moon and the Unification Church: An In-Depth Investigation of the Man and the Movement* (Nashville: Abingdon, 1977).
[8]Ibid., p. 119.

references in her *O* magazine, and it will soon be obvious words like *spiritual, faith, truth* and *God* do not mean to her what they do to historically orthodox Christian believers. To properly understand how words are used, we must always investigate their significance, denotation and connotation in a given context.

Another helpful communication theory of word use begins with landmark publications by general semanticists. Although these philosophers of communication do not generate the same kind of contemporary interest that they once did in the 1960s and 1970s, their work still has insightful applications for our use of words. Noted rhetorical theorist I. A. Richards, while not known as a general semanticist, nevertheless wrote about a concept that was coined by general semanticists: *feedforward*. Every college student in a public speaking course soon learns about *feedback* (reactions to a speech from an audience as they hear it for the first time). However, *feedforward* asks a communicator to anticipate reactions from an audience and adapt accordingly. If we can anticipate positive or negative feedback, we should be able to prevent misunderstandings that could occur. Just as I am learning to delay sending a knee-jerk e-mail response to someone on campus, *feedforward* calls us to consider in advance how our message will be heard or understood by the receivers.

Alfred Korzybski's *Science and Sanity*, considered a seminal general semantics theoretical text, devises tools for improving the understanding of human communication.[9] The mantra of general semanticists is "the map is not the territory," meaning that a word, drawing or image is a product of "perception," not necessarily an accurate description of a real, empirically verifiable reality. Maps exist in our minds; territories exist in the real world and can be experienced. General semanticists have problems with belief in God because for them "God" is a map, not a territory. Still, the Bible attempts to bridge this difficulty by claiming that Jesus Christ is the "image of the invisible God" (Col 1:15). Jesus also makes the claim that "anyone who has seen me has seen the Father" (Jn 14:9). Christians must realize that discussions with postmoderns are going to go back and forth about maps and territories. Christians would endorse the no-

---

[9]Alfred Korzybski, *Science and Sanity* (Lakeville, Conn.: Non-Aristotelian Library, 1947).

tion that the Bible is the map and Jesus, the visible expression of the invisible God, is the territory. Skeptics, however would say their fluid interpretations of reality are the territory and their narratives are the maps. But it would be insensitive and also an example of misperception to dismiss general semanticists' theories, because they only embrace things that can be verified empirically, and God cannot be.

Semanticists want senders and receivers of messages to distinguish between signals and symbols. Signals and symbols give information, but they may illustrate the legacy of Babel in creating more confusion than clarity. So general semanticists try to isolate or conceptualize meanings by their concreteness. Can a word or concept be visualized? Because stereotyping, grouping and overgeneralizing mitigate against accurate and fair descriptions of reality, semanticists suggest that we use *extensional devices* or techniques "for neutralizing or defusing the emotional connotations that often accompany words by adding information that makes my meaning clear" to others.[10] So, rather than fostering a war of words and hurt feelings over theological perspectives, we need to speak to avoid terms like *predestination* or *free will*, which only continue a war of words. Christians see systematic theology in terms of their own interpretive frame of reference as they read and study the Bible. Perhaps the key to finding semantic devices to help us explain our understanding should also include a humble admission that we don't know how seemingly paradoxical theological positions can be solved through theological study. The ultimate Word, now in glory, will one day make it all clear to us.

Besides extensional devices, general semanticists suggest that we also incorporate other devices to help us understand context and perceptions in our word choices. *Indexing* means narrowing a claim about a group to a specific subordinate group, with added descriptive information. For example, a claim may be true of *some* members of a group, perhaps even true at a stage of development, but certainly not true of the whole group as currently configured. *Dating* also helps by linking descriptions to a year or time; *dating* reminds us that meanings can evolve over time. "Some Christians in the South during the 1990s be-

---

[10]Larson, *Persuasion*, p. 126.

lieved that young people who read Harry Potter books would be at-tracted to witchcraft" is an example of an argument that includes *index-ing* ("some Christians" and "the South") and *dating* ("during the 1990s"). To remove the extensional devices completely is to make the argument an overgeneralization and probably false.

Semanticists also like to advocate the use of "et cetera" when the whole story cannot be told about any person, event, place or thing. Christians need to access this concept when they get involved in con-versations that lead to questions like, What happens to those who have never heard of Christ? Or, If God is good, why did the hurricane kill so many innocent children? There are no quick answers to those ques-tions. Theologians for centuries have wrestled with the issues. If et cetera suggests that multiple meanings or outcomes could be viable in biblical interpretations, it does not necessarily follow that the concept makes certainty unknowable. Bible study essentially calls believers back to investigations as we mature spiritually. For example, does 1 Thes-salonians 4:13-18 mean that "the dead in Christ" refers to deceased believers whose earthly bodies will be elementally and cellularly recon-stituted as they rise from the graves or could it mean that the "dead in Christ" refers to Old Testament saints redeemed by Christ's death and resurrection, or could the passage means something else? Et cetera means that we can't give all possible explanations about something, but a dialogue will continue the discussion.

Finally, semanticists advocate using *quotation marks* around flag words or concepts that do not necessarily indicate the orator's perspec-tive. Interestingly enough, we have a nonverbal signal we use for quota-tion marks when we speak aloud that employs the index and middle fingers of both our hands in a clipping gesture that attempts to show quotation marks.[11]

At this point, we could surmise that as long as we learn to control and discipline what comes out of our mouth, we will be a consistent, authentic and ethical communicator. Unfortunately, that would be an incorrect assumption because Jesus Christ does not give us that option.

---

[11]See Samuel I. Hayakawa, *Through the Communication Barrier: On Speaking, Listening, and Un-derstanding* (New York: Harper & Row, 1979), pp. 75-79.

Allow me to use a poker metaphor in a spiritual application. Jesus ups the ante for all of us. In the Sermon on the Mount, Jesus makes it clear that merely refraining from uttering certain words doesn't free us from transgression. "I tell you that anyone who looks at a woman lustfully has already committed adultery with her in his heart" (Mt 5:28). The desire is formulated in our brains. And Jesus says the desire itself is sinful, and wrong desire often leads to a sinful act.

Jesus has even more to say about words later on in his sermon: "When you pray, do not keeping on babbling like pagans, for they think they will be heard because of their many words. Do not be like them, for your Father knows what you need before you ask him" (Mt 6:7-8). So, long-winded prayers do not necessarily get God's approval. Conciseness and getting to the point quickly with less verbiage is considered a virtue.

Jesus concludes his sermon with some other advice about motives, intent and perceptions:

> Not everyone who says to me, "Lord, Lord," will enter the kingdom of heaven, but only he who does the will of my Father who is in heaven. Many will say to me on that day, "Lord, Lord, did we not prophesy in your name, and in your name drive out demons and perform many miracles?" Then I will tell them plainly, "I never knew you. Away from me, you evildoers!" (Mt 7:21-23)

So, if you judge others by how they sound and the words they use, you may be surprised; some of them may not have the same relationship with God that you have. We have much to learn from the general semanticists about the clarity and intent of genuine communication.

The epithet "Christians are all hypocrites!" hurts true believers, but hypocrisy would have no meaning if the counterfeit version could not be compared to the genuine. So, all Christians cannot be hypocritical, otherwise there would be nothing to compare them to. That being said, we need to adjust our gullibility radar to be the first to expose those who say, "Lord, Lord" but give no evidence of following the example and modeling of Jesus Christ.

In the 1970s and 1980s, Rollen Stewart was a strange spokesperson for Christianity. At major sporting events he would maneuver himself in front of television cameras with his John 3:16 T-shirt and his rain-bow-colored Afro wig. Even though he continues to espouse the return of Jesus Christ in bodily form and the coming apocalypse, the words ring hollow because Rollen Stewart is serving three life-sentences for taking hostages. He has been married four times, and the last wife says he tried to choke her for holding his sign in the wrong place. "No one can meet my standards, but I don't recall ever hitting her," Stewart says.[12] Now in prison for also bombing churches and newspaper offices, he remains in the minds of many an inventive spokesperson for Jesus Christ. He used coded biblical references and symbols to make people, especially Christians, believe he was sincere in promoting the kingdom of God on earth, but his actions are evidence that he only uses the words of Christianity for self-promotion.

SYMBOLIC INTERACTIONISM THEORY AND WORD USAGE

Herbert Blumer coined the term *symbolic interactionism*, based on the writings of his mentor George Herbert Mead. "Conversing with one other" is the most naturally human activity that people can engage in and three core principles of this theory involve meaning, language, and thought."[13] First, *meanings* are assigned to people, events and actions, and word choices and the context of human dialogue are the means to this end. Second, meanings are discovered in the social interaction people have with each other. Our *language* usage helps clarify meaning but only through dialogue; meanings are in people, not in objects. There is a true sense that we negotiate and interpret meaning by active engagement with others; this is the interactionism effect. Meaning seems to be accentuated by the ability to "name" things. It was one of the first gifts granted to Adam by God in the Garden of Eden.[14] Third, meanings are modified by an individual's interpretation of symbols us-ing his or her own thought processes. In this highly intellectual activ-

---

[12]Rollen Stewart, quoted in Jerry Crowe, "Rainbow Man, Once Ever-Present, Shows His Dark Side," *Los Angeles Times*, May 19, 2008, sports sec., p. 2.

[13]Herbert Blumer, *Symbolic Interactionism* (Englewood Cliffs, N.J.: Prentice-Hall Publishers, 1969), pp.1-89.

[14]Em Griffin, *A First Look at Communication Theory*, 7th ed. (Boston: McGraw Hill, 2009), p. 61.

ity, we all understand more about those we have dialogue with, but perhaps we learn more about our own self. Interaction with others means that our interpretations and assigned meanings to words have an effect on how we think about ourself.

Since we primarily exercise this symbolic interactionism by words, what practical applications does this theory hold for us? There is a strong sense that by espousing words that link or identify us with Jesus Christ, we will follow his modeling and his teaching, found in the Bible. The active Christian involved in fellowship with other believers and Bible study will embrace an identity that is consistent with the reality of faith. We understand best how to fellowship, grow and mature in our faith as we walk a mile in the shoes of our fellow Christians. As Em Griffin says, "[George Herbert] Mead would have liked the wrangler who said the only way to understand horses is to smell like a horse, eat from a trough, and sleep in a stall. That's participant observation! Undoubtedly, the *Horse Whisperer* was a symbolic interactionist."[15]

Since the concept of naming is so essential to a sense of self, the names we call each other help as well as hurt. Perhaps no one shoots their wounded quite like active churchgoers. What needs to emerge from actively pursuing a symbolic interactionist perspective in our churches is a greater ability to listen, learn, pray, empathize and be involved in the healing process. We have a great role model. To a gathering of men ready to stone a woman caught in adultery Jesus Christ said, "If any one of you is without sin, let him be the first to throw a stone at her" (Jn 8:7). Jesus made it quite clear that only those without sin could "shoot" this wounded woman. Ironically, the only one without sin chose to forgive her and learn more about her through shared interaction and meanings.

CONCLUSION

So, words, words, words—we get in trouble using them, but we can't exist without them. We expand our ability to create meaning in life when we exercise the capacities that words allow. Using words as meta-

---

[15]Ibid, p. 63.

phors or similes gives us context and deeper understanding. Using words with care and sensitivity while embracing honesty and truthfulness may prove to be more daunting, but nevertheless it is our quest.

It is discouraging to admit that we probably spend more time explaining ourselves than saying what we intend accurately, truthfully and with sensitivity from the outset. Yet there is something profound in the thought that "in the beginning was the Word." To be fully imagined, something must be described with words. The very act of using words links us to the image of God, because using words is essentially creative.

A popular Christian worship song by MercyMe is titled "I Can Only Imagine." The lyrics express the inexpressible in an attempt to worship God Almighty. It must resonate with God because he delights in our praise, and words are the component we use to mount that praise. God uses so many passages to remind us of the power of words for good and for evil purposes. How we choose to use our words links us to the creative image of God.

Secular theorists can help us understand the semantic dimensions of our word choices, but only God can transform our choices into meaningful expressions that not only allow us to worship him but also to draw others toward him. Symbolic interactionism can help explain why we so desperately need to communicate to each other as well as with God, because in active and engaging dialogue we model God's relationship with us. But today the true power of our ability to communicate with others is merely a shadow of what we were created to do. Our roots lie with people, all people, who at one time spoke the same language and will do so again in another dimension—so Christians believe.

I like the concluding expressions that self-taught longshoreman and philosopher Eric Hoffer offered on these notions of understanding, clarity and meaning: "Quite often in history action has been the echo of words. An era of talk was followed by an era of events. . . . [However] action can give us the feeling of being useful, but only words can give us a sense of weight and purpose."[16]

---

[16]Eric Hoffer, *The Passionate State of Mind* (1955; reprint, New York: Buccaneer Books, 1998).

Paul tells us that after encountering the awesome living God an appropriate response is to try to persuade others of what we have come to know and experience (2 Cor 5:11). Yet, how can our attempts at persuasion be effective without being manipulative? We will explore the art and science of persuasion in chapter four.

Persuasion

Spiritual Power or Manipulation and Rhetorical Tricks?

"My message and my preaching were not with wise and
persuasive words, but with a demonstration
of the Spirit's power, so that your faith
might not rest on man's wisdom, but on God's power."

1 Corinthians 2:4-5

"I say this in order that no one
may delude you with persuasive argument."

Colossians 2:4 NASB

At the beginning of each new session of a required communication course titled "Persuasive Communication," I (Todd) read two passages (1 Cor 2:4-5 and Col 2:4) in which Paul apparently denigrates persuasive rhetoric. "So," I ask the students, "should we just all drop out of the class right now and not waste our time? Paul says that 'persuasion' is tantamount to manipulation or delusion, and as Christian leaders we should avoid it." The ensuing conversation with the students leads to a more enlightened discussion of Paul's own educational experience and what he was attempting to condemn.

Paul is certainly not condemning the practice or art of persuasive speaking, but rather the abuse and deceptions of rhetorical tricks. Since it was a core of the educational process for all first-century Roman citizens, Paul, a Roman citizen, would have been educated in the tenets of Greco-Roman rhetorical theories. But Paul cautions all Christians that the ability to use language devices to manipulate others to do whatever we want them to do is not remotely related to the true sharing of the Christian message. In this chapter we attempt to link persuasion-theory options to a fair and reasonable promotion of the gospel's life-changing concepts, primarily through evangelism, but not exclusively. Christians need to consider persuasive attempts to instill a quiet time or the better care of their own physical bodies or sexual purity or commitment to social or environmental justice. These resolutions are certainly worthy of consideration, but they need to be centered on the commitment to communicating consistently with the power of the Holy Spirit, not human wisdom.

EARLY CHRISTIAN RHETORICAL INFLUENCES

Duane Litfin, president of Wheaton College, makes the reasonable supposition that "if Paul was first educated in the Hellenistic university of Tarsus, a university that was known for its teaching in rhetoric, then this alone would be more than enough to account for the modicum of understanding we see in Paul."[1] Paul wanted to separate himself and his approach to public speaking from the notions of eloquence, snooty stylistic vocabulary words and arrogance that permeated the open-air pronouncements of sophists and local orators.[2] Paul would probably have known about Plato's accusations that rhetoric was mere flattery and was used by many sophists to manipulate court proceedings so that payments from opposing clients could find their way into greedy pockets.[3] Paul may have even encountered sophists in his travels that used

---

[1]Duane Litfin, *St. Paul's Theology of Proclamation: I Corinthians 1-4 and Greco-Roman Rhetoric* (Cambridge: Cambridge University Press, 1994), p. 139.

[2]Donald R. Sunukjian, "The Preacher as Persuader," in *Walvoord: A Tribute*, ed. Donald K. Campbell (Chicago: Moody Press, 1982), pp. 292-96.

[3]See Plato's scathing indictments of sophists in Plato *Gorgias*, trans. W. R. M. Lamb; and Plato *Phaedrus*, trans. H. N. Fowler, quoted in *Readings in Classical Rhetoric*, ed. Thomas W. Benson

"decorative rhetoric" to deceive the immediate audience.

It would be grossly unfair to characterize all sophists as inherently manipulative tricksters with a rhetorical turn of phrase. Despite Plato's indictments, some sophists taught and used their oratorical abilities with a commitment to truth and accuracy. Aristides, a sophist, spoke out in opposition to Plato's blanket indictments, emphasizing that the capacity to choose from among many persuasive options—"all that is better to be said"—brings rhetoric back to an ethical base.[4] When I finish up the conversation with my students about Paul's true intent in the Corinthians and Colossians passages, I immediately move to the classic definition and ethically based commitment to persuasion espoused by Aristotle as a counter to Plato's perspective: "Rhetoric is the faculty of observing in any given situation the available means of persuasion."[5] Paul thus is really saying that he does not want to be confused or linked in any way with the sophists of his day (or of ours, for that matter) who will lie and deceive to get people to follow their lead. "Your faith should not rest on the wisdom of men, but on the power of God," Paul reminds his listeners.

In attempting to emulate Paul's commitment to truth, the challenge for the Christian persuader today lies in the same tensions that faced Paul's use of first-century public speaking as the primary mode of mass communication. Litfin says that first-century audiences

> enjoyed the merely decorative [rhetoric] as well as the genuinely persua-
> sive and probably did not distinguish over much between the two. Both
> were considered powerful. . . . [So the task of the orator] was to discover
> and manipulate the mix of rhetorical possibilities inherent in the audi-
> ence, subject, and occasion that his purpose would be accomplished . . .
> to come as close to success as circumstances might allow.[6]

How relevant is this discussion of the tricks of sophistry? Today, the term *rhetoric* (usually accompanied by the adjective *mere*) embraces the clearly non-Aristotelian and non-Pauline notion that rhetoric is vacuous,

---

and Michael H. Prosser (Boston: Allyn & Bacon, 1969), pp. 3-42.
[4]Aristides *To Plato in Defense of Oratory* 185; cf. 382, quoted in C. H. Behr, *Aelius Aristides and the Sacred Tales* (Amsterdam: Adolf M. Hakkert, 1968).
[5]Aristotle *Rhetoric*, trans. W. Rhys Roberts (New York: Modern Library, 1954), p. 24.
[6]Litfin, *St. Paul's Theology of Proclamation*, pp. 133-34.

empty and distant from reality or truth. One political rival without the oratorical gifts and charisma of an opponent will play the "mere rhetoric" card, implying that there is no truth or substance to his or her pronouncements or plans. But even well-meaning Christians jettison the primary rhetorical notion of freedom-of-choice response, if the end result of their evangelism is saying the magic words: "I accept Christ as my personal Savior and Lord," no matter the means to get to that statement.

We must reembrace the decidedly pro-rhetoric and anti-sophistry notions that Paul addresses in his readers. There can be no manipulations or deceptions on behalf of Christ, because to use these tricks is to deny the power of God and the Holy Spirit. There are many who continue to say that they speak for Christ in our day, but the message of grace and mercy through faith in Christ can be skewed to unimportant decorative rhetorical rabbit trails that potentially lead people away from a meaningful relationship with Christ.

The current media darlings for evangelical Christians may have broad smiles on their faces and offer soothing encouragement, but we must constantly be on guard that what is pleasing to the ears and to the eyes needs to hold up to the standard of biblical truth and application. We often wish that intelligent and thoughtful Christians were interviewed on subjects of national interest or concern. I cringe at some sound bites from people who say they speak for Christianity when interviewed in the media. If we intend to restore true rhetoric and persuasion to its ethical and insightful base, we cannot offer "Christianity Lite" to talk-show hosts and TV reporters. We must be vigilant in our commitment to truth in our rhetoric seasoned with grace, not resorting to deception or rhetorical tricks. We must maintain the commitment to adapt to audiences using "all the available means in a given situation" with ethics and integrity of purpose. But while we do not want to use tricks to deceive people for a greater cause, we have to guard against boring our audience with trite and predictable jargon or marketing devices.

PRINCIPLES FOR UNDERSTANDING PUBLIC PERSUASION

Contemporary Christians, attempting to adapt persuasive efforts in our mass-communication-driven situations, are all too often rightfully criticized for being reactionary rather than proactive. We borrow heavily and without shame from popular culture with T-shirts, bumper stickers, music, Christian talk-show formats and the like. And our redundancy and predictability have repercussions for our attempts at persuasion.[7]

HIGH PREDICTABILITY LEADS TO LOW INFORMATION

Our culture now knows and is familiar with such terms and phrases as *born again, accept Jesus as personal Savior, get saved* and *God loves you and has a wonderful plan for your life*. It is common knowledge that the fish sign on our bumpers, especially the one eating the Darwinian fish, is a symbol for evangelical Christian. In our efforts to be separated from the world, we have created a smugness that has not enhanced our image, especially for the Mosaic generation (born 1984-2002) and the Busters (born 1965-1983). With the predictability of our messages and strategies has come the low or meager informative engagement with our culture.

David Kinnaman and Gabe Lyons provide groundbreaking research from the Barna Group in their book *UnChristian*, and the candid summaries of the research dismay all of us who believe in Christ.[8] Mosaics and Busters are skeptical of and object to evangelicalism because of these typical evangelical attitudes and behaviors, which are obstacles to persuasion as well:

- *Hypocrisy.* Christians give off an air of virtuous living, yet do not act accordingly with their own value systems.

- *Convert obsessed.* Though *evangelical* inherently suggests that Chris-

---

[7]See John Fiske, *Introduction to Communication Studies*, 2nd ed. (New York: Routledge, 1990), pp. 9-16. While "redundancy" can be helpful up to a point for review or reminders, "entropy" or "maximum unpredictability," as described by Fiske, halts communication. What makes communication artistic, however, is finding the formula to juxtapose redundancy and entropy so that insightful commentary surprises an audience with new information, couched in terms that sound predictable but are in reality novel and refreshing.

[8]The Barna Group is a highly respected research and resource organization located in Ventura, California. This organization, founded by George Barna, has designed and analyzed nearly five hundred projects for various clients, including the Billy Graham Evangelistic Association, Campus Crusade for Christ, Focus on the Family, InterVarsity Christian Fellowship, NBC-Universal and Time-Life.

tians tell others of their faith, the non-Christian feels like a "target," not a "person" who should receive care.

- *Hostility to homosexuals.* Outsiders believe that Christians are homophobic, bigoted and only want to transform homosexuals into heterosexuals.

- *Isolated/sheltered.* Outsiders think Christians do not understand the complexities of reality and only offer simplistic solutions without care or concern for others.

- *Politically conservative bias.* Extreme right-wing philosophy in politics is perceived as the only acceptable political response.

- *Judgmental.* Outsiders think that Christians evaluate others unfairly and seem smug and negative about others who are different.[9]

Rightfully or wrongfully, outsiders assume these themes will be evident in their communication styles and strategies of Christians. That outsiders have been hurt or misunderstood further exacerbates the problem of perception and seems to continue the stereotyped notions.

When Christians use insider language or jargon with outsiders, this highly predictable behavior conveys low information, failing to share the depth of what Christ offers to all who would accept his offer of grace and mercy. When Christians promote "Christian" movies with biblical story lines, altar calls or stereotypical conversions by felons on Death Row, the response of non-Christians is dismissal or "I've heard it before." Pop culture enhances this predictability when secular movies or contemporary songs (e.g., the conversion scene in the movie *There Will Be Blood* or the pop song "Believe") present the Christian message as hypocritical, irrelevant or innocuous.

The Christian effort to change perceptions is difficult because once we identify ourselves as Christians, the assumptions kick in immediately. Our persuasive task then must embrace another principle, which suggests an alternative approach.

---

[9]David Kinnaman and Gabe Lyons, *UnChristian: What a New Generation Really Thinks About Christianity . . . and Why It Matters* (Grand Rapids: Baker, 2007), pp. 29-30.

LOW PREDICTABILITY LEADS TO HIGH INFORMATION

Christians need to adopt a communication approach that is low in predictability and high in information. Notice that the principle is not "no predictability." The principle's value would be nullified if we were weird just to be weird. Being "off the wall" may only serve to convince outsiders that Christians are stupid and naive, incapable of even coherent intellectual dialogue or engagement.

Jesus Christ is the greatest example of the "low predictability, high information" principle at work. The Pharisees assumed that the Messiah would be a warrior king, the conqueror of Rome, wealthy and status-oriented, and especially grateful to the religious groups who maintained order while they awaited his arrival. Some of this thinking even affected Christ's followers. Judas seems to have determined that Jesus needed to be prodded to assume this political warrior and savior role in order to establish the Jewish kingdom on earth, and his betrayal was merely seen as a means to get Jesus moving in that direction. But Jesus did not come with high predictability; even his parables were layered with meaning, and it was not until he explained their meaning or the disciples brooded over their interpretation that this form of communication became clear.

Jesus demonstrated low predictability and high information by being a "friend of sinners" (Mt 11:19), especially tax collectors, prostitutes, lepers and the lower-caste members of his society. The Bible can't contain all of the stories and narratives that Jesus told or exemplified. His birth in Bethlehem, his encounter with the priests at the temple when he was twelve, his Sermon on the Mount, his raising of Lazarus from the tomb, his brutal scourging and death on the cross, his resurrection—all these and more instances reveal that Jesus' life was far from predictable, but he had untold amounts of information to share.

So how can we be persuasive without being highly predictable? As we share aspects of the Christian worldview, we will not be so pedantic and preachy that we provide answers to every possible question about personal salvation and devotion. I love the title of Bruce Bickel and Stan Jantz's 2008 faith-engaging book *I'm Fine with God . . . It's Christians I*

Can't Stand: Getting Past the Religious Garbage in the Search for Spiritual Truth.[10] You can laugh (or wince) at the examples of how we Christians are represented in the marketplace of ideas, but you have to admit that we sometimes are horrible ambassadors for the truth we so love.

Our evangelistic devices fail because they attempt to do too much. They should create opportunities for dialogue and discussion that can eventually lead to more prescriptive changes. Evangelistic devices are sometimes called *rhetorical artifacts* (e.g., sermons, Christian logo clothing, movies, TV shows, music lyrics) because they seem to be automatic means to persuade others with our important messages. We must move away from the notion that an artifact itself "saves" or "draws people to Christ." Human interaction, nonverbal encounters, symbolic gifts with no strings attached, dialogue, question-and-answer periods, and even admissions of ignorance (with the caveat of seeking to know the truth) allow the high-informational view of Jesus Christ to be shared and ultimately understood.

I love to hear about evangelical churches and groups that serve their communities with no expectations of reciprocal church attendance, donations or sitting through evangelistic meetings. My own church in Whittier, California, has for the past several years set aside one weekend in which the usual preaching services are not offered and the entire congregation is given the opportunity to volunteer to serve in hundreds of nonpaid projects throughout the community. Outsiders have asked, "Why are you doing this for free? What do you want from us?" We reply, "Nothing. We want to share the truth we believe and now practice that Jesus Christ came to serve others. This weekend we practice what we preach." What began as a single church experiment has been picked up by many other churches in our community. They give bottled water to runners in marathon races or mow peoples' lawns or give financial assistance and food to the homeless. The national press is taking notice as well, mentioning our church in news reports about volunteerism during economic downturns.[11] The low-predictability factor

---

[10]Bruce Bickel and Stan Jantz, *I'm Fine With God . . . It's Christians I Can't Stand* (Eugene, Ore.: Harvest House, 2008).

[11]"Last weekend, 1,100 of the Whittier Area church's 1,800 adult members were signed up to

(e.g., no expectations for attending church or raising their hands to be saved) leads to the high-information factor (e.g., perhaps there is something deeper to these Christians than at first glance; tell me more about this Jesus you serve). Our creativity and desire to reach people for Christ must now embrace the notion that sometimes we must commit ourselves to serving first, volunteering to solve social justice concerns, then gaining a respect to be heard at a later time.

THEORIES OF ATTITUDE CHANGE: IMPLICATIONS FOR CHRISTIAN PERSUASION

Within the academic study of communication one of the most appealing theories of attitude change leading to persuasion is the social-judgment theory. First espoused by Carolyn W. Sherif, Muzafer Sherif, Roger E. Nebergall and Carl I. Hovland,[12] the social-judgment theory proposes that attitude change can be seen as moving along a hypothetical continuum from various "latitudes" of rejection to noncommitment to acceptance:

/___/___/___/___/___/___/___/___/___/___/___/___/
-5   -4   -3   -2   -1   0   +1   +2   +3   +4   +5
Rejection   Non-Commitment   Acceptance

This theoretical explanation for attitude change is important for Christian persuaders to understand. For example, an evangelistic effort to present the claims of Christ may have begun with an individual whose cognitive response is at -4. After observing us and listening to our articulation of what it means to become a Christian, he or she may

---

help with more than 112 service projects in areas schools, hospitals, homeless shelters and other public sites." See Cathy Lynn Grossman, "In Times Like These, More People Are Going to Church for Help," *USA Today*, March 29, 2003 <www.usatoday.com/news/religion/2009-03-29-churches-helping_N.htm>.

[12]See Carolyn W. Sherif, Muzafer Sherif and Roger E. Nebergall, *Attitude and Attitude Change* (Philadelphia: Saunders, 1965); Muzafer Sherif and Carl I. Hovland, *Social Judgment: Assimilation and Contrast Effects in Communication and Attitude Change* (New Haven, Conn.: Yale University Press, 1961); Muzafer Sherif and Carolyn W. Sherif, "Attitude as the Individual's Own Categories: The Social Judgment-Involvement Approach to Attitude and Attitude Change," in *Attitude, Ego-Involvement, and Change*, ed. Carolyn W. Sherif and Muzafer Sherif (New York: Wiley), pp. 105-39.

have responded to an invitation to accept Christ with a "No, thanks," but cognitively moved from -4 to -3. Has this person embraced Christ as Lord and Savior? No, but persuasion has occurred because the hostility is not so pronounced. How many persuasive efforts will it take to have a person reach +5 and accept Christ? The answer is unknown and certainly not guaranteed, but multiple efforts can be normative prior to any persuasive conclusion.[13] What happens cognitively to persuasive efforts regarding evangelism over time? Obviously, not everyone who hears the gospel responds affirmatively, but the "still small voice" of the Holy Spirit can remind people of previously heard messages. Dormant arguments for faith in Christ may be remembered or accessed by an individual at a distant time period; dormant arguments can be powerfully self-persuasive at times.[14] We should never assume that an attempt at persuasion, especially one that seems to end in failure, is in the long term unsuccessful. Moving along the theoretical latitudes of rejection or acceptance takes time, but is most certainly progressive.

Charles E. Osgood and Percy H. Tannenbaum suggested that the theory of congruity, referring to the realm of agreement, correspondence or harmony, could be a natural beginning to persuasion and prediction of attitude change.[15] Congruent circles look like those in figure 4.1.

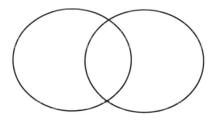

Figure 4.1. Congruent circles

[13]Robert Zajonc's 1968 hypothesis is that repeated exposure to a stimulus results in more favorable evaluation of that stimulus. Twenty-five repetitions seem to be the maximum for this "mere exposure" hypothesis before a point of diminishing return. (Now we know why certain television commercials get repeated so often.) See Charles Larson, *Persuasion: Reception and Responsibility.* 12th ed. (Boston: Cengage Learning, 2010), pp. 106-8.

[14]Larson, *Persuasion*, pp. 97-98.

[15]Charles E. Osgood and Percy H. Tannenbaum, "The Principle of Congruity in the Prediction of Attitude Change," *Psychological Review* 62, no. 1 (1955): 43.

The area of overlap represents the area of congruity. The theory of congruity supposes that if we begin with that overlapping area of agreement, we can work to increase the volume of agreement (overlapping congruency) in the future. Add to the overlapping area the notion offered up by psychologist Robert Zajonc that "repeated exposure to a stimulus results in more favorable evaluation of that stimulus" and we have a means to dialogue with people who share core beliefs.[16] This has particular insights for evangelical Christians who dialogue with devout members of a religious group that embraces similar but not all their theological positions. By emphasizing shared theological beliefs, the move to the next level of difference (e.g., outside the congruency) seems to be filled with less tension or resentment. To use another application, repeated exposure to Christian music heard on the radio or on iPods could influence a nonbelieving "music lover" to pay more attention to grace-infused lyrical content.

In our persuasive efforts with someone from another faith, the concept of *inoculation* is instructive.[17] The medical analogy implies that if we are given a nonlethal dosage of a foreign component, our body will build up resistance to the foreign component (e.g., counterarguments). The basic procedure for inoculating people against persuasive attacks consists of providing advanced knowledge of a counterargument, perhaps even an apologetic response. The theory posits that someone "inoculated" with a weaker form of the original argument should be less susceptible to future arguments and persuasive efforts.[18] Thus Christian apologetics is not merely useful as a means of countering an opponent's argument, but to strengthen our own faith through the concept of inoculation.

There is, however, a "dark side" to the inoculation theory. Some people are introduced to a form of Christianity, but not the essence of the faith. They are wooed to the faith by hit-and-run linguistic prom-

---

[16]Ideas presented in Larson, *Persuasion*, p. 106.

[17]W. J. McGuire, "Inducing Resistance to Persuasion: Some Contemporary Approaches," in *Advances in Experimental Social Psychology*, ed. L. Berkowitz (New York: Academic Press, 1964), 1:191-229.

[18]James B. Stiff and Paul A. Mongeau, *Persuasive Communication* (New York: Guilford Press, 2003), p. 287.

ises or T-shirt claims and offers, but some representatives of the faith do not consistently model the tenets of spiritual practice. The result is that some people may be inoculated with a strain of Christianity that may be inaccurate and incomplete, thus making future attempts at persuasion difficult. The scar tissues of previous links to something that passed for Christianity deflect persuasive efforts. Those inoculated against the true Christian faith resist efforts to embrace the message of true spiritual relationship with Christ.

Herbert Kelman offers another insightful persuasion theory for attitude change by means of the process of compliance, identification and internalization.[19] This process has implications for Christian persuasion especially. Kelman lays out the conditions for attitudes to occur as well as continue. At first, all that is asked for is basic *compliance.* Parents tell their young children to do something and the children obey. Compliance can be achieved later in life by accompanying rewards or opportunities to escape punishment. Private beliefs are irrelevant at this stage and many young people go to Bible studies or youth activities at the compliance stage. They like the group dynamic, they like the people in the group, or they like what the group offers them (e.g., food and fun activities).

Next, *identification* describes the attraction necessary for the attitude to continue as the compliant individual begins to find relational reasons to continue to attend the group. A special person or even a subgroup offers security, belonging or a sense of fulfillment not understood or achieved in other group settings.

Finally, *internalization* provides the individual with a supportable and ingrained attitude or even value congruency.[20] A genuine commitment to Christ as personal Lord and Savior would seem to occur at the internalization part of the process, but the reality of most Christian attempts at persuasion means that many dialogic encounters will be at pre-Christian compliance and identification stages. The danger for

---

[19]Herbert C. Kelman, "Processes of Opinion Change," *Public Opinion Quarterly* 25 (1961): 57-78.

[20]Raymond S. Ross and Mark G. Ross, Understanding Persuasion (Englewood Cliffs, N.J.: Prentice-Hall, 1981), pp. 92-93.

Christians is that many people can speak the vocabulary of committed Christianity at the compliance or identification stage, but true commitment does not occur until belief in Christ has been inculcated into the value system of the new convert.

Homeowners are approached by compliance-seeking salespersons who attempt to sell them products to enhance the value of their home. Some of these enhancements are merely replacements for worn-out original features of the home; other enhancements attempt to sell technological advances that are now standard in new homes. As I pondered two bids from competing vinyl-window-replacement companies recently, I realized that the "elaboration likelihood model" (ELM) of persuasion was being demonstrated in my living room.[21] Social psychologists Richard Petty and John Cacioppo indicate that "elaboration" in ELM refers to the conscious scrutiny and questions we ask in making an evaluative judgment about information we are given. We process this information on a *central route* with a slow, deliberate, well-reasoned thought process. (I asked many questions and listened to the sales appeals over an hour and a half period for each company.) We also may have a persuadable trait called the "need for cognition" (NFC) that ranges from those who love asking questions to those who just want to avoid thinking about the sale. At the opposite end of the elaboration continuum, people being persuaded use the *peripheral route* of information processing, which may seek out mental shortcuts, rules of thumb or even knee-jerk responses, seeking to make the persuasion process as brief as possible. The first window salespersons did not want me to hear a bid from a second company. They wanted me to access my peripheral route of information and make the decision to buy their windows *now!* The peripheral route of information approach is difficult to deny when the spokesperson is glib, handsome, slick and insistent, but the NFC factor probably needs to lean more toward the central route when important (and expensive!) issues are at hand.

---

[21]See Richard E. Petty and John Cacioppo, "Effects of Forewarning of Persuasive Intent and Involvement on Cognitive Responses and Persuasion," *Journal of Personality and Social Psychology* 37 (1979): 1915-26; Richard Petty and John Cacioppo, *Communication and Persuasion: Central and Peripheral Routes to Attitude Change* (New York: Springer-Verlag, 1986).

There are well-meaning Christian and evangelistic groups that act more in accord with the peripheral route approach, because they want as many people to come to Christ as possible, and time is of the essence. Still, a well-reasoned decision for Christ should, just as in buying windows, never be short-circuited or sped through.[22]

Fear and guilt appeals seem to be the preferred techniques for many Christian groups, but the residual negative reactions bode ill for attempting to rely on these approaches for persuasion and attitude change. Are there things we should be afraid of? Yes, of course there are. Imminent danger has a potent persuasive appeal. While the dosage of minimal, moderate and extreme fear messages has been studied since 1953, the reproduced findings vary, based on people's perceptions of the ability to handle the threat of fear, now called *efficacy*.[23] Certainly there seems to be little disagreement that minimal-fear appeals (e.g., merely talking about the dangers without going into graphic detail) have meager impact. The traditional view that moderate-fear appeals work best most often has to be tempered with the notion that sometimes strong, graphic imminent-fear appeals only work if the efficacy notion provides a means to overcome the obstacle containing the fear.[24] If there is a strong fear-appeal message coupled with a low-efficacy possibility (i.e., people truly feel threatened) then people respond with defensive *avoidance* or *denial*. So the Christian groups that attempt to literally "scare the hell out of their young people" by showing the graphic

---

[22]I did not yield to the appeal to make an immediate decision but waited for the second window bid. The second window bid had a comparable window, perhaps not as many "bells and whistles," but still a good window, and came in at $6,000 less than the first bid. We were thrilled with the second bid and love the windows *and* the money we saved by reasoned considerations of the information made available to us.

[23]Larson, *Persuasion*, p. 102.

[24]Jesus spoke more about hell than heaven. In Luke 12:5 he says, "I will show you whom you should fear: Fear him who, after the killing of the body, has power to throw you into hell. Yes, I tell you, fear him." The appeal is not graphic but certainly imminent and powerful and obviously truthful. Jonathan Edwards gained renown for his sermon "Sinners in the Hands of an Angry God." But understood in context that sermon uses a logical "method of residues" approach to dismiss all excuses for rejecting salvation through Christ until all that remains ("the residue") is to embrace the offer of salvation. The fear appeal of imagining that God holds us like a spider on a thin strand of web over the flames of hell resonated with a Calvinistic audience that already had heard about election and predestination. That appeal to fear had a basis in logical persuasion even more than an emotional reaction to an overt description of hell at its most graphic depiction.

Burning Hell movie or offer up *hell houses* for Halloween alternatives with torture chambers, aborted fetal materials, screams and general mayhem do more damage, sending young people away with scarred memories of what "Christians" are really about.

While fear appeals attempt to persuade through concern for the future, guilt appeals tend to focus on the omissions or practices of the past. Guilt appeals may result in immediate compliance, but rarely does this technique lead to identification and internalization levels of Christian commitment. Why do we let guilt have such a vice grip on our feelings and actions? Because we know our own past better than anyone. Timothy Borchers defines guilt as "a psychological feeling of discomfort that arises when order is violated."[25] We know that we have violated God's moral code. Only the jaded and cynical person refuses to admit that he or she has lived a perfect life. The very words we choose to use in interpersonal relationships tend to have built-in confrontations with what we should do and haven't done. "When we do what our language says is wrong, we experience guilt."[26] Guilt can be experienced individually or on a societal level. But if, as Kenneth Burke argues, guilt is created through language, we need to acknowledge that it is language choices that will help us manage our guilt.[27] Many Christian communicators feel free to use guilt-inducing language to gain compliance and behavioral changes, but they frequently leave out the means to manage and ultimately mollify the guilt. The language of repentance, acknowledging our guilt and desire to turn from our past, can be best understood when the source of the message is internal (i.e., a *conviction* about misconduct that originates from the Holy Spirit's work within us). The notion of good guilt must be redefined as an internalized guilt-management message that desires to make a person new, not suffer for past indiscretions or moral lapses. Christians who confuse their guilt-inducing messages with a desire to do the work of the Holy Spirit may be guilty themselves of usurping a vital role that

---

[25]Timothy A. Borchers, *Persuasion in the Media Age*, 2nd ed. (New York: McGraw-Hill, 2005), p. 195.

[26]Ibid.

[27]Kenneth Burke, *Language as Symbolic Action: Essays on Life, Literature, and Method.* (Berkeley: University of California Press, 1966), p. 16.

God's Spirit plays in each individual. A key notion is to listen to the still small voice, speaking internally about moral lapses, and ignore the external attempt to alter behavior.

Theories are only as useful as their practical applications. The theories mentioned in this section seem to have important applications for every Christian who would consider the role and activity of persuasion as essential to living out the Christian faith. But these theories have the potential for manipulation if not practiced or exercised with the overriding notion that everyone is free choose to accept or reject, without coercion, the offer of eternal salvation, personal physical care and well-being, and ultimate spiritual maturity. The ends never justify the means, even if the ends are couched in spiritual terminology. "Scaring the hell out of people" rarely occurs without serious and often misguided perspectives on God's nature. We all know people who sounded like committed Christians, but their language merely told us what we wanted to hear. To be genuine, persuasion must always be offered with the caveat that it is a personal choice. If Jesus was willing to let the rich young ruler walk away, so too must we be willing to let those we are attempting to persuade walk away, even when we know what the result of rejecting Christ's message will be.

CHARISMA

Aristotle names three modes of persuasion *(ethos, pathos* and *logos)* and these factors are instrumental in many different scenarios for influence and attitude change.[28] *Pathos* or emotional proof has the power to effect change, even immediate change, due to effective fear or guilt appeals. *Logos* tends to be reliant on statistics, testimonies, empirical evidence and personal narratives. *Ethos*, on the other hand, relies on the rather amorphous concept of source credibility and trustworthiness. Aristotle deemed *ethos* as the most powerful mode of persuasion, and a special subset of this concept, called *charisma*, can illustrate the power of this form of influence.

I focused my doctoral dissertation on a rhetorical study of charis-

---

[28]Aristotle *Rhetoric*, pp. 19-23.

matic communication and faith healers, building a rhetorical theory that attempted to garner explanations of the power of charisma from such fields as communication, psychology, sociology and history.[29] While I support the notion that charisma occurs only in the midst of a situational crisis that is social, religious or political in nature, there is also a notion that some leaders have such rhetorical gifts and they can use their dynamic delivery to influence people and persuade them to consider options, even if the situational crisis has not restricted choice options or perceptions. Specialized perceptions of a charismatic leader require that all possibilities in a social, religious or political crisis be so focused that following this leader is the only option an audience has. This occurs in times of war, economic depression, social upheaval, societal or political collapse, and medical terminal illness. Other societal occurrences that describe problems or issues of meaninglessness could generate a minicrisis that might create a smaller environment for a charismatic leader to emerge that would be less universal but nevertheless important. I believe that speakers can develop aspects of this charisma that truly do assist in the persuasive effort.

There is evidence that people respond well to beautiful and handsome people. People with reputations or family associations to greatness gain charisma by fiat. People able to articulate in simple but direct language that they have a vision for the future gain followers. The delivery pattern for most charismatic speakers tends to use shorter syllabic word choices, rapid delivery, short pauses, varied pitch patterns, volume variety and engaging dramatic personas. People with acting in their background bring with them to the speaker's rostrum a sensitivity to audience responses and the abilities to engage audiences in responsive opportunities.[30]

CONCLUSIONS

We have come full circle in a sense. The apostle Paul was concerned that no one judge his oratory by the standards of contemporary sophists

---

[29]Todd V. Lewis, "Charismatic Communication and Faith Healers: A Critical Study of Rhetorical Behavior" (Ph.D. diss., Baton Rouge: Louisiana State University, 1980). See also Todd V. Lewis, "Charisma and Media Evangelists: An Explication and Model of Communication Influence," *Southern Communication Journal* 54 (1988): 93-111.

[30]Ibid.

who might use tricks and devices to influence people. A highly charismatic leader/speaker can sound Christian but be heretical or deficient in depth of spiritual maturity or understanding of theology. Paul understood enough about rhetorical standards to attempt to adapt to his audience with references to their own cultural understandings. He does this admirably in the Mars Hill Address, even quoting the Greeks' own poets to build his case for Christianity. The Acts 17 reference indicates that Paul's persuasive effort had various effects: some sneered, some merely wanted to hear him again, but some men and women joined Paul and believed that what he said was the truth. Our own attempts to engage our popular culture will meet with similar responses, but we can increase the likelihood of being heard again if our attempts embrace the principle that "low predictability leads to high information."

We must not assume that even when we prayed for persuasive success that our observations or reliance on verbal-nonverbal responsiveness can be accurate because we do not know how the power of the Holy Spirit is working within the minds of our listening audiences. We may have been the means to move them along a continuum that brings them nearer to accepting Christ as Savior. We may have become the first evangelical to explain the congruent elements of true faith that can suggest that a more mature and correct faith awaits the true seeker. We must realize that, in particular, young people who may have come to our churches as compliant, identity-seeking pre-Christians may be waiting for us to bring the full knowledge of a commitment to Christ to their attention. Some people are so afraid of the future that they have difficulty living in the present, and yet we have the message of hope, grace and joy.

Some people may need to let go of the past and its guilt messages. We may be the means to help some people move on with their lives without dwelling on the imperfections of their past. If the term *Christian* was originally intended to mean "little Christ," then perhaps we should ask God to make us into the kinds of people who sound and act more like Christ, and less like highly predictable pseudosaviors with our own selfish motives driving our persuasion efforts. I'd love for someone to say to me, "He sounds like he's been with Jesus!" Then, I would know that my persuasive efforts were well-founded and clearly articulated.

PART TWO

APPLYING COMMUNICATION

5

BEFORE THE SUN SETS

CONFLICT AND CHRISTIAN UNITY

Jesus knows his death is imminent. Within hours a series of events will begin to quickly unfold: personal betrayal by a disciple, two hastily convened trials, scourging, public humiliation and crucifixion. To prepare, he gathers his disciples together for one last meal. During this time together, Jesus delivers his final instructions to them, commonly called the "Upper Room Discourse." While each of the Gospel writers mentions the significance of this time, only John goes into depth, sharing specifics of what Jesus said. A pivotal moment comes when Jesus tells his disciples: "A new command I give you: Love one another. As I have loved you, so you must love one another" (Jn 13:34).

The command to love others was far from new. The Old Testament commanded individuals to love others as they loved themselves and to even extend that love to foreigners (Lev 19:34). What was new is the focus of this love: Jesus' love for them. The love each of the disciples had experienced while following Christ would now serve as a standard of Christian love. Jesus tells them that the authenticity of their love for him would now be judged by their mutual love for each other. "By this all men will know that you are my disciples, if you love one another" (Jn 13:35). New Testament scholar Merrill Tenney sums up this startling claim: "The attitude of love would be the bond that would keep them united and would be the convincing demonstration that they had partaken of his own spirit and purpose."[1]

Jesus' command to love each other has relevance for all Christians. The central identifying feature of devotion to Christ is how we diligently pursue unity and resolve interpersonal conflicts that threaten it. Even if believers cannot fully resolve differences, how can conflict be managed in such a way that our witness is preserved? In light of Christ's command all believers have a vested interest in learning how to understand and resolve conflict.

INTENDING TO PURSUE CHRISTIAN UNITY

What will it take to foster the unity described by Christ? In his book *Renovation of the Heart*, Christian philosopher Dallas Willard argues that personal transformation is dependent on three necessary factors: vision, intention and means.[2] *Vision* refers to what a person wants to accomplish, be it learning a foreign language, losing weight or following Christ. The vision Christ lays out for us in the Upper Room Discourse is one of authentic love and unity among his believers. Jesus prays that present and future believers "all . . . may be one" (Jn 17:21). However, more than mere vision is required. *Intention* is the purposeful decision to bring a vision into reality through personal resolve and action. If Christian unity is to become a reality we must all intend to diligently resolve, to the best of our ability, our differences. *Means* are the practical instrumentalities needed to follow through on our intentions and accomplish our vision. A teenager's desire to pursue a driver's license (vision) will entail necessary means such as enrolling in driving school, going on practice runs with a parent and using a study guide for the driver's test.

If Christians are serious about addressing conflict within the Christian community, then we must have access to means that will help us

---

[1]Merrill C. Tenney, *John*, Expositor's Bible Commentary 9, ed. Frank E. Gaebelein (Grand Rapids: Zondervan, 1981), p. 142.

[2]Willard offers a useful acronym to remember vision, intention and means: "To keep the general pattern in mind, we will use the little acronym 'VIM.' As in the phrase, 'vim and vigor.' 'Vim' is a derivative of the Latin term *'vis'* meaning direction, strength, force, vigor, power, energy, or virtue; and sometimes meaning sense, import, nature, or essence" (Dallas Willard, *Renovation of the Heart: Putting on the Character of Christ* [Colorado Springs: NavPress, 2002], p. 85).

accomplish the vision of Christian unity. While Christ provides the vision, students of communication can provide the means for conflict resolution by defining conflict, understanding the role communication climates play in conflict and offering communication strategies that integrate biblical insight with communication theory.

Before defining conflict, a word should be said concerning the negative view many of us have of conflict and what communication scholars call the *inevitability of conflict*.

First, our perception of conflict influences how we approach disagreements with others. At marriage conferences I (Tim) often ask conferees to tell me the *first* word they think of when hearing the word *conflict*. Before I reveal what my conferees say, write down five words that come to mind when you think of conflict.

Are the words you've written negative, positive or neutral? Through the years the most common responses from people attending my marriage conferences are *war, hate, battle, lose, argument, rejection, explosion, sadness, anger* and *failure*. It is particularly interesting when individuals describe conflict by comparing it with something else like wars, battles or explosions. Samuel Hayakawa comments that the power of metaphors reveals how we think about something or someone.[3] If individuals perceive conflict as a battle or an explosion, then it is not surprising that they'll avoid conflict at all costs.

Instead of avoiding conflict, the Scriptures encourage believers to deal with conflict promptly. Paul admonishes us that if anger exists between two believers they should not "let the sun go down" while they are angry (Eph 4:26). Jesus tells a crowd that if while they are presenting an offering they remember that their "brother has something against you," they are to leave the gift and seek reconciliation (Mt 5:23).

Second, how we view conflict is important in light of what communication scholars call the *inevitability of conflict*. Studies focusing on conflict have centered on relationships between college students, family members, coworkers, friends, dating partners and spouses, to name a few. Their conclusion is that conflict is common, and in a sense, in-

---

[3]Samuel I. Hayakawa, *Language in Thought and Action*, 4th ed. (New York: Harcourt, Brace, Jovanovich, 1978).

evitable to all relationships. The inevitability of conflict means "that we should cease our efforts to find perfect people and learn how to manage the conflicts we are sure to have with those closest to us."[4] Due to this inevitability, we should not be surprised to see occasional conflict within the Christian community. Even though Paul exhorts the Philippians to "make my joy complete by being like-minded" and be "one in spirit and purpose" (Phil 2:2), he still has to intervene in a disagreement between Euodia and Syntyche and ask them to "agree with each other in the Lord" (Phil 4:2). Paul tells believers at Corinth that they have been called to be holy "together with all those everywhere who call on the name of our Lord Jesus Christ" (1 Cor 1:2). Yet, nine verses later he writes that he has learned there are "quarrels among you" (v. 11). Paul himself experienced conflict with Peter over Peter's decision to separate from Gentile Christians and eat only with Jewish Christians (Gal 2:11-14). Just as there are no perfect people outside the church, there are none inside.

The presence of conflict among believers, though regrettable, should not be entirely unexpected. Believers must also keep in mind that conflict resolution may not always be possible in every situation and is not the only goal. Relational communication scholars Joyce Hocker and William Wilmot describe four different goals central to interpersonal conflict: *content goals* focus on what individuals want; *relational goals* involve the type of relationship participants want to maintain or foster during conflict; *identity goals* focus on who participants want to be as they work out differences; and *process goals* include the communication strategies or means used to manage or resolve conflict.[5] Often, believers may strongly disagree on the content goal—what they hope to gain—while engaging in conflict with another.

In the early 1990s my wife and I (Tim), along with two other couples, lived in Vilnius, Lithuania, teaching at Vilnius University during the day and leading Bible studies at night. Lithuania had just broken free of Soviet

---

[4]Roxane S. Lulofs and Dudley D. Cain, *Conflict: From Theory to Action*, 2nd ed. (Needham Heights, Mass.: Allyn & Bacon, 2000), p. 11.
[5]William Wilmot and Joyce Hocker, *Interpersonal Conflict*, 5th ed. (Boston: McGraw-Hill, 1998), p. 56.

domination and there was an unprecedented interest in the spiritual aspect of life. For the first time, students and faculty could openly inquire about God, faith and Christianity. As the year progressed, we soon had a large number of students and faculty attending Bible studies (strictly forbidden under Soviet rule) all across campus and in our homes. With this growth came a strong difference of opinion between two couples on how to organize these groups and the content of the studies. These differences were rooted in differing theological convictions and ministry philosophies. These two couples viewed their convictions as incompatible and their objectives (content goals) as oppositional. Many late nights were spent trying to forge a compromise.

Yet, even in the midst of our team's disagreement, we still needed to pursue common relational goals (relating to each other as brothers and sisters united in a common faith) and identity goals (living and acting as disciples of Christ). Peter reflects relational and identity goals when he writes: "All of you, live in harmony with one another; be sympathetic, love as brothers, be compassionate and humble" (1 Pet 3:8). By struggling to keep all these goals in focus—not just ministry preferences (content goals)—we were able to keep the group intact as we sought to meet the spiritual needs of others.

Understanding conflict is not merely for those involved in ministry or for those living overseas. If you have roommates who have different standards for cleanliness, if you are required to do a group presentation for a class and feel some aren't carrying their load, if you have a falling out with other student leaders in your campus ministry, if you disagree with your parents about how you'll spend your summer, then it's crucial to understand how inevitable conflict can be managed and resolved. For individuals interested in resolving conflict, the first step is to carefully define it.

DEFINING CONFLICT

Building off the work of other theorists, Ronald Adler, Lawrence Rosenfeld and Russell Proctor offer this useful definition of conflict: "Conflict is an expressed struggle between at least two interdependent parties who perceive incompatible goals, scarce rewards, and interference from the other party in achieving their goals."[6] Each part of this definition warrants our attention.

Expressed struggle. From a communication perspective interpersonal conflict exists only if it is recognized or expressed by participants. For example, in writing to the church at Philippi Paul urges Euodia and Syntyche to work out their differences, which leads us to believe their disagreement was a public one (Phil 4:2-3). Yet, what if Euodia was angry with Syntyche but never communicated it? For the conflict to exist she must have communicated it in some manner. Communicating that she is angry can be done through both verbal ("I'm angry with you") or nonverbal (angry looks, walking out of the room when other person comes in, avoiding eye contact, tone of voice) ways. "One way or another, both people must know that a problem exists before it fits our definition of conflict."[7]

Perceived incompatible goals. We often view conflict through the lens of winners and losers. If you get what you want, it will come at my expense. Much attention has been given to a debate known as the "worship wars." Some members of a church want a praise band up front singing modern worship songs, while others argue for traditional hymns, choir and the inclusion of liturgy. While compromise is always an option (traditional service Sunday morning and contemporary service at a different time) conflict flourishes when individuals perceive only an either-or outcome.

Scarce rewards. Conflict is also fostered when individuals believe that there is a shortage of a particular psychological, emotional or material resource. Relational scholars Kathryn Rettig and Margaret Bubolz identified seven resources that couples value in long-term romantic relationships. In order of importance they were love, status, service, information, goods, money and shared time.[8] Dissatisfaction and conflict occurred when individuals perceive a shortage in one or more areas. While their research primarily focused on romantic relationships

---

[6]Ronald B. Adler, Lawrence B. Rosenfeld and Russell F. Proctor, *Interplay: The Process of Interpersonal Communication*, 10th ed. (New York: Oxford University Press, 2007), p. 334.
[7]Ibid.
[8]Kathryn D. Rettig and Margaret M. Bubolz, "Interpersonal Resource Exchanges as Indicators of Quality of Marriage," *Journal of Marriage and the Family* 45 (1983): 497-509.

the resources they identify are relevant to most interpersonal relationships. The resource of status, along with his own hurt ego, was at the heart of King Saul's conflict with David. After a young David kills Goliath, he is given a prominent place in Saul's army. When the Israelite army returns, they are met by women singing, "Saul has slain his thousands, and David his tens of thousands" (1 Sam 18:7). Saul views this adoration of David as a threat to his status and ego. He considers status a type of limited commodity that is being taken from him by David's growing popularity and becomes angry, resulting in a bitter conflict with David.

Interference from the other party. "However antagonistic they might feel, the people in a conflict are dependent upon each other. The welfare and satisfaction of one depends on the actions of the others."[9] To the disciples who heard the Upper Room Discourse, independence was not an option. The only way Christ's new commandment could be fulfilled—loving each other as Christ loved them—was through an interdependence with each other that focused on the welfare of the other.

From this definition of conflict several points can be made. First, if disagreements exist between followers of Christ, they need to be expressed. We seek to resolve conflict with other believers because we are "all members of one body" (Eph 4:25). We are called to be proactive in resolving tensions or disagreements that would harm our collective unity. When the conflict came up among the six of us teaching and ministering at Vilnius University, it was not an option for us to simply ignore our conflict and go about our business. Since we were "members of one body" we needed to express our differences and seek a resolution. While resolution is not always possible, we needed to address—and hopefully repair—our Christian unity. Our decision to follow Christ is *also* a decision to form relationships with fellow believers. The apostle Paul's favorite metaphor for this community of believers is the *human body*: "For we were all baptized by one Spirit into one body—whether Jews or Greeks, slave or free—and we were all given the one Spirit to drink" (1 Cor 12:13). Paul's image of a body implies a vital relational

---

[9]Adler, Rosenfeld and Proctor, *Interplay*, p. 335.

interconnectedness between those of us who make up Christ's body.

Second, believers must acknowledge and embrace our interdependence. Adler, Rosenfeld and Proctor note "many conflicts remain unresolved because the people fail to understand their interdependence."[10] The spiritual interest of students on that Lithuanian campus forced us to recognize that we needed to work together as a team to meet those needs. If we splintered into separate groups, or couples, then our effectiveness would be greatly diminished.

To keep the church body healthy and unified we must all make a commitment to recognize and address conflict. A first step to resolving conflict is to acknowledge the crucial role communication climates play in interpersonal conflict.

COMMUNICATION CLIMATES

As soon as two people begin to communicate, a communication climate begins to take shape. "The term communication climate refers to the emotional tone of a relationship."[11] Climates can either be positive or negative and are determined by "the degree to which people see themselves as valued."[12] If a communication climate is overly negative or disconfirming, then not only is conflict magnified but attempts to resolve conflict are greatly compromised. The research of Jack Gibb identified six forms of communication that moved individuals toward a defensive climate and six that produced a more supportive climate.

Evaluation versus description. We tend to become defensive when our thoughts are quickly critiqued or evaluated. Alternatively, when our opinion is talked about in a descriptive fashion, that is, by describing actions or values without passing judgment, we are more likely to feel safe and supported. For example, "You seem to be angry lately" (descriptive) as compared to "You are being too emotional" (evaluative).

Neutrality versus empathy. When speaking with a person, we can become defensive if we perceive our thoughts, passions, experiences

---

[10]Ibid.
[11]Ibid., p. 302.
[12]Ibid., p. 303.

and convictions are met with a type of detached, distant neutrality. However, when our views are met with empathy and acknowledgment of hurts or struggles, we feel valued.

Strategy versus spontaneity. Strategy language is evidenced by manipulation and control. We understandably feel manipulated when we sense the other person is involved in a type of mental chess match. Every response is a calculated part of some overarching plan that will ultimately benefit the other. In contrast, the central characteristic of spontaneous communication is openness and honesty resulting in a conversation that is unpremeditated or contrived.

Controlling versus problem orientation. Similar to a strategy approach, controlling communicators attempt to manipulate the conversation and force their perspective on others. Problem-oriented communicators seek, as much as possible, to discover solutions that are beneficial and equitable to everyone.

Certainty versus provisionalism. Certainty language, Gibb noted, is laced with a dogmatism that asserts that a communicator's views and beliefs are unshakable and absolute. Provisionalism communicates openness to the views and perspectives of others. While certainty language discourages alternative views, provisionalism welcomes such views by expressing a willingness to reconsider long held positions and convictions.

Superiority versus equality. Most of us feel more comfortable when interacting with other individuals who treat us with a sense of equality rather than inferiority. We become defensive when we encounter others who project an attitude of superiority.

Gibb concluded that evaluation, neutrality, strategy, controlling, certainty and superiority would foster a defensive climate, while description, empathy, spontaneity, problem-orientation, provisionalism and equality would create a positive one.

In addition to the communication styles identified by Gibb, scholars have also isolated a key feature of communication climates—trust. To understand the important role trust plays in communication climates, stop reading and think of a person you trust completely: a parent, sibling, best friend or spiritual mentor. Now, think of a person you don't trust; a person whose intentions or motives you can never really trust. Do you see the difference? For this reason, researchers continually identify trust as a foundational characteristic of healthy communication climates and relationships.[13]

The problem is that the circle of people we trust is tragically becoming smaller. With alarming regularity various media report on politicians, clergy, sports figures and presidents being caught in lies. Young athletes have grown up in the steroids era and now look at sports heroes with a suspecting eye. The cumulative result, suggests Ronald Arnett, is a hermeneutic of suspicion. "A hermeneutic of suspicion is the result of a generalized lack of trust in existence that encourages us to interpret daily communication actions from a vantage point of mistrust and doubt."[14] A lack of trust becomes deeply problematic for communication when it becomes the "interpersonal norm, rather than an occasional response."[15] If the communication climate is marked by mistrust a person "begins to question what is stated and looks for an unstated real answer, which begins a cycle of distrust and suspicion in everyday existence."[16]

If a lack of trust exists between individuals, any attempt to effectively communicate or resolve differences will be compromised. For this reason Paul writes to the believers at Ephesus that they should "put off falsehood and speak truthfully" to others (Eph 4:25). He reminds the Colossian church that since they have taken off the old self they should "not lie to each other" (Col 3:9). The valuing of truthfulness is presented in the book of Proverbs, which contrasts honesty with lying. Referring to a Persian custom of trusted friends greeting each other with a kiss, an "honest answer is like a kiss on the lips" (Prov 24:26).[17]

---

[13]See Jill Doner Kagle, "Are We Lying to Ourselves About Deception?" *Social Service Review*, June 1998, pp. 234-44; Joseph Veroff, "Marital Commitment in the Early Years of Marriage," in *Handbook of Interpersonal Commitment and Relationship Stability*, ed. Warren H. Jones and Jeffery M. Adams (New York: Plenum Press, 1999), pp. 149-62.

[14]Ronald C. Arnett, "Existential Homelessness: A Contemporary Case for Dialogue," in *The Reach of Dialogue: Confirmation, Voice, and Community*, ed. Rob Anderson, Kenneth Cissna and Ronald Arnett (Cresskill, N.J.: Hampton Press, 1994), p. 238.

[15]Ibid.

[16]Ibid.

[17]William McKane, *Proverbs: A New Approach* (London: SCM Press, 1970).

In contrast, a lying tongue both hurts and hates the recipient of the lie (Prov 26:28).

Anyone desiring to address conflict with another must first assess and adapt communication goals to the existing communication climate. The writers of Proverbs state that an "offended brother is more unyielding than a fortified city" and the dispute between individuals can be as formidable as "the barred gates of a citadel" (Prov 18:19). In commenting on this verse, Old Testament scholar Derek Kidner notes that interpersonal disputes can create walls that are easy to erect yet hard to demolish.[18] Any attempt to resolve conflict with this offended brother would not only be futile in such a negative climate but could make the climate more disconfirming. The overall communication climate described in this proverb must be addressed first before most conflict resolution strategies can be utilized.

Having defined conflict and examined the importance of communication climates, we are now ready to focus on how conflict can be addressed and hopefully resolved.

COMMUNICATION PRINCIPLES FOR CONFRONTING CONFLICT

While it is impossible to go into detail concerning the plethora of communication principles useful in addressing interpersonal conflict, three will be considered: conflict assessment, writing the third story and empathy.

Conflict assessment. "Preparation is the most extensive and, in many ways, the most important stage of the confrontation process."[19] The actions we take before engaging in conflict with another person will largely determine the outcome. Key to our preparation is what conflict experts Roxane Lulofs and Dudley Cahn describe as *conflict assessment*. The first step is to write a description of the conflict from your perspective. This narrative should reflect both the content and relational levels of communication mentioned in chapter two. Once this narrative

---

[18]Derek Kidner, *Proverbs*, Tyndale Old Testament Commentaries 15, ed. D. J. Wiseman (Downers Grove, Ill.: InterVarsity Press, 1964).

[19]Rory Remer and Paul de Mesquita, "Teaching and Learning the Skills of Interpersonal Confrontation," in *Intimates in Conflict: A Communication Perspective*, ed. D. Cahn (Hillsdale, N.J.: Lawrence Erlbaum, 1990), p. 229.

is written, four broad categories and corresponding questions should be answered. For example, in considering the background of the conflict the following should be considered:

1. What set off the conflict?

2. Explain the conflict from your perspective.

3. Explain the conflict from the other person's perspective.

4. What kinds of emotions does the conflict arouse in you?

5. Why do you think you feel the way you do about the conflict?[20]

A significant benefit of taking time to assess conflict before bringing up conflict with a person is that it provides a person distance from the conflict in order to gain perspective and let powerful emotions settle.[21]

The importance of conflict assessment became apparent to me (Tim) when tension arose between me and a copresenter at a conference on creativity. While the woman I was speaking with was a talented speaker, we disagreed concerning how we should prepare for our presentation. She valued spontaneity and wanted to work from a loose outline, while I wanted to work from a manuscript that clearly broke up the material. Tension turned to conflict as the conference approached. Before we met to talk it out, I found it beneficial to work through the questions suggested by Lulofs and Cahn.

The question I found particularly helpful was, "Why do you think you feel the way you do about the conflict?" As I thought about this question, I remembered a speaking engagement in which I felt unprepared and hurried. The month leading up to the event had been packed with family and professional responsibilities resulting in my speaking from a legal pad filled with scribbled, disjointed thoughts. From my perspective the presentation was disappointing. My performance made me think of a humorous quote concerning public speak-

---

[20]For a complete list of categories and questions see Lulofs and Cain, *Conflict*, pp. 360-63.

[21]Caryl E. Rusbult, "Responses to Dissatisfaction in Close Relationships: The Exit-Voice-Loyalty-Neglect Model," in *Intimate Relationships: Development, Dynamics, and Deterioration*, ed. Daniel Perlman and Steve W. Duck (London: Sage, 1987).

ing: "Do you ever think that your speech is a boring dinner party you can't leave, because you're the one giving it?" The thought of speaking at another conference from a loose outline on a topic outside my expertise made me relive the emotions of that night. Doing a conflict assessment helped me recognize and later articulate why I was opposed to my copresenter's preferred speaking style.

Once we reflect on the specific conflict situation and analyze choices of how to approach conflict, we must carefully decide how to bring up the conflict to the other person. How we broach conflict with another person is crucial and is often a struggle for many of us. Members of the Harvard Negotiation Project offer a useful strategy described as "the third story."

The third story. Professional mediators Douglas Stone, Bruce Patton and Sheila Heen suggest that most of us make a mistake in resolving conflict with another person in how we *start* a conversation:

> Often, we start from inside our own story. We describe the problem from our own perspective and, in doing so, trigger just the reactions we hope to avoid. We begin from precisely the place the other person thinks is causing the problem. If they agreed with our story, we probably wouldn't be having this conversation in the first place.[22]

The authors argue that in every dyadic conflict there are three stories, not two. Every disagreement includes each participant's story and an invisible third story. The third story is "one a keen observer would tell, someone with no stake in your particular problem."[23] The key to starting a difficult conversation is to begin with your version of the third story. "Specifically, this means describing the problem between parties in a way that rings true for both sides simultaneously."[24]

Telling the third story from your perspective entails risk. The third story will only be effective if you describe the problem in such a way that acknowledges the complexity and validity of the other person's

---

[22]Douglas Stone, Bruce Patton and Shelia Heen, *Difficult Conversations: How to Discuss What Matters Most* (New York: Penguin Books, 1999), p. 148.

[23]Ibid., p. 150.

[24]Ibid., p. 151.

intentions, desires and goals. If the third story comes across as favoring the position of the one giving it, then the third story could actually turn a disconfirming communication climate even more negative. For example, consider the disagreement I had with my copresenter at the creativity conference. A third story would perhaps sound like this:

> Both of us are excited about speaking at the conference and we both want to do well. Each of us wants to be prepared, but we have different ideas of what that preparation looks like. Neither of us is comfortable with the other's approach.

If the third story is told in a manner that acknowledges the validity of both perspectives it can be powerfully confirming. "Confirmation does not mean that one is simply treated nicely, or that one is always agreed with, or that anything one does is OK and that one is never corrected or punished. Confirmation means, simply yet profoundly, being recognized."[25] The confirmation found in a well-told third story can greatly increase a positive communication climate and in turn make conflict resolution strategies more effective.

Empathy. Sally Planalp argues that emotions are a powerful indicator of how we view the world.[26] The more powerful the emotion the more strongly we feel that something isn't right or that an injustice has been committed. If our emotions or perspective is ignored, conflict resolution will become increasingly unlikely. In light of this, scholars regard empathy as the "pinnacle of listening" and argue that empathy can facilitate successful conflict resolution.[27] While definitions of empathy can be complex, Adler and Rodman's definition is useful: "Empathy is the ability to re-create another person's perspective, to experience the world from the other's point of view."[28] The call to empathy is vividly expressed by the writer of Hebrews in encouraging believers to

---

[25]Rob Anderson, Kenneth Cissna and Ronald Arnett, "Dialogue's Confirmation," in *The Reach of Dialogue* (Cresskill, N.J.: Hampton Press, 1994), p. 71.

[26]Sally Planalp, *Communication and Emotion* (Thousand Oaks, Calif.: Sage, 1999).

[27]See Mark H. Davis, *Empathy: A Social Psychological Approach* (Boulder, Colo.: Westview Press, 1996); Elaine Hatfield, John T. Cacioppo and Richard L. Rapson, *Emotional Contagion* (Cambridge: Cambridge University Press, 1994).

[28]Ronald Adler and George Rodman, *Understanding Human Communication*, 9th ed. (New York: Oxford University Press, 2006), p. 43.

empathize with persecuted Christians. We are called to not only "remember those in prison" who are mistreated but to do so "as if you yourselves were suffering" (Heb 13:3). We are directed to imagine prison life, and all the emotions associated with it, through the perspective of those imprisoned.

Empathy powerfully communicates to the person you are having conflict with that you care about him or her and the emotions the conflict is surfacing for him or her. Remember that Gibb noted that defensive climates take shape when our perspectives are met with detached neutrality that fails to acknowledge our emotions or passions. Stone, Patton, and Heen of the Harvard Negotiation Project advocate that acknowledging someone's emotions means "letting the other person know that what they have said has made an impression on you, that their feelings matter to you, and that you are working to understand them."[29]

When my copresenter and I met to address our differing ideas of preparation, empathy played a key role in understanding each other's views. She explained to me that she had spent years studying creativity and was greatly looking forward to sharing her views at this conference. Because she had so much to say, she feared that scripting our comments would restrict her from sharing her passions and that a talk on creativity might come across flat and *uncreative*. Acknowledging her fears and emotions and seeing the conflict through her perspective helped me appreciate her side of the disagreement. Once she felt heard, we were able to agree on a compromise that combined both our preferences. Our presentation was a success.

The ability to effectively utilize the communication principles described earlier will be greatly challenged by the reality and presence of sin in the very individuals seeking to resolve conflict.

THE EFFECT OF SIN ON COMMUNICATION

God's intention for our world is shalom. "Shalom," notes theologian Cornelius Plantinga Jr., "means universal flourishing, wholeness, and

---

[29]Stone, Patton and Heen, *Difficult Conversations*, p. 106.

delight."[30] When Old Testament prophets spoke of a coming new age marked by shalom, they envisioned human communities knit together in affirming, flourishing relationships. Sin then is a "disruption of created harmony."[31] This disruption of shalom is evidenced by human sins of commission and omission. Sins of commission consist of actions God has prohibited, such as sexism, racism, misogyny, violence, deceitfulness and lying. Sins of omission comprise actions God requests of us—generosity, neighbor love, social justice, truth telling, compassion—that we refuse or neglect to do. It should not surprise us that in a world where God's shalom has been ruptured, humans would experience relationships marked by conflict and an absence of peace.

Quentin Schultze, a communication scholar focusing on religious communication, notes that sins of commission and omission have characterized our communication in a world devoid of shalom. "We commit sins of omission when we fail to communicate what and when we should."[32] Specifically, in our communication with others we are "gripped with laziness or fear, we stay out of conflicts and awkward situations. Sometimes we even abusively refuse to communicate with people we consider inferior or unworthy. We repeatedly fail to speak when we should, blithely assuming that time will heal the injury."[33] Sins of commission occur in communication when we "spread distorted, selfish, and manipulative information. We lie, defame, verbally abuse, and gossip."[34] Schultze concludes, "Unless we recognize the reality of sin, we will wrongly assume that all we need for better communication is a bit more common sense, greater education, or additional practice."[35] A Christian view of communication must seriously acknowledge how the reality and presence of sin disrupts our ability to resolve or manage conflict and speak the truth in love.[36]

---

[30]Cornelius Plantinga Jr., *Not the Way It's Supposed to Be: A Breviary of Sin* (Grand Rapids: Eerdmans, 1995), p. 10.

[31]Ibid., p. 5.

[32]Quentin J. Schultze, *Communicating for Life: Christian Stewardship in Community and Media* (Grand Rapids: Baker Academic, 2000), p. 75.

[33]Ibid., p. 76

[34]Ibid.

[35]Ibid., p. 75.

[36]Schultze makes an interesting comment concerning truth (a powerful precondition for con-

CONCLUSION

Years before Jesus' last meal with his disciples he stood on a mountainside and delivered to the crowd what would later be called the Beatitudes. In them Jesus reveals that there is one activity that if undertaken would earn individuals the title "sons of God." What activity could possibly earn such an affirmation? "Blessed are the peacemakers," Jesus declares (Mt 5:9). When Christians love each other with Christ's love, diligently seek to resolve conflict and engage in peacemaking, those outside our community will take notice and know we are followers of Christ.

To be effective peacemakers requires that we learn to embrace God's forgiveness and pass it on to others. As we will see in chapter six, granting forgiveness is often a challenge. "Every one says forgiveness is a lovely idea," notes C. S. Lewis, "until they have something to forgive."[37]

---

flict): "The discernment of truth is a hassle that gets in the way of our pragmatic needs for success and self-fulfillment, and grow increasingly callous to the impact of our deceptive communication with our neighbors. . . . Veracity is disappearing from public life. We emphasize effectiveness over truthfulness, impact over honesty" (ibid., p. 85).

[37]C. S. Lewis, *Mere Christianity* (New York: Macmillan, 1960), p. 89.

6

COMMUNICATING FORGIVENESS

L. Gregory Jones, professor of theology and dean of Duke University Divinity School, reminds us that

> the purpose of forgiveness is the restoration of communion, the reconciliation of brokenness. Neither should forgiveness be confined to a word to be spoken, a feeling to be felt, or an isolated action to be done; rather, it involves a way of life to be lived in fidelity to God's Kingdom.[1]

According to Jones, noted theologian Dietrich Bonhoeffer understood that the act of asking for and giving forgiveness was at root level "a craft that must be learned . . . and embodied over time as people seek to become holy in communion with God and one another."[2] The certainty of forgiveness can only be known to the person asking and the person receiving when an act is communicated or written. And forgiveness is most definitely heard and understood by a fellow believer from within a community of Christians.[3] The ramifications are overwhelming: when Christians demonstrate that they can forgive each other, others in the vast communities of unbelievers will take note of something remarkable and unusual, to say the least.

As noted in chapter five, the ongoing task for the community of

---

[1]L. Gregory Jones, *Embodying Forgiveness: A Theological Analysis* (Grand Rapids: Eerdmans, 1995), p. 5.

[2]Ibid, p. 13.

[3]Dietrich Bonhoeffer writes, "As the open confession of my sins to a brother insures me against self-deception, so, too, the assurance of forgiveness becomes fully certain to me only when it is spoken by a brother in the name of God" (Dietrich Bonhoeffer, *Life Together*, trans. J. W. Doberstein [New York: Harper & Row, 1954], pp. 116-17).

Christians is to seek divine guidance and assistance in resolving or managing conflict, actively seeking to make peace with one another. This, of course, frequently leads to the need to communicate forgiveness with one another.

For about twenty-five years I (Todd) taught a communication course titled "Pragmatic Social Theories of Communication." One of the pragmatic topics in this course was "communicating forgiveness." I had no idea how this topic would illustrate the tedious journey of navigating the tensions of Christian communication. And little did I realize how many old as well as recent "wounds" I would reopen by delving into this deeply personal topic. But over the years I received more letters and e-mails thanking me for broaching the subject than for any other class I taught.

In this chapter I will juxtapose academic commentary about the act of forgiveness along with several of my own personal stories to focus attention on giving as well as receiving forgiveness among the body of Christ.

INITIATING THE COMMUNICATIVE ACT OF ASKING FOR FORGIVENESS

Formulas on asking for forgiveness are necessarily fluid and nonprescriptive. If we merely followed a three- or four-step process, the result might all too frequently sound disingenuous and trite. Marriage and family therapist Terry Hargrave offers this basic definition of forgiveness: "Generally, the word *forgive* means to cease to feel resentment against an offender."[4] Educational psychologists Robert Enright and David L. Eastin researched theological, philosophical and psychological writings to discover that the idea of forgiveness includes "the casting off of deserved punishments, the abandonment of negative reactions, the imparting of love toward the other person, self-sacrificial nature, the potential restoration of the relationship, and positive benefits for the forgiver."[5] That definition sounds ambitious and perhaps naive as well. But there are some communicative acts that assist the forgiveness process.

Assuming that both parties acknowledge and agree on what the in-

---

[4]Terry D. Hargrave, *Families and Forgiveness* (New York: Brunner/Mazel, 1994), p. 339.
[5]Robert D. Enright and David L. Eastin, "Interpersonal Forgiveness Within the Helping Professions: An Attempt to Resolve Differences of Opinion," *Counseling and Values* 36 (1992): 88.

fraction was (not always something that can be assumed but must be indicated), both parties must provide the opportunity for a damage report as well as the opportunity for some type of apology from the offender for the damage caused.[6] Psychologists Michael McCullough, Everett Worthington and Kenneth Rachal found strong evidence to suggest that a verbal apology is needed before the relationship can be renegotiated.[7] But not all researchers, counselors and writers agree that a verbal apology is necessary or even likely in some cases. A possible alternative might be a nonverbal apology that has one person look the other in the eyes, hug him or her, and behave differently or act nicer.[8] Lewis Smedes expects that perpetrators of pain must truly understand "the reality of what they did to hurt you."[9] But short of a blow-by-blow apology, Smedes indicates that no two people in the history of misunderstandings have ever remembered their painful experience in the same colors and the same sequences, because no two people have experienced the same hurt in precisely the same way. . . . [However,] they must feel the hurt that you feel.[10]

Whether or not a direct apology is offered, communication forgiveness strategies must involve the forgiver *directly* addressing the offense with the offender. This is accomplished by such things as discussing the issue, having the forgiver express forgiveness to the offender, and possibly using a third party to mediate the issue.[11]

How do we know that discussions by forgiver and offender have led to a positive result and change in behavior? Kelley indicates that participants in the forgiveness process knew they had been forgiven when the relationship returned in time to a state of normalcy. Time is a key

---

[6]Douglas L. Kelley, "Communicating Forgiveness," in *Making Connections: Readings in Relational Communication*, ed. Kathleen M. Galvin and Pamela J. Cooper, 3rd ed. (Los Angeles: Roxbury, 2003), p. 225.

[7]Michael F. McCullough, Everett L. Worthington, and Kenneth C. Rachal, "Interpersonal Forgiving in Close Relationships," *Journal of Personality and Social Psychology* 73 (1997): 321-36.

[8]Julia T. Wood, *Relational Communication: Continuity and Change in Personal Relationships*, 2nd ed. (Belmont, Calif.: Wadsworth, 2000), p. 234.

[9]Lewis Smedes, *Forgive and Forget: Healing the Hurts We Don't Deserve* (New York: Pocket Books, 1984), p. 52.

[10]Ibid.

[11]Kelley, "Communicating Forgiveness," p. 227.

element because in many cases time is needed to restore the trust factor in the relationship.[12]

Both offender and forgiver have much at stake in the process of forgiveness. Using interpersonal communication discussion opportunities to identify the sources of hurt, acknowledging that hurt was imparted and desiring to restore a relationship makes forgiveness possible. And it does so for a very good reason. As R. P. Walters states, "When we have been hurt we have two alternatives: be destroyed by resentment, or forgive. Resentment is death; forgiving leads to healing and life."[13]

FORGIVING OURSELVES AND OTHERS IS A PROCESS

I received a personal letter in 2008 from a 1988 graduate who needed to apologize and ask my forgiveness for a "sin" he felt he committed some twenty years earlier. He said that he had called me "fat and ugly" under his breath, but I had honestly never heard the comment. The student went on to acknowledge his anger issues while a student and said that he felt the need to put someone else down to feel better about himself. He acknowledged that he was better adjusted now, but back in 1988 everything about his life was such a mess. He thanked me in advance for "forgiving him."

I felt terrible for this young man after reading his letter. He had carried this burden for such a long time—and the reality is I don't remember the incident, nor do I remember the context for such comments. He never hurt my feelings or caused me harm, because I never knew about the comments. I wrote him back and told him it was time to let this go, to move on with his life and that, most certainly, I forgave him.

> Please, please let this go now. You've held onto this thought, this memory for almost twenty years, and I give you permission to let it go. Experience fully the grace that God has always wanted you to feel in this matter.

---

[12]Ibid., p. 230.
[13]R. P. Walters, "Forgiving: An Essential Element in Effective Living," *Studies in Formative Spirituality* 5 (1984): 366.

I am convinced that we must begin to communicate forgiveness by obviously asking God's forgiveness for our sin, but since he desires to impart his grace to us, we must also learn to *forgive ourselves*. In his most uplifting, deeply life-changing book titled *What's So Amazing About Grace?* Philip Yancey reminds us of the faithfulness of God to forgive sin when we ask for it. What is more difficult to understand is why we tend to be harder on ourselves than God is. We expect God to forgive us because he says he will. But we punish ourselves far too long for sins that have been forgiven and are frequently forgotten by the one harmed. In order to live healthy lives we must communicate intrapersonally that we forgive ourselves and can now move on with life.

Marshall Rosenberg, conflict mediator for the Center for Nonviolent Communication, imagines what that kind of intrapersonal communication might sound like:

> We ask ourselves, "When I behaved in the way which I now regret, what need of mine was I trying to meet?" I believe that human beings are always acting in the service of [personal] needs and values. This is true whether the action does or does not meet the need, or whether it's one we end up celebrating or regretting. . . . Self-forgiveness occurs the moment this empathic connection is made.[14]

I ask my students two related questions: How do you feel when God forgives you? How do you feel when you forgive others? The responses to the first question typically are "clean," "relieved," "unworthy," "too easy." The responses to the second question were similar with a couple of exceptions: "unsatisfied," "glad I made them feel better, but I still feel the same," "distrustful; I still remember the pain." Lewis Smedes breaks down the communication process for forgiveness into stages that would require a separate chapter each (as they do in his book), but seeing the process as a whole reminds us that *communicating forgiveness is a process, not merely an act*.[15] Smedes reminds us that people forgive slowly, with a little understanding, in confusion, with anger left over, a little at a

---

[14]Marshall B. Rosenberg, *Nonviolent Communication: A Language of Life* (Encinitas, Calif.: PuddleDancer, 2005), p. 133.
[15]Smedes, *Forgive and Forget*, pp. 125-58.

time, freely, or not at all, with a fundamental feeling.[16] A communicative process has no prescriptive formula or timetable. I ask my students another question: What hope is there for you if you are in the middle of a situation where you cannot forgive right now? Are you hopelessly deadlocked forever? When students answer those questions with "I'm not ready to forgive right now. I wish I was, but I'm not. I still hurt and hate too much to want to forgive," I follow up with another question: Do you want to stay inert forever, or would you truly like to find some way to take a first step toward forgiveness? Most answer yes, and I reply with

> You've just taken your first step. God can help you along the process now because you have expressed a desire to have him help you make some kind of move. It doesn't have to be resolved tonight by 9:45 p.m., at the end of class, but the Lord will move you along the process now that you've asked for his help.

In chapter four, on persuasion, I mentioned the social-judgment theory and the latitudes of acceptance, rejection and noncommitment attitude-change variables (see pp. 88-89). I believe that a person should be encouraged that movement in the process to forgive him- or herself or others can move incrementally along the latitude line, even if complete forgiveness has not been offered or experienced. First steps in a process of forgiveness are not evidence of inertia or nonprogress; just the opposite, those first steps may be the most important changes made in the forgiveness process.

Consider this true story from one of my students about being caught in process but not yet having resolution to the pain. The student sent me a note through Biola's house mail, indicating how grateful she was that we had a class session on forgiveness. She told me that she was reminded of someone whom she had never really forgiven. She told me she didn't want to forgive her, wanted to punish her, yet the only one who was hurting was she herself, not the offender. She wrote to me that, even after our class, she still felt miserable, but after many tears she had to admit she wasn't willing to forgive just yet. However, she

---

[16]Ibid., pp. 95-117. (These are all chapter titles in part three of Smedes's book.)

knew she was closer to forgiveness than ever before, so she thanked me and asked me to pray for her.

Believe me, I prayed for her and continue to pray for so many others just like her who are stuck but never incapable of moving along the forgiveness continuum to resolution and recovery.

WHAT IS FORGOTTEN IN THE FORGIVENESS PROCESS

Once we forgive, how do we forget? A communication axiom clarifies this for us: *We never forget the incident. If over time we have truly forgiven the person who has unjustly wronged us, we forget the acuteness of the pain we felt.* God cannot possibly forget that we sinned. He is omniscient; he knows everything and is incapable of *not* knowing something. What God's grace communicates to us is that the sin will no longer separate us from a relationship with him. Did we sin? Yes. Does God remember the sin we committed? Yes. Will he hold it against us even though we have asked for forgiveness? No.

When people hurt us, we can't help but remember the incident, but when they ask for forgiveness, and we provide it for them in some communicative format, we eventually forget that the incident hurt us. That is the power of forgiveness and grace. God does not have "holy amnesia" when it comes to the specifics of sinful actions. We should never become so naive that we act as if no incident ever occurred. But grace received and provided to others eventually makes the hurt and pain fail to hurt us any longer, if we learn to let it go. This process probably will not be as speedy as we might like, but God promises by his own example that it can indeed occur. We have a deeply communicative relationship with God because he desires the relationship more than he desires to remember the hurt and pain of separation due to sin.

WHAT FORGIVENESS IS NOT

We must also address what forgiveness is not: *Forgiveness is not a license to be treated as a doormat.* You should never allow anyone to wrong you over and over again, even flaunting the fact that you should forgive him or her. God never called us to remain victims but to do all we can to embrace the notion of being a victor over circumstances. Part of forgiveness may mean establishing a boundary for the oppressor.[17] Kelley also discusses when the forgiveness option is clearly conditional. For example, when a father asks forgiveness of his son as part of his alcohol recovery program, the son may offer forgiveness on the condition that alcoholic consumption will no longer be tolerated inside the home.[18]

Forgiveness does not mean we condone or rationalize offenses.[19] We will not dismiss the action but will begin the process of making sure that the offense does not continue to hurt us. Smedes says it succinctly: Excusing is not forgiving.[20]

Confronting someone who needs to ask us for forgiveness does not guarantee that the person will see it our way. The person who wronged us may not acknowledge that an incident needs forgiveness. As the wronged party, we can forgive ourself, gain satisfaction from communicating that we were hurt, but then we must move on with our life.

A dead person or a person no longer a part of our life cannot offer forgiveness, but we can determine to not let the pain of this unresolved situation do further damage to our life. Some people have found help by writing and mailing a letter to a dead person. The symbolic gesture actualizes release from pain for many who desire to no longer let the "monsters" in their life control and detract from the joy and happiness they wish to experience with a growing relationship with God and fellow believers.

FORGIVING GOD

Part of the process of healing from hurt and pain may require a confrontation with God. No believer will be eternally damned for briefly addressing God's role in the process of hurt. *We can learn to forgive God.* Forgive God! That smacks of blasphemy to some. But the reality is that we do not know or may never know the role that God plays in events, except that he wants us to heal and mature once the process is complete.

---

[17]Grace Ketterman and David Hazard, *When You Can't Say "I Forgive You": Breaking the Bonds of Anger and Hurt* (Colorado Springs: NavPress, 2000), pp. 70-71.
[18]Kelley, "Communicating Forgiveness," p. 227.
[19]Ibid., p. 71.
[20]Smedes, *Forgive and Forget*, pp. 61-66.

If we think that the mere concept of forgiving God is an unforgivable sin, we need to take another look at David's venting in the Psalms:

Awake, O LORD! Why do you sleep?
　　Rouse yourself. Do not reject us forever.
Why do you hide your face
　　and forget our misery and oppression? (Ps 44:23-24)

I am worn out calling for help;
　　my throat is parched.
My eyes fail,
　　looking for my God. (Ps 69:3)

Why, O LORD, do you reject me
　　and hide your face from me?
From my youth I have been afflicted and close to death;
　　I have suffered your terrors and am in despair.
Your wrath has swept over me;
　　your terrors have destroyed me. (Ps 88:14-16)

I pour out my complaint before him [the Lord];
　　before him I tell my trouble. (Ps 142:2)

David certainly understood that God could handle his venting. You can't help but notice that David eventually changes his attitude about God in other psalms too, such as Psalm 130:2-4:

O LORD, hear my voice.
Let your ears be attentive
　　to my cry for mercy.
If you, O LORD, kept a record of sins,
　　O LORD, who could stand?
But with you there is forgiveness;
　　therefore you are feared.

I love this poem by Norman C. Habel, who also discovered that perhaps an early step on the road to forgiveness is to forgive God. Habel vents this prayer and accusation to God in contemporary terms, with blame and accusations that clearly echo the angry and frustrating cries of David in his psalms:

I want you to listen
when I yell at the sky . . .
kick the ground,
throw stones at the stars,
slam doors,
or swear at the world.
Perhaps that's not giving
all glory to God . . .
But it means I trust you with the truth—
all the Truth.[21]

God understands implicitly why some people need to vent, yell, scream or perhaps even profanely confront him. A person caught up in such a hurtful period eventually realizes what a great listener and counselor God is. God says, in effect, "Let me have it. I can take it. And then we will begin the process of making you whole once again." God desires relationship, but he will let a believer work through a confrontational process while he or she discovers that God has been there all along to provide comfort in the midst of so much misunderstanding and loss. It's ironic that a person who yells at God does so with a communicative attempt to establish dialogue, and God desires it so much that he is willing to wait for us to come around and reestablish the relational link!

WHEN THE WRONGED PARTY DOES NOT KNOW THE OFFENSE

Something that is difficult to discern is whether or not we ought to ask forgiveness of someone who does not know or realize that we wronged him or her. We might risk making the relationship less credible if we bring it up in order to be forgiven. During my first year of teaching at Biola, a student I did not know came to my office door and said, "I need to talk to you. I need you to know that I've hated you. And now I am sorry and I want to ask you to forgive me." I was dumbfounded. I didn't know what to do at first. Apparently, this student had attended some kind of training seminar that asked the attendee to remember all past sins and seek out the person wronged to make it right. Seriously, I did not

---

[21]Norman C. Habel, "All Glory to God," *Interrobang* (Minneapolis: Fortress, 1969).

know this student, and I certainly did not know he "hated me." Of course, I forgave him, but as he left relieved, I was left feeling dumped on and the gnawing question of why he hated me was never resolved. To be honest, this student did not need to be forgiven by me because I did not know or feel the offense. He certainly needed to ask God for forgiveness and for the desire to forgive himself. There is an appropriate communication element that accompanies the desire to ask for forgiveness. The one who grants forgiveness should never feel dumped on or second-guess the decision to forgive because the request was inappropriately presented.

But are there unknown offenses that should be made known, even if trust is broken? Counselors, pastors and communication professionals have widely different viewpoints on this kind of disclosure, and not everyone agrees with me. I believe that there are a few cases where disclosure is necessary, but again, every situation must be analyzed separately. The spouse that cheats but desires restoration of the marriage relationship will have to hurt the other spouse with the truth. If the vow to be faithful means anything in the wedding ceremony, then disclosure of an infidelity must be considered. I'm convinced that trust between a husband and a wife demands the truth, even when it could hurt the spouse who knew nothing. Hiding a sin, even a sin that has been forgiven by God, may eventually prove more hurtful when the past sin is revealed (but not in a context of asking for forgiveness). There are sins that damage trust, but true forgiveness allows us to move on in godly relationship even when trust has been momentarily impaired. I cannot imagine the emotional betrayal that was felt by Gayle Haggard and her children when Ted Haggard, a pastor and the president of the National Association of Evangelicals, admitted his indiscretions with a male prostitute to the media and to his family. But even the most insensitive cynic had to take notice of Gayle's offer of forgiveness to her husband, uttered in the press and on the *Larry King Live* show a year later.[22] Such expressions, bred in hurt, pain and betrayal, exemplify

---

[22]See Todd V. Lewis, "Rhetoric and the Process of Splitting: A Critical Analysis of Rev. Ted Haggard," a paper presented to the Religious Communication Association/National Communication Association, Chicago, November 16, 2007, pp. 1-21; Larry King, "Interview with Ted and Gayle Haggard," *Larry King Live*, January 29, 2009.

grace and mercy given to the undeserving.

And how strange was it that God told the Old Testament prophet Hosea to marry a prostitute who would continually cheat on and be unfaithful to him? Not strange at all when you realize that God was demonstrating through his prophet Hosea the on-again, off-again relationship between God and the nation of Israel. Forgiveness, even when trust has been impaired, can once again restore relationship.

FORGIVENESS CAN RESTORE UNITY

As we seek ways to resolve and manage conflict within the body of Christ, we must embrace the notion that forgiveness is the primary means to restore the unity we so long for. David reminds us, "How good and pleasant it is when brothers live together in unity!" (Ps 133:1). When we get it right with our brothers and sisters in Christ, we get noticed by a world that thinks forgiveness is ludicrous or at best a sign of weakness. On my bookshelf I have at least six different interpersonal communication textbooks that explain conflict resolution and conflict management, but seldom if ever mention forgiveness. The concept of forgiveness is only just beginning to make the index in many secular interpersonal communication textbooks.[23] The world around us will be astounded when we start practicing the communicative process of forgiveness.

CONCLUSION

I began this chapter with some true stories from my students. I want to end it with one more. This particular student wrote me a note after class, indicating that although he didn't pipe up in class to share any

---

[23]The topic of "forgiveness" is emerging primarily in specialized communication textbooks for advanced interpersonal and theory courses that focus on relational communication or family issues. See Em Griffin, "Accountability and Forgiveness," in *Making Friends* (Downers Grove, Ill.: InterVarsity Press, 1987); Em Griffin, *A First Look at Communication Theory*, 7th ed. (New York: McGraw Hill, 2009), pp. 70, 293, 326-27, 337, 417, 474; Julia T. Wood, *Communication Mosaics: A New Introduction to the Field of Communication* (Belmont, Calif.: Wadsworth, 1998), p. 187; Julia T. Wood, *Relational Communication: Continuity and Change in Personal Relationships*, 2nd ed. (Belmont, Calif.: Wadsworth, 2000), pp. 232-34; Marshall B. Rosenberg, *Nonviolent Communication: A Language of Life* (Encinitas, Calif.: PuddleDancer, 2005): 133-34; Vincent R. Waldron and Douglas L. Kelley, *Communicating Forgiveness* (Thousand Oaks, Calif.: Sage, 2007).

thoughts, he actually had a thousand thoughts and emotions, but he was having trouble articulating exactly what he felt. However, he told me, he was definitely listening. And then, as he returned to his dorm room and began to check his e-mails, he found out about God's timing. An ex-girlfriend who had hurt him nine months earlier wrote to him, and all of the hurt and pain returned in the form of an intense stomachache. But in response to our class discussions he was prepared to forgive her and wish her well—and it would be for real this time. Oh, and yes, he did tell me that her e-mail was a request for forgiveness. I loved the concluding sentence he sent to me: "How good is God, huh?"

I think it is *very* important as well as *insightful* that God began the process of forgiveness before the other person asked for it. I've discovered over the years that he frequently works that way.

Life does not get any better than forgiving others and knowing you too have been forgiven. The verbal and nonverbal signs may be slight at first, but there will be evidence you have been forgiven, such as a touch or eye contact, an ability to treat the offense as if it no longer hurt, or an open discussion about how the offended person has moved on with life. No one needs to carry unresolved guilt over forgiveness issues. And closure comes when forgiveness is offered but not accepted. At least we have done what we need to do. God supplies the wounded with eventual healing. There is mercy. There is grace. There is a rediscovery of relationships as they were meant to be experienced. It does not get any better than this.

7

COMMUNICATING ABOUT
AND EVALUATING THE MESSAGES
OF POPULAR CULTURE

While sitting in my office at Biola University one morning in the fall of 2007, my secretary received a frantic telephone call from the English department. "We just read on Facebook that Todd Lewis died this morning." My secretary assured the person on the other end of the line that she was looking directly at me and that I was very much alive and agitated about this information, which of course was news to me. I had never accessed Facebook on my computer, but I needed to establish the fact that I was *not* dead. (It may have been the only time in my life I could accurately do my impression of the classic line from *Monty Python and the Holy Grail:* "I'm not dead!") As I maneuvered through this online website, I found the source of the rumor. There was a Southern California high school teacher named Todd Lewis who in one particular photo bore a somewhat striking resemblance to me and had, indeed, recently died. I sent out an e-mail to all of the university, quoting Mark Twain ("The report of my death was an exaggeration."), and I actually had a very reassuring day with friends and colleagues sending greetings that indicated they were happy I was still alive. But I decided I needed to establish a presence, with a photograph and biography, on Facebook, and thus began my computer-mediated relationship with this ubiquitous form of interpersonal communication.

While I stumbled on this new form of communication within our popular culture in order to establish my physical presence and current well-being, it became apparent to me that Christians cannot ignore this format or any other message-centered aspects of our popular culture. In this chapter, I will address options we have as we engage, comment on and critique the various centers for messaging in pop culture.

COMPUTER-MEDIATED COMMUNICATION, SOCIALIZATIONS AND A CHRISTIAN RESPONSE

There were no less than fifteen sessions regarding communicative management of online networking sites (e.g., Facebook, MySpace, YouTube, etc.) at the 2007 National Communication Association Convention, and predictions are that the number of such analytical sessions will increase in the coming years. After my introduction to Facebook, I attended one of these sessions to find out how online communicative relationships are sustained.[1] I was surprised to discover that individualized personal websites, replete with photos and text-message conversations, emphasized interpersonal privacy matters more than I had anticipated. Faculty members who teach interpersonal communication courses are signing up for these sites as well, but self-disclosure aspects can enhance or detract from student-teacher relationships. "I facebooked you!" shows that the computer-mediated websites have even created new verb forms that expect reciprocal responses.

Apparently, in some schools, admission decisions are made after viewing a prospective student's website on these social networks. If non-Christian faculty members report that they encourage their students to rethink and in some cases take down compromising photos and commentary, how much more should Christians, whether faculty or students, consider what they want to say on these online networks?

For some Christians, the answer is to separate themselves from the taint of scandal and innuendo in the secular Internet realm by joining an ostensibly "Christian-only" socialization Internet site. The website ChristiansOnDemand.com is one countercultural site that provides

---

[1]Alycia Ehlert and Amy Trombley, "Socialization Networks as Learning Tools: Examining Harms and Benefits of MySpace and Facebook Use by Students in the Communication Classroom," National Communication Association Convention, Chicago, November 15, 2007.

this service. The website states: "At ChristiansOnDemand our purpose is to encourage ordinary Christians to fellowship and Network with other Christians while glorifying God in their professional lives." But the Christian-only site seems to offer internalized banter and streamed video clips for Christians who understand the jargon and in-house language of those who have grown up in the evangelical community. It seems it would be better for a Christian student to download video, photographs, commentary, well-reasoned debate and dialogue that provide avenues for discussion with non-Christian as well as the Christian communities.

When a website is designed to be separate from the secular, our ability to integrate our faith through it seems minimal. Contextually, Paul's thoughts in 2 Corinthians 6:17 ("'Therefore come out from them and be separate,' says the Lord") call for separation with unbelievers in binding relationships, such as a marriage. Paul is certainly not advocating that we create separate means to communicate with other believers, to the exclusion of interaction with those who need to know Christ. I have certainly been encouraged by the occasional video clip on YouTube and have found it a means to engage in dialogue with those outside my own personal faith.[2] We must guard against merely copying secular social networks for Christian fellowship. Instead we should embrace the more difficult task of engaging the popular culture with our faith-driven worldviews offered in reasonable and civil responses.

INSIGHTS FROM RHETORICAL THEORIES ON THE POPULAR CULTURES OF FILM AND TELEVISION

For the Christian communication studies student, understanding rhetorical theories is an essential component of the educational process.

---

[2]My wife and I were privileged to sing in a five-hundred-plus mass choir made up of church and public school choral members at the 2007 Disneyland Candlelight Christmas Concert, hosted by the amusement park. Someone videotaped the concert and placed it on YouTube, and we were able to tell all of our friends, Christians and non-Christians, about our involvement and how they could access the concert on the Internet. Not only was the experience a life-changing moment for us, we appreciated the opportunity to sing and dialogue with people of all ages, especially those who represented choirs from secular high schools in the Southern California area.

But merely knowing the component parts of a rhetorical theory is pointless unless the student can apply the theory elements, which will in turn create opportunities for *evaluative* commentary. To illustrate this point, let's look at several rhetorical theories of Kenneth Burke, one of the twentieth century's great philosophical and rhetorical minds. Burke's most famous evaluative theory would have to be the "dramatic pentad."[3]

Seeing virtually all communicative situations as inherently dramatic, Burke calls on the rhetorical critic to look at the artifacts[4] of public speaking, public entertainment or virtually any communicative encounter as consisting of five distinct elements.[5] *Act* is the artifact itself: the speech, the film, the event. *Agent* is the primary communicator of the artifact: the speaker, the actor, the leader. *Agency* is the channel or mediated means to share the act: public presentation, filmed or televised presentation, interpersonal communication. *Scene* identifies the historical context for the act and perhaps also identifies elements as descriptions of the immediate or universal audiences. *Purpose* describes the message intent as the rhetorical critic understands it. I have just *described* the five elements of the pentad; what the rhetorical critic must do is provide reasoned and arguably supportable notions of each element to offer *evaluation*, which can then serve as a beginning for discussion and debate.

The primary reason for doing a Burkean critical analysis is to inductively determine why the speaker or writer made certain rhetorical choices and to comment on the motivation for those decisions. The answers generated by that inductive process move the rhetorical critic to make *evaluative* assessments: Is each stage or element effective or not? Can a motivation for action be assessed at each stage/element or not? The evaluative critic must answer why or why not. *Description*

---

[3]The dramatic pentad later become a six-pointed hexad, with the addition of "attitude."

[4]"The artifact is the data for the study—the rhetorical act, event, or product you are going to analyze . . . a song, a poem, a speech, a work of art, or a building, for example" (Sonja K. Foss, *Rhetorical Criticism: Exploration and Practice*, 4th ed. [Long Grove, Ill.: Waveland, 2009], pp. 9-10).

[5]Kenneth Burke, *A Grammar of Motives* (Berkeley: University of California Press, 1969), pp. xv-xxiii.

without *evaluation* is an incomplete academic discipline that would merely measure definitional objectives. *Evaluation* added to the initial *description* moves the student to *assessment*, and this provides the Christian student the opportunity to integrate Christian worldview options as possible interpretive ways to engage the popular culture.

Burke believes that "ratios" can link key terms together to uncover motives for communicative acts. There are twenty different ratio possibilities, but the most common ones rhetorical critics use for evaluation are *act-scene* and *act-agent*. *Act-scene* critical commentary focuses on how the *act* (e.g., a prominent speech) cannot be understood apart from the *scene* (e.g., historical or immediate context of events). *Act-agent* reveals the links between the artifact (e.g., a prominent speech) and the oratorical gifts and abilities of the *agent* (e.g., speaker).

Without doing a full-fledged Burkean pentadic analysis, I will use Barack Obama's Philadelphia speech on race, published on March 18, 2008, as an example of how the pentad can provide evaluative insights. *Act* would first describe and then evaluate the composition and ideas contained in the speech itself. The speech references America's "original sin of slavery," the impact of race on the election itself, Obama's clear denunciation of Rev. Jeremiah Wright, his former pastor, for his racial divisiveness, yet Obama's continuing loyalty to Wright, who introduced him to the Christian faith. The speech primarily establishes that race will not be a distraction from the true concerns that need to be addressed and solved in the United States. A Burkean analysis of the *act* would evaluate motives and critique the means of Obama's perspectives. *Agent* would first describe Obama's delivery style and oratorical techniques, then the critic evaluates their effectiveness. Part of this evaluation would focus on pace of delivery, word choices, use of vocal force for emphasis and Obama's own personal *ethos* as a part of source credibility, dynamism and trustworthiness.

Agency would describe the differences between *reading* the speech and *viewing* or *hearing* the speech, then the critic can evaluate whether or not television, radio or print journalism changes the perception of the content. For example, television would reveal Obama's nonverbal gestures and facial expressions, whereas the speech on radio or in print might emphasize the purposeful syntax and word choices Obama used to form his thoughts.

Scene describes background of the rationale for giving the speech, probably focusing on the link between Obama and his pastor, then the critic would evaluate why the speech was necessary in the context of the political campaign. Most rhetorical critics would note that the Jeremiah Wright controversy, with its accompanying anti-American sound bites, would not disappear from the context of the campaign for the presidency. Obama needed to use the Philadelphia scene to make what he hoped would be the definitive and final commentary on racially inflammatory language. That the immediate scene included a reference to American history occurring "in the [Independence] hall that still stands across the street" is helpful in generating evaluative commentary for the rhetorical critic. Did Obama choose this particular context and scene to make this important speech for a reason? What nuanced meaning comes from delivering this particular speech in Philadelphia and not New York or Washington, D.C., or Chicago?

Purpose first describes the intent of the speech, then the critic offers an evaluation, quoting other sources to determine how successful the *agent* was in delivering the *act*.[6] A pentadic criticism would focus most of the evaluation on whether or not the *agent* actually achieved the intended *purpose*. Since Burke was interested in the study of motives, the critic can also elaborate on the likelihood that Obama's motives were achieved by this defining moment of the campaign. In the evaluative aspects of the pentad commentary the Christian rhetorical critic would include the religious context of the controversy surrounding the racial comments by Obama's pastor as well as political and social concerns.

This example of the Obama speech is skeletal at best, merely providing aspects that would need much more amplification to be considered

---

[6]Rhetorical critics can discover commentators who will assist them in building arguments to support their evaluative claims. For this Obama speech on race, a good example of commentary might be Bob Herbert, "With a Powerful Speech, Obama Offers a Challenge," *New York Times*, March 25, 2008 <www.nytimes.com/2008/03/25/opinion/25herbert.html?ex=1222056000&en=d39f172e2f078b28&ei=5087&excamp=GGOPobamaspeech&WT.srch=1&WT.mc_ev=click&WT.mc_id=OP-S-E-GG-NA-S-obama_speech>.

an important and rigorous evaluation.[7] Using Burke's seminal theory of the dramatic pentad should never be considered a quick and easy cookie-cutter approach to insightful evaluation. The five points of the theory organize the amplification structure but should never be used as a shortcut to mere descriptive investigation. Amplification that offers tangible responses to the so-what question moves the rhetorical critic toward meaningful evaluation.

Two additional theories espoused by Kenneth Burke allow the Christian student to provide evaluative commentary on popular cultural artifacts such as films or television series that intentionally interact with faith issues: *terministic screens* and *the rhetoric of rebirth*.[8]

In her discussion of Kenneth Burke's theoretical basis for critical application of *terministic screens*, Sonja K. Foss says,

> Rhetoric does not simply provide a name for a situation, however. It also represents a creative strategy for dealing with that situation or for solving the problems inherent in it. Rhetoric offers commands or instructions of some kind, helping individuals maneuver through life and helping them feel more at home in the world. . . . A rhetorical act or artifact provides assistance to its audience in a number of ways. It may provide a vocabulary of thoughts, actions, emotions, and attitudes for codifying and thus interpreting a situation.[9]

Although some rhetorical critics believe that Burke's writings fall under the all-encompassing notion of *dramatism*, I believe Sonja K. Foss, Karen A. Foss and Robert Trapp correctly separate some Burkean theories from the dramatism rubric.[10] Burke refers to *terministic screens* as filters, frames or focused encasements that direct attention to reality perspectives, which by definition exclude other viewpoints. "Much that

---

[7]A more developed and amplified pentadic evaluation would be better served in an academic journal as an independent essay rather than the primary focus of this chapter.

[8]Burke's life provides little evidence that he was an active practitioner of any religious faith, although his writings indicate a fascination with theological notions and their impact on philosophical interpretations of rhetoric. He seems to have had an encounter with Catholicism, because his religious terminology patterns the Catholic viewpoint of the soul's progression from birth to death to purgatory to heaven.

[9]Foss, *Rhetorical Criticism*, p. 64.

[10]Sonja K. Foss, Karen A. Foss, and Robert Trapp, *Contemporary Perspectives on Rhetoric* (Prospect Heights, Ill.: Waveland, 1985), pp. 153-88.

we take as observations about 'reality' may be but the spinning out of possibilities implicit in our particular choice of terms."[11] Burke advises critics to "track down the kinds of observation implicit in the terminology" that are used in the rhetorical artifact, whether the "choice of terms was deliberate or spontaneous."[12] Foss extends this Burkean analysis to advocate that critics explore "cues to rhetors' worldviews and meaning" by charting or narrowing obvious ingredients of perceived terministic screens.[13] Foss insightfully empowers the rhetorical critic when she states that "the equations or clusters that a critic discovers in a rhetor's artifact generally are not conscious to the rhetor."[14]

What this means for the Christian critic of popular films and television series is that a particular terministic screen, once identified, can provide a means to evaluate the artifact's message from a Christian perspective. But it doesn't necessarily take a Christian movie critic to point out the terministic screen. Notice the following commentary from Carina Chocano, movie critic for the *Los Angeles Times:*

> [In the film *Horton Hears a Who!*] the moral, or one of them, . . . is that every voice counts. . . . "A person's a person no matter how small" is a lovely sentiment—which also happens to strangely echo one side of the abortion debate.[15]

Chocano may or may not be a Christian, but she would not make this comment if she was not *aware* of the Christian worldview, which espouses the sanctity of life; she intuitively offers an interpretation of the movie's "moral" through a Christian terministic screen.

Lost, one of the most popular television series over the past several years, has developed a cult-like following with its own websites and its own "encyclopedia" of possible interpretations. This series embodies the postmodern culture we live in and attempts to touch on virtually all major religions with references, intertextual commentary, visual sym-

---

[11]Kenneth Burke, *Language as Symbolic Action: Essays on Life, Literature, and Method* (Berkeley: University of California Press, 1966), p. 46.
[12]Ibid., p. 47.
[13]Foss, *Rhetorical Criticism*, p. 71.
[14]Ibid., p. 72.
[15]Carina Chocano, " 'Horton' Here Isn't a Hoot," *Los Angeles Times*, March 14, 2008, E1.

bols and philosophical or spiritual statements about the "reasons" why things happen. The show has spawned video games, jigsaw puzzles, Internet reality games, toy action figures, short videos for mobile phones, novelized books and even religious and cultural criticism in printed texts.[16] Even though some religious interpretations have been denied by the creative team, a rhetorical artifact may have subconscious terministic screens, perceived by objective observers who interpret the information through a different lens.[17]

Today, churches and other religious groups are forming social gatherings to discuss the themes found in *Lost*. A church in suburban Atlanta is offering a class featuring discussion themes from *Lost*, such as "Numbers and Symbols," "Light and Darkness," "Others," "Fate and Reason" and "Purgatory."[18] The religious terministic screens are appearing as discussion items to facilitate message interpretations in the postmodern world that has so many interpretive options and possible meanings.

The creators of *Lost* have determined to set 2010 as an expiration date for the series. Themes and terministic screens will have further refinement as the series closes. Will all the mysteries be revealed? The answer is difficult to say. Since the very notion of interpretation is key to the power of message criticism, there always may be room for other perspectives, even religious ones.

In another rhetorical theory, "the rhetoric of rebirth," Kenneth Burke uses language that parallels the Catholic view of the religious journey. For Burke there are three stages in this spiritual rhetoric: *pollution, purification* and *redemption*.[19] At stage one, a life is polluted with sensations of

---

[16]John Ankerberg and Dillon Burroughs, *What Can Be Found in LOST?* (Eugene, Ore.: Harvest House, 2008); Joley Wood, *Living Lost: Why We're All Stuck on the Island* (New Orleans: Garret County Press, 2007); Todd V. Lewis, " 'I Once Was *LOST*, but Now Am Found . . .': Rhetorical Religious Terministic Screens in the Television Show, *LOST*," paper presented to National Communication Association Convention, San Diego, November 2008.

[17]J. J. Abrams, creator and originator of the *Lost* series has gone on record as debunking the notion that the *Lost* island represents purgatory, but he also said that "he claimed to like the idea." http:tv.zap2it.com/tveditorial/tve_main/1.1002.271%7C94107%7C1%7C,00.html (March 14, 2005). See also Lewis, "*LOST*, but Now Am Found . . .," p. 5.

[18]Brandy Wilson, "Community of Faith: News from House of Worship: The Religious Themes of 'Lost,' " *Atlanta Journal-Constitution*, February 2, 2008.

[19]Burke's theory is presented by combining his commentary from two texts: *The Rhetoric of*

guilt, anxiety, social tension, unresolved tension, even embarrassment. In order to survive, the pollution must be purged. There must be catharsis; without it there can be no sense of forgiveness. At stage two, the language units that created our guilt become the means to purge ourselves. We seek "purification" by the symbolic action of *victimage* and *mortification*. Victimage is the process in which guilt is transferred to a vessel or vessels outside of the rhetor. (Another term for this concept is *scapegoat*.) Mortification means that we make ourselves suffer for our guilt or sins. This self-inflicted punishment occasionally leads to self-sacrifice. Stage three is redemption, which represents a temporary respite that signifies symbolic rebirth. Redemption provides a new identity, a different view on life or a momentary gain in pursuit of perfection.

Signs, the 2002 blockbuster movie starring Mel Gibson and directed by M. Night Shyamalan, reveals the journey of a minister's loss and regaining of faith in God through harrowing experiences with aliens and near-death encounters.[20] We realize early in the film that ex-Father Hess has taken off his clerical collar and has turned to farming and fathering his own two children and younger brother after the "accidental" death of his wife (stressed through reoccurring flashbacks to the accident scene).

Stage one Burkean examples of guilt and tensions occur as Hess declines to be called "Father" and the crop signs in his field become associated with an alien invasion. David Elliott, movie critic for the *San Diego Union-Tribune*, comments that

> Hess, he of lost faith, walks around like a hunk zombie, his posture and dead-locked face indicating his tragic grief. The outline shadow of a cross remains on his wall (why didn't he just paint it over?) and we know he will answer its call again—that the global alien crisis has little meaning except to make Hess put on his collar again, after nearly losing his family.[21]

Religion: Studies in Logology (Boston: Beacon Press, 1961), and *Permanence and Change: An Anatomy of Purpose*, 3rd ed. (Berkeley: University of California Press, 1984).

[20]The following commentary is based on Todd V. Lewis, "Loss of Faith Rhetoric in *Signs:* A Burkean Analysis of Rhetorical Rebirth," paper presented at the National Communication Association Convention, Miami, November 20, 2003.

[21]David Elliott, "Alien, Get Thee Behind Me," *San Diego Union-Tribune*, August 1, 2002, Entertainment p. 11.

Critic Robert Wilonsky correctly notes that Hess is racked with guilt, "though it's a sentiment never expressed directly, only hinted at."[22] Shyamalan's attention to detail in his films cannot be ignored, and the remaining visual of the cross both at the beginning of the film and triumphantly at the end indicates an initial sense of guilt, an inability for Hess to actually act on his verbal statements of denial of God's existence. (That this same symbol becomes the means to reveal his cathartic purgation and return to faith at the end of the film is fascinating rhetorically.) This commitment to showing the difficulties for faith in the midst of grief and fear raises *Signs* above the B-movie alien invasion film. Critic Frank Gabrenya argues that Gibson's choice as an actor "downplays the bitterness, letting the viewer weigh the severity (or credibility) of the ex-priest's retreat. Has he reached a point of irredeemable despair, or does his salvation still hang in the balance?"[23]

At stage two of the "rhetoric of rebirth," a person allows *mortification* and *victimage* to occur as a part of suffering. If a person suffers long enough, the resulting "process" will lead to a regained sense of the divine and an embracing of the elements of grace and spiritual understanding. In *Signs* the assignation of a "Last Supper" (with cheeseburgers as the entrée) due to the alien invasion, leads to an outburst of anger and denial about God's presence and care, but the scene in the film also resonates with a sense of the cry of personal pain as well from the Mel Gibson persona. Later on in the film as it appears that Hess's son will die because he cannot breathe, Hess screams out to God, "I hate you! Don't do this to me again!" From the conclusion of this scene until the end of the film, as the aliens are conquered by simple elemental faith and insights from a daughter with a fixation on water and cryptic near-death hallucinations from Hess's wife, God's intervention in the affairs of human beings is acknowledged. A flashback to an earlier statement by Hess reveals that there are "two groups of people"—those who see events as miracles and those who see them as random acts of nature.

---

[22]Robert Wilonsky, "Signs of Faith: Mel Gibson Has a Close Encounter with God—or Just a Mean E.T.," *New Times Los Angeles*, July 25, 2002, n.p.

[23]Frank Gabrenya, "Close Encounters with Crop Circles Bring Out Best of Shyamalan, Gibson," *Columbus (Ohio) Dispatch*, August 2, 2002, 10F.

That God's intervention is not always initially interpreted as spiritual reveals the dimensional levels of belief and the commitment to working through despair to embrace faith, once all the information is placed in its proper context. The apostle Paul said, "Now we see through a glass, darkly; but then face to face" (1 Cor 13:12 KJV). Faith, resulting from victimage and mortification, ultimately can lead to purification.

This stage three in the film occurs when all of the cryptic messages find new meanings and the film's director artistically shows Mel Gibson once again donning his collar to return to his work as an Episcopal priest; we also see the outline of the cross on the bathroom door. Prior to this shot, the highly rhetorical comment is made by Hess that "there are no coincidences," which leads to the cathartic embracing of faith once more. No dialogue offers a reason, but the conclusion of the film suggests that the priest left behind his despair and moved onto a deeper level of faith and understanding due to his trials and even his bout with death and denial.

Film critic Donna Britt states that "some who see the wonderful new movie 'Signs' will be shocked to hear its ex-priest hero (Mel Gibson) whisper to God, 'I hate you,' when his family is endangered. Others like me were stunned to hear a film character speak to the Deity at all."[24] Britt's comments remind us that Hollywood has returned on occasion to a subgenre of film messages that deal with the "loss of faith and the regaining of faith." *Signs* will not be the final film to create interest among gifted filmmakers desiring to share a message as well as entertain.

Signs was being filmed during and after the events of September 11, 2001, and there is a sense that no American can be the same since those horrific days. "Everything about *Signs* reflects and responds to the confused spirit of universal threat, the need for national unity and the search for a renewed faith aroused by the events of 9/11."[25] Even as we return to normality, films continue to explore the inherent need for

---

[24]Donna Britt, "Far Too Often, Religion Isn't Even a Subject," *Washington Post*, August 2, 2002, B01.

[25]P. French, "Fields of Screams: The Sixth Sense's Director Captures the US National Mood in a Polished if Simplistic Tale of Menace and Faith," *The Observer*, September 15, 2002, Observer review pages, 9.

spiritual answers to deep-seated questions, even as they attempt to entertain us. *Signs* could be interpreted as a story of alien invasion that happened as a result of God's way to help people like Graham Hess work out

> his relationship with God, his kids, his brother, his dead wife and the man who accidentally killed her. Shyamalan suggests throughout that to hate God is at least to acknowledge the existence of a higher power. In *Signs* something comes from above, only it may not be little green men, just a Big Guy who doesn't need spaceships to make contact.[26]

Rhetorical criticism gives Christian students the means to offer up counterintuitive framing mechanisms to begin the intentional integration of faith perspectives with nonbelievers. Seeing the potential will come from a developmental process of study and prayerful insights. It is not an impossible task, however. The capacity to see redemptive and spiritual themes in popular culture, especially in movies and television series, can be enhanced by a commitment to studying the classic narrative stories of our time. Redemptive narratives resonate with audiences even if they do not want to admit that the redemption motif has its roots in Jesus Christ. The opportunity for every Christian student of rhetorical criticism is to provide an alternative perspective that reminds everyone that embedded in all stories and themes is the desire to discover redemption.

But how can a Christian evaluate an aspect of popular culture with a unique critical perspective? Foss suggests that

> seasoned rhetorical critics, however, engage in rhetorical criticism using a different process . . . without following any formal method of criticism. This kind of criticism is generative in that you generate units of analysis or an explanation from your artifact rather than from previously developed, formal methods of criticism.[27]

Generative criticism identifies the major features, noticing the frequency and intensity of allusions to these features. Theory building

---

[26]Wilonsky, "Signs of Faith," n.p.
[27]Foss, *Rhetorical Criticism*, p. 387.

requires structure and identifiable components, explained with references to the identifiable features.[28] Suppose a Christian rhetorical critic wanted to develop a rhetorical theory of explicit sexual content in contemporary motion pictures, commenting on the gratuitous as well as efficacious nature of nudity or sexuality. Such a theory would have to have a description of features of explicit sexual content and whether or not frequency, context or intensity changed the communicative perceptions. Such a generative theory would also have to have a thorough discussion of the contribution that such an analytical approach would make to rhetorical theory practice.

For example, I would like to challenge Christian students to theoretically generate a means to evaluate the use of nudity in motion pictures. Could the Franco Zeffirelli's usage of male nudity, sensitively filmed from a distance, in *Brother Son/Sister Moon* (1972) actually deliver the important message of leaving behind materialism to embrace a life of faith (e.g., Francis of Assisi stripping off his expensive clothes and walking naked out of the Italian village to become a monk)? Does the full-frontal male nudity of *Monty Python's Life of Brian* (1979) merely allow the Monty Python troupe to offer gratuitous profanity (e.g., Brian revealing his naked self from a window)? Does the nudity in Steven Spielberg's *Schindler's List* (1993) express the moral degradation more than prurient sexual interests? Or does sexual explicitness depend solely on the whims of the director or the screenwriter? Christian rhetorical critics need to take a critical communication look at such a ubiquitous popular culture phenomenon as sexual explicitness.

CONCLUSION

In response to popular culture Christians should never embrace separation and disengagement. Our culture needs Christian attorneys, Christian professors at secular universities, Christian actors, Christian politicians as well as Christian Internet supervisors and programmers. We need Christian plumbers, TV repairmen, nurses, doctors, supermarket checkers and car attendants. Abdicating a vocation because it is inher-

---

[28]See Leonard C. Hawes, *Pragmatics of Analoguing: Theory and Model Construction in Communication* (Reading, Mass.: Addison-Wesley, 1975).

ently immoral or unredeemable will create a self-fulfilling prophecy. Our culture may be prurient and obsessed with immorality, but if Christians stop engaging the ideas, stop critically analyzing messages and stop offering alternative perspectives, the world will only grow worse. Though modernists or postmodernists dismiss Christian viewpoints as "nice for you, but not for me," to be consistent they must listen to the Christian story. The Christian story competes quite well with any story that the world can offer. We gain a hearing because our message and our evaluation of popular culture offer something that resonates with every person: Hope!

Christian communicators provide alternative perspectives not only to the issues of pop culture but to those being debated in the university. Communication scholars call those providing alternative perspectives "counterpublics," which we will examine in chapter eight.

RESIDENT ALIENS

CHRISTIANS AS COUNTERPUBLICS

"God Almighty has set before me two great objects,
the suppression of the slave trade and the reformation of manners."

WILLIAM WILBERFORCE

Playing a key role in ending the slave trade in Great Britain came at great cost for William Wilberforce. He was mocked in newspapers as a self-righteous moral do-gooder and staunchly opposed by businessmen, ship owners and the politicians who represented their economic interests. In the late 1700s abolitionists were viewed as a threat to the English ruling class and a booming economy that was built around the slave trade. On many occasions Wilberforce had to hire personal bodyguards to ensure his safety. After one particularly bitter defeat—where Wilberforce's antislavery bill fell short by four votes because his opponents bribed Wilberforce supporters with opera tickets the night of the vote—he had a nervous breakdown. Confined to his bed, he despaired that change would never happen. His diary records tortured prayers begging God to end the plague of slavery. Eventually, his prayers were answered.

From his first antislave-trade speech in Parliament in 1789 to the Abolition Act becoming law in 1807 to the abolishment of slavery in the British Empire on July 26, 1833, Wilberforce worked to change political and public opinion. Before the Abolition Act was passed, anti-slavery bills were defeated year after year. But the tide turned, slowly. In 1814 Wilberforce and his carefully assembled coalition "gathered one million signatures, one-tenth of the population, on 800 petitions, which they delivered to the House of Commons."[1] Unfortunately, three days after the historic vote to end British involvement in slavery, Wilberforce died.

To Christians interested in having a voice within the field of communication, Wilberforce serves as a powerful example of a *counterpublic*. Nancy Fraser writes that "members of subordinated social groups" serve as counterpublics when they "invent and circulate counterdiscourses to formulate oppositional interpretations of their identities, interests, and needs."[2] Counterpublics operate within mainstream culture to challenge the dominant culture's understanding of their beliefs and the messages they advance. Counterpublics emerge "in response to exclusions within dominant publics" and the desire to "expand discursive spaces."[3] When Wilberforce and other abolitionists first started challenging Britain's participation in the slave trade, many viewed "abolitionists as radical and dangerous, similar to French revolutionaries of the day."[4] As a member of a counterpublic Wilberforce wanted to change how abolitionists were viewed. He wanted abolitionists to be seen not as treasonous revolutionaries seeking to overthrow the government, but as reformers who wanted to help the existing government be righteous in the eyes of God. The success of his rhetoric depended on this change of perception.

As Christians interested in communication we can sometimes find ourselves at odds with our discipline's embracing of theoretical or moral positions that challenge our beliefs. In order to effectively communicate our views we need to understand the characteristics of a counterpublic

---

[1] Richard Pierard, "Little-Known or Remarkable Facts About William Wilberforce and the Century of Reform," *Church History* 16, no. 1 (1997).

[2] Nancy Fraser, "Rethinking the Public Sphere: A Contribution to the Critique of Actually Existing Democracy," in *Habermas and the Public Sphere*, ed. C. Calhoun (Cambridge, Mass.: MIT Press, 1992), p. 123.

[3] Ibid.

[4] Pierard, "Little-Known or Remarkable Facts," p. 2.

and how we can appropriately affirm and challenge the dominant discourse within our field.

Counterpublics

Communication scholar Daniel Brouwer identifies three key features of counterpublics: oppositionality, withdrawal and engagement.

Oppositionality. Oppositionality occurs when a group of individuals resist, reject or dissent from the dominant culture's narrative. Brouwer writes, "It is important to recognize that oppositionality is primarily perceptual; that is, counterpublics emerge when social actors perceive themselves to be excluded from or marginalized within mainstream or dominant publics and communicate about that marginality or exclusion."[5] As individuals committed to a Christian worldview we'll sometimes find ourselves at odds with the dominant ideology embedded within the field of communication studies. Ideology refers to a set of foundational ideas that shape how a group or culture views and defines reality. While a group or culture may contain competing ideologies, "the dominant ideology of a culture is the one that has the greatest power and the adherence of the greatest number of people at a given moment in the life of a culture."[6] For example, a significant number of students in university classes and the professors who teach them embrace a form of postmodernism which asserts that all knowledge is relative to a particular culture.[7] Simply put, there is no unifying truth that transcends a person's community or culture. Christian philosopher J. P. Moreland summarizes this view:

> On a postmodern view, there is no such thing as objective reality, truth, value, reason, and so forth. All these are social constructions, creations of linguistic practices, and as such are relative not to individuals, but to social groups that share a narrative.[8]

---

[5]Daniel Brouwer, "Communication as Counterpublic," in *Communication as . . . Perspectives on Theory*, eds. Gregory Shepherd, Jeffery St. John, and Ted Striphas (Thousand Oaks, Calif.: Sage, 2006), p. 197.

[6]Julia T. Wood, *Communication Theories in Action*, 3rd ed. (Belmont, Calif.: Wadsworth, 2004), p. 276.

[7]Postmodernism will be fully explored and critiqued in chapters 9-10.

[8]J. P. Moreland, *Kingdom Triangle* (Grand Rapids: Zondervan, 2007), p. 77. While Moreland's

This puts individuals within our field who hold to certain faith traditions in a difficult position. Specifically, followers of Islam, Judaism and Christianity maintain that their particular religion makes absolutist truth claims that apply to all people not merely followers of that religion. For example, Muslims maintain that Allah's final revelation is found in the holy Qur'an. While elements of truth may be found in Christian and Jewish texts, the Qur'an is authoritative for all. To maintain that the truth claims of one faith tradition apply to *all* means that followers of those faith traditions dissent from the dominant ideology of our field concerning a postmodern view of truth.

However, our dissent is not relegated to philosophical debates of the nature of truth. As Christians within the field of communication we join with other spiritually interested communication students and scholars to advocate for the valuing of religious knowledge and inquiry. Yale law professor Stephen Carter argues that in secularized Western culture religion is tolerated so long as it remains a personal interest that does not influence political or academic judgments. He writes: "One good way to end a conversation—or start an argument—is to tell a group of well educated professionals that you hold a political position (preferably a controversial one, such as being against abortion or pornography) because it is required by your understanding of God's will."[9]

In a culture (or university) committed to secular or naturalistic assumptions "religion is not the sort of thing that can be true. Religion is merely a cultural, social phenomenon to be analyzed by sociologists."[10] Having our religious commitments viewed as a type of intellectual hobby has a powerful silencing affect. I (Tim) remember attending a divisional meeting of the Religious Communication Association (RCA)

---

description of postmodernism is useful, we must be careful not to assume that everyone who holds to a social constructionist view necessarily has a relative view of truth or is postmodern. One can believe that a culture's view of masculinity, femininity, courtship, friendship, leadership, race or beauty is socially constructed, yet still hold to an objective view of truth. Many of the scholars quoted in this book, including Christian scholars, would to varying degrees consider themselves social constructionists. The issue at question is a postmodern view of truth that runs counter to a biblical notion of truth rooted in God's good character that applies to all cultures, at all times.

[9]Stephen L. Carter, *The Culture of Disbelief: How American Law and Politics Trivialize Religious Devotion* (New York: Basic Books, 1993), p. 23.

[10]Moreland, *Kingdom Triangle*, p. 31.

at a National Communication Association convention and listening to a colleague share that coming out of graduate school he was warned not to join the RCA because he would not be considered a serious scholar. While there are encouraging signs that this view is changing, evidenced by increased participation in the religious communication and spiritual communication divisions of NCA and religious communication scholars whose work is valued across the discipline, students and scholars serious about their faith can still run into this view.

Students and scholars serious about their faith are not arguing that religious knowledge is all that matters. However, we agree with the biblical writer who affirmed that the "beginning of wisdom" (Prov 9:10) starts with an acknowledgment and respect for God. Wheaton College president Duane Litfin argues that it make sense to start with God because the "cosmos God created is not simple. It is multi-faceted. It has physical, spiritual, and moral dimensions to it, but each dimension is fully real because its reality is anchored in the fact that it is part of what God knows to be the case."[11] Because the spiritual dimension is just as real as the physical dimension, communication scholars with faith commitments are equally interested in both. Litfin continues:

> Humans can come to know that something is the case because God has told them by special revelation (for example, that Jesus is God's Son); or they can know something is the case by discovering it for themselves— that is, by applying their God-given capacity for apprehension to those dimensions of the created order that are available to them (for example, that the earth revolves around the sun).[12]

One of the problems secular scholars have with Litfin's statement is the idea that special revelation is uncritically accepted by religious followers and is beyond investigation, testing or objective verification. While this critique may be valid concerning religions such as Hinduism or Buddhism—which value inner experience over objective verification—it does not apply to Christianity. Apologist Craig Hazen ar-

---

[11]Duane Litfin, *Conceiving the Christian College* (Grand Rapids: Eerdmans, 2005), p. 89. Litfin offers a useful definition of reality: "As a shorthand definition we can think of reality as simply things as God knows them to be" (ibid., p. 88).

[12]Ibid., p. 91.

gues that Christianity is unique "in that it actually *invites* people to investigate carefully its claims about God, humankind, the universe, and the meaning of life."[13] To support this assertion Hazen points readers to a shocking statement made by the apostle Paul. To the church in Corinth he writes: "If there is no resurrection of the dead, then not even Christ has been raised. And if Christ has not been raised, our preaching is useless and so is your faith" (1 Cor 15:13-14). In this statement Paul links the validity of his—and our—faith to an event open to historical verification. Hazen concludes, "I have not been able to find a passage in the Scriptures and teachings of the other great religious traditions that so tightly links the truth of an entire system of belief to a single, testable historical event."[14] Far from fearing scholarly inquiry, Christians invite it. This invitation is extended not just by Christian apologists but also Christians interested in human communication.

For example, those of us interested in marital communication know that there are communication practices that both help and hurt a couple's relational culture. These practices are identified by communication scholars who spend time carefully observing how couples interact. However, the Scriptures tell us that the most important resource a couple (or anyone) can utilize is prayer. Paul tells his readers that we should, in all things, pray (Phil 4:6). Jesus told his followers that prayer could uproot a mountain and cast it into the sea (Mk 11:23-24). Christian communication scholars not only value information gleaned from both observation and revelation, but sometimes combine the two. Baylor University's Institute for Studies in Religion is currently conducting a national study to ascertain if prayer makes a difference for couples in increasing perceived happiness and decreasing a fear of divorce. Participating couples commit to praying together for five minutes a day for forty days and recording their perceptions.

When we resist our discipline's move toward postmodernism or devaluing of religious knowledge, we act as counterpublics and enter into

---

[13]Craig Hazen, "Christianity in a World of Religions," in *Passionate Conviction: Contemporary Discourses on Christian Apologetics*, eds. Paul Copan and William Lane Craig (Nashville: B & H Academic, 2007), p. 143.
[14]Ibid.

what cultural critic Stuart Hall identifies as the "theatre of struggle."[15] Hall reminds us that culture and ideology are always fluid and often contested. Within every culture and group is a struggle to resist, redefine or challenge the dominant ideology. Christians within our discipline are part of that ideological struggle.

As Christian counterpublics it is crucial that we understand we do not need to win every argument concerning postmodernism or the valuing of religious knowledge. Nor does it mean that a Christian student needs to sit in the front row with a large leather-bound Bible sitting on his or her desk. Rather, our goal should be to have the Christian worldview taken seriously by communication professors and students within our discipline. Making our beliefs plausible will happen through taking time to understand the theoretical insights of others and offering insightful and respectful critique.

Withdrawal. All counterpublics, notes Brouwer, deal with the tension brought on by a dialectic of inward communication with fellow counterpublics and outward communication with dominant publics. "Those who constitute oppositional communication need to speak among themselves in moments of retreat, regrouping, reflection, or rejuvenation."[16]

This idea of coming together for collective times of rejuvenation, reflection and preparation is a constant theme in the history of the early church. Luke tells us that believers "devoted themselves to the apostles' teaching and to the fellowship, to the breaking of bread and to prayer" (Acts 2:42). Like the early church, Christian counterpublics need to retreat together to accomplish three objectives: encouragement, intellectual preparation and prayer.

Encouragement. The writer of Hebrews warns believers not to "give up meeting together" but rather to come together to encourage fellow believers and "spur one another toward love and good deeds" (Heb 10:24-25). One key element of this encouragement is that witnessing the faith of others builds our faith. When reading the letters of Paul it

---

[15]Stuart Hall, "The Problem of Ideology—Marxism Without Guarantees," *Journal of Communication Inquiry* 10, no. 2 (1986): 28-44.
[16]Brouwer, "Communication as Counterpublic," p. 197.

is striking how much he is encouraged by learning of the growing faith of others. While under house arrest and awaiting trial in Rome (Acts 28:30) he writes to the church at Ephesus and tells them that since hearing of their faith and love for the saints he has not "stopped giving thanks" for them (Eph 1:16). This is a common pattern in Paul's ministry—he hears of the faith and obedience of others and is strengthened in his faith and obedience (Rom 1:12; Phil 1:25; Col 2:7; 1 Thess 3:10; 2 Thess 1:3). The early church needed these times of encouragement since they were often small communities in the midst of pagan religions, moral decline and political forces opposed to their cause.

As counterpublics, Christians often find themselves in the same situation as the early church. They are part of a minority opinion in a department that runs counter to a traditional Christian worldview. Communication researchers Nancy Eckstein and Paul Turman note that many students with religious convictions are often silenced in the university classroom. Their research focused on the communication styles of professors that caused students to feel uncomfortable with sharing religious views. "To be able to openly express potential controversial views, the student needs to feel the support from the teacher—not necessarily for the ideas—but for the right to express it."[17] The communication style of the professor plays a crucial role in determining the communication climate of the classroom. Through a professor's use of *naming* (starting a conversation by saying, "Those in this class who are born-again Christians"), *not naming* (referring to God as "her" rather than "him") and *smoothing over* (quickly tabling religious discussion), religiously minded students learn, to quote Fine, "The price of success is muting one's voice."[18] Christians acting as counterpublics need to meet frequently to encourage each other to "stand firm" in the faith (1 Cor 16:13) and strategically voice their Christian worldview. This meeting and regrouping can happen in small groups (a Christian study group or Bible study) or at regional or national conventions.

---

[17]Nancy Eckstein and Paul Turman, "Children Are to be Seen and Not Heard: Silencing Students' Religious Voices in the University Classroom," *Journal of Communication and Religion* 25 (2002): 177.
[18]Ibid.

Intellectual preparation. In addition to meeting for encouragement and fellowship, believers need to gather regularly to prepare to engage others on a scholarly level. There are many in academia today who believe that conservative Christians (or any person who claims to have the truth) embrace a type of anti-intellectualism fostered by faith commitments. Nothing could be further from the truth, argues Michael Green in his book *Evangelism in the Early Church*. Green argues that one of reasons the early church grew at such a rapid rate was the ability of Christian intellectuals to out-think opponents. He writes:

> Armed with these [biblical] convictions, the early Christian intellectuals from Paul and John to Clement and Origen glow with the confidence of having found the key to understanding the universe, of having arrived while other philosophers were only stumbling along the way. There was, therefore, no need for Justin to remove his philosopher's garb after his conversion.[19]

The same applies to those of us interested in communication studies. Our allegiance to Christ does not mean that we have to take off our scholarly garb and set aside our interest in communication theory. To the contrary, we need to take seriously the purpose of the series this book is a part of—to integrate our faith into our studies at a high academic level. We agree with communication and media-ethics scholar Clifford Christians who writes that "unless we come to grips with our field's core—its intellectual life—our impact will be partial and ineffective."[20] He argues that while our personal conduct should at all times reflect Christ, it must be accompanied by scholarly books and research projects if the field of communication is to be transformed for the long run. "We need a powerful stream of Christian thinking that academia as a whole cannot ignore. Because the Bible opens up all of life, scriptural truth is a white light that shines through a prism of *intellectus* into a spectrum of colors, not merely illuminating a narrow road

---

[19]Michael Green, *Evangelism in the Early Church* (Grand Rapids: Eerdmans, 2003), p. 172. Green notes two other compelling reasons the church grew: its outreach to social outcasts and living corporately in the Spirit's power.

[20]Clifford Christians, "Christian Scholarship and Academic Pluralism," *Journal of Communication and Religion* 27 (2004): 12.

to heaven."[21] Christians is echoing a sentiment held by C. S. Lewis:

> The difficulty we are up against is this. We can make people (often) attend to the Christian point of view for half an hour or so; but the moment they have gone away from our lecture or laid down our article, they are plunged back into a world where the opposite position is taken for granted. As long as that situation exists, wide-spread success is simply impossible. . . . You can see this most easily if you look at it the other way round. Our Faith is not very likely to be shaken by any book on Hinduism. But if whenever we read an elementary book on Geology, Botany, Politics, or Astronomy, we found that its implications were Hindu, that would shake us.[22]

Lewis concludes that what "we want is not more little books about Christianity, but more little books by Christians on other subjects—with their Christianity latent."[23] Imagine if a freshman or sophomore picked up a book on social justice, feminist theory, interpersonal communication, gender or rhetoric and found that it was written by a professor committed to exceptional scholarship and a Christian worldview. As counterpublics our desire is to increase discursive spaces to include the finest scholarship in any field of inquiry.[24]

Prayer. As Christian counterpublics we understand that our ability to effectively change the perceptions and beliefs of others is not just a matter of crafting persuasive and intellectually stimulating conference papers, journal articles or sound research projects. Unlike secular counterpublics, we know that there is a spiritual dimension to our task that can only be addressed through prayer. There is no better example of the need for prayer than Christ himself. Often, while in the midst of in-

---

[21]Ibid., p. 13.

[22]C. S. Lewis, "Christian Apologetics," in *God in the Dock: Essays on Theology and Ethics* (Grand Rapids: Eerdmans, 1970), p. 93.

[23]Ibid.

[24]Charles Malik, former Lebanese ambassador to the United States, voiced the same concern as Christians and Lewis in his dedication of the Billy Graham Center in Wheaton, Illinois: "Who among evangelical scholars is quoted as a normative source by the greatest secular authorities on history or philosophy or psychology or sociology or politics? Does the evangelical mode of thinking have the slightest chance of becoming the dominant mode in the great universities of Europe and America that stamp our entire civilization with their spirit and ideas?" ("The Other Side of Evangelism," *Christianity Today*, November 7, 1980, p. 40).

tense ministry, Jesus "withdrew to lonely places and prayed" (Lk 5:16; see also Mt 14:23; 26:36; Mk 6:46; Lk 6:12; 9:28). Christ knew that the effectiveness of his mission was contingent on moving the Spirit via prayer. Following his example, Christian counterpublics need to pray for the Spirit's guidance and power as we seek the change hearts and minds.

While withdrawing for times of renewal, learning and intercession is crucial for counterpublics, there is a danger to a prolonged time of retreat. It feels good to be among those who share our convictions and worldview. The longer we isolate ourselves from those who disagree with us, the easier it is to grow comfortable and draw increasingly inward. Soon we are publishing exclusively with Christian publishers, joining professional Christian societies and presenting papers at Christian conferences on how to be an effective counterpublic. Counterpublics must not be merely content to discuss strategies of engagement, we must actually engage.

Engagement. Brouwer argues that central to the idea of counterpublics is engagement with dominant publics. "In this view, radical exclusions such as forced exile or chosen separatism, in which social actors cannot or do not address other publics, do not constitute counterpublicity."[25]

Building off of our discussion of persuasion (chap. 5) we offer some thoughts of how Christian counterpublics can engage those around us. First, while the primary feature of our role as Christian counterpublics is to advocate for the truth even if it runs counter to the dominant discourse or ideology, we do not have to always go it alone. In fact, there are many issues in which we can link arms with other counterpublics in our discipline. For example, at a National Communication Association convention I (Tim) took part in a panel discussion in front of a packed auditorium that explored how faith and scholarship inform each other. One panelist explored the connection between Islamic values and ethics in communication. Another shared how her Buddhism influenced her teaching and scholarship particularly concerning the Buddhist con-

---

[25]Brouwer, "Communication as Counterpublic," p. 197.

cept of mindfulness (being fully present in the moment). A Jewish scholar gave a fascinating presentation on how the Talmud helped broaden his understanding of rhetoric. A few of us on the panel represented the Christian perspective. Despite our religious differences, all panelists acted as counterpublics, arguing that religious commitments did not limit our scholarship but enhanced it. Linking arms with these scholars reminded me of C. S. Lewis, who said in order for friendship to thrive, it must be about something, "even if it were only an enthusiasm for dominoes or white mice." Why? "It is when we are doing things together that friendship springs up—painting, sailing, praying, philosophizing, fighting shoulder to shoulder." "Friends," concludes Lewis, "look in the same direction."[26] The thing I remember most about that panel was "fighting shoulder to shoulder" with other counterpublics to argue for the value and intellectual weightiness of faith commitments.

Second, being on the panel with other Christians allowed us to share distinctive features of our faith tradition and counter negative perceptions of what Christians care about. Em Griffin, a Wheaton College communication professor emeritus, shared that Jesus in both word and deed presented himself as the truth. Griffin explained that Christ embodied the truth. "I'm therefore skeptical of an overriding skepticism, or any approach which automatically dismisses metanarratives—whether religious or secular."[27] I had the opportunity to address the perception that Christians are not really interested in issues of social justice except those that directly impact our own community. I told the audience my faith supports our discipline's call for social justice for everyone and reminds me that God defends the fatherless, the widow and the alien in all walks of life (Deut 10:18). The genesis of chapter twelve on social justice in this volume came from the thoughts shared that day.

RESIDENT ALIENS

As Christians, serving as counterpublics is part of our history. In He-

---

[26]C. S. Lewis, *The Four Loves* (New York: Harcourt, Brace, 1988), p. 98.
[27]Em Griffin, "A Believer's Efforts to Integrate Faith and Scholarship," *Journal of Communication and Religion* 27 (2004): 26.

brews 11 the writer describes people of faith as "aliens" and "strangers" (v. 13) on earth who look toward a "better country—a heavenly one" (v. 16). Pastor and author Timothy Keller notes that the term *alien* in Greco-Roman culture carried with it a very specific social status. Aliens who had taken up permanent residence in a city were considered resident aliens, neither visitors nor citizens. Because these individuals were permanent residents, they had a vested interest in the success and flourishing of a city that would never fully embrace them. Keller points out that this is the tension Christians have had to negotiate through the ages.[28] To some extent, Christians will be out of place in any society. A second-century document describes early Christians as individuals who "inhabit their own country, but as sojourners: they take part in all things as citizens, and endure all things as aliens: every foreign country is theirs, and every country is foreign."[29]

As Christians and counterpublics in the field of communication we need to embrace both aspects of being a resident alien. First, as individuals committed to a Christian worldview we will never be fully embraced by our discipline. We will always need to resist aspects of the dominant ideology that shape communication studies. Second, as resident aliens we are committed to the advancement of our discipline. With all communication students and scholars we recognize the vital importance communication plays in what it means to be and to flourish as a human. We enthusiastically participate in a discipline that will never fully receive us.

Today, a powerful challenge facing Christian counterpublics is the postmodern worldview, which has deeply influenced many in the field of communication. What is it that postmoderns believe that could undermine our deepest Christian convictions? In chapters nine and ten we'll introduce five ideas that have changed how many of our fellow scholars and classmates view reality, truth and God.

---

[28]Timothy J. Keller, "City of God: Hebrews 11:13-16; 13:10-16," sermon preached on May 1, 2005, Redeemer Presbyterian Church, New York.

[29]Quoting the anonymous Epistle to Diagnetus, in Kenneth Wuest, *Wuest's Word Studies from the Greek New Testament* (Grand Rapids: Eerdmans, 1973), 2:203.

9

Postmodern Times and Christian Counterpublics, Part 1

In *The Matrix*, a science fiction blockbuster of 1999, a pivotal scene occurs when Neo (played by Keanu Reeves) is offered a chance to come face-to-face with a reality that has been strategically hidden from him. Up to this point Neo, a computer programmer and underground hacker, has believed that everything he touches, sees, eats and experiences is real. A mysterious stranger named Morpheus offers him the opportunity to see beyond the illusion by taking a red pill. Neo accepts and the rest is cinema history. Along with Neo, we learn that humans have been tricked into believing that everyday experiences are real when in actuality they are part of a virtual reality created by machines to pacify humans. Once pacified, human body heat and electrical activity are used as fuel by the machines. The Matrix Trilogy along with movies such as *The Truman Show* and *Dark City* were part of a wave of movies designed to shake our confidence in what we perceive.[1]

In the discipline of communication there are a growing number of postmodern scholars that, like Morpheus, want us to question taken-for-granted assumptions about reality. While it's wise to place a question mark over long-held assumptions, these scholars want to call into question beliefs central to our faith. How should Christian counterpublics respond? In the next two chapters we'll examine five key ideas that postmodern theorizers want us to *reconsider* and how Christians

---

[1]The hit Broadway musical *Wicked* does this as well, telling the "true" backstory of the characters in *The Wizard of Oz*. *Wicked* concludes that evil may be a perception that compares greater with lesser evils.

within the field of communication should respond.

Before we look at these key ideas, a word should be said about how Christians should approach postmodernism as a whole. In the introductory chapter of this book, J. P. Moreland and Francis Beckwith note that throughout church history followers of Christ have with great discernment been open to learning from the wisdom of other cultures and belief systems. "To imagine none can teach you but those who are themselves saved from sin," argues John Wesley "is a very great and dangerous mistake."[2] When we encounter postmodern ideas coming from professors or fellow classmates, we should not immediately be defensive. Rather, we should seek to understand and, when appropriate, learn from postmoderns. Theologian Millard Erickson wisely titled his introductory book on postmodernism *Truth or Consequences: The Promise and Peril of Postmodernism*. While the perils of postmodernism have been well documented, few seek to explore the promise of this worldview. Erickson notes that when it comes to understanding the relationship between knowledge and power, the importance of narratives, the role of communities, and the value of suspicion, the postmodern worldview is penetrating and insightful. In my own work I (Tim) have found the writings of postmodern thinkers to be useful in understanding issues of gender, race and identity.

While postmoderns and Christians often differ on the answers to key philosophical questions such as the existence of truth or the moral grounding of social justice, we agree that questions surrounding these issues are crucial. Having similar points of interest, not similar conclusions, can be starting points for authentic dialogue. C. S. Lewis notes: "The man who agrees with us that some question, little regarded by others, is of great importance can be our friend. He need not agree with us about some answer."[3]

In the following critique we will start by noting points of common concerns or interests shared with postmoderns. After establishing points of connection we will offer areas of concern for our postmodern friends and colleagues to consider.

---

[2]John Wesley, *A Plain Account of Christian Perfection* (London: Epworth Press, 1952), p. 87.
[3]C. S. Lewis, *The Four Loves* (New York: Harcourt, Brace, Jovanovich, 1960), p. 96.

So, it is with both openness and discernment we now turn in this chapter to two ideas foundational to postmodernism. These two pivotal ideas lay the foundation in how reality is conceptualized. As postmodern author Walter Truett Anderson fondly states, "Reality isn't what it used to be."[4]

POSTMODERN IDEAS

Idea 1: Metanarratives are oppressive. In his foundational work *The Postmodern Condition*, Jean-François Lyotard states, "Simplifying to the extreme, I define postmodern as incredulity toward metanarratives."[5] A metanarrative is an overarching or totalizing story a culture or society tells about itself that presents its particular values, beliefs and practices as natural and right. A metanarrative serves as an organizing framework for independent local narratives. "A metanarrative is a *story* of mythic proportions, a story big enough and meaningful enough to pull together philosophy and research and politics and art, relate them to one another, and—above all—give them a unifying sense of direction."[6] Lyotard cites the Christian, Marxist and Enlightenment stories as examples of totalizing narratives. Central to metanarratives is the assumption that one view or narrative possesses a "truth fixed and beyond mere human conjecture."[7]

Postmodern theorists oppose metanarratives for several reasons. Their first concern is ethical; that is, metanarratives are viewed as inherently authoritarian and oppressive. Who has the right to determine what is good, right or moral for the rest of us? Each community, society or culture should be free to craft stories or myths that represent their unique take on life, art, love, justice and so forth. Metanarratives, by their very nature, repress and supplant local narratives. Consequently,

---

[4]Anderson's phrase is the title of his thought-provoking introduction to postmodernism *Reality Isn't What It Used to Be: Theatrical Politics, Ready-to-Wear Religion, Global Myths, Primitive Chic, and Other Wonders of the Postmodern World* (San Francisco: Harper & Row, 1990).

[5]Jean-François Lyotard, *The Postmodern Condition: A Report on Knowledge*, trans. Geoff Bennington and Brian Massumi (Minneapolis: University of Minnesota Press, 1984), p. iv.

[6]Walter Truett Anderson, "Introduction: What's Going On?" in *The Truth About the Truth: Deconfusing and Re-constructing the Postmodern World*, ed. Walter Truett Anderson (New York: Tarcher/Putnam, 1995), p. 4.

[7]Ibid.

Lyotard declares "war on totality" and compares narratives that claim a universal perspective to crimes against humanity.[8] Oxford literary critic Terry Eagleton attacks metanarratives for a "secretly terroristic" desire to perpetuate and legitimate the "illusion of a universal human history."[9] The desire for one point of view to triumph over another must be abandoned. Even the most established metanarratives cannot avoid this blistering critique. "Science and philosophy must jettison their grandiose metaphysical claims and view themselves more modestly as just another set of narratives."[10]

Another problem with metanarratives is that in their refusal to tolerate alternate views they close us off from the diverse perspectives of others. Postmodern scholars like Jacques Derrida value and promote an ongoing openness to the *other*. The recognition of other perspectives forces us to loosely hold onto our beliefs as we playfully explore the narratives of those who view the world in different ways. Lyotard views the consensus created by a metanarrative as being impossibly restrictive to creativity, diversity and invention.

These totalizing narratives not only inhibit creativity but foster intellectual arrogance and laziness. Christopher Falzon argues that the totalizing thinking central to metanarratives is "condemned to a sterile, tautologous repetition or affirmation of its basic categories, categories which themselves remain entirely unquestionable within this system of thinking."[11] The result is a "dogmatic slumber" that places a person into "a kind of claustrophobic, airless confinement in which everything is repetition, and nothing new can enter to break the spell."[12] When a person feels that his or her culture's view is in possession of the truth, there is no longer a need to explore the views of others. A possessor of the truth closes him- or herself off from criticism and intellectual exploration.

Areas of agreement. The apprehension postmoderns have toward

---

[8]Lyotard, *Postmodern Condition*, p. 82.
[9]Terry Eagleton, "Awakening from Modernity," *The Times Literary Supplement*, February 20, 1987, p. 194.
[10]Ibid.
[11]Christopher Falzon, *Foucault and Social Dialogue* (New York: Routledge, 1998), p. 19.
[12]Ibid.

metanarratives and dogmatic claims to truth should be taken into consideration for several reasons.

First, a main concern for thinkers like Lyotard or Falzon is that when people think they possess the truth, they are inclined to approach others' views with arrogance or a rigid close-mindedness. To be honest, in many cases they're right. Many within the Christian community lock themselves into what Falzon identifies as a "dogmatic slumber" and refuse to consider or acknowledge the insight of those outside the walls of the church. As students and faculty committed to the pursuit of knowledge, we must be open to diligently and authentically study the views of others. The first steps in receiving an education are to listen and seek to understand. "There is a deeply concealed impatience, if not open arrogance," writes Christian apologist Os Guinness, "in the attitude characterized by instant replies and irrelevant judgments."[13]

Second, postmoderns are right to remind us that any belief system and the metanarrative that might accompany it cannot remove all uncertainty concerning its validity. Christians are convinced that we possess a metanarrative that correctly describes and unifies reality, yet we cannot remove all doubt that our beliefs are true. "While we may possess absolute truth, it is quite a different matter to say that we understand it absolutely. Because of our human limitations, our beliefs will always contain an element of the uncertain and the merely probable."[14] Such a statement should not be overly disconcerting to followers of Christ. Paul reminds us that in this life we'll walk by "faith, not by sight" (2 Cor 5:7) and the writer of Hebrews states that "without faith it is impossible to please God" (Heb 11:6).[15] Christians have sound intellectual arguments and powerful personal experiences that firmly buttress our belief in God and Christ. Yet our arguments and experi-

---

[13]Os Guinness, *Doubt* (Downers Grove, Ill.: InterVarsity Press, 1976), p. 152.

[14]Millard Erickson, *The Postmodern World: Discerning the Times and the Spirit of Our Age* (Wheaton, Ill.: Crossway, 2002), p. 88.

[15]To live a life of faith is not to say that we cannot pursue Christ with passion and conviction. The writer of Hebrews states that "faith is being sure of what we hope for and certain of what we do not see" (Heb 11:1). What the writer is describing is not proof-positive belief void of faith, but rather a settled belief. To use a poker analogy, faith is that moment when a player, based on keen observations of other players, intuition and knowledge of the game, goes *all in* even though he or she cannot be absolutely certain his or her bet will work.

ences will never remove all uncertainty or make faith unnecessary. In a sense, every human is forced to live by faith and wrestle with doubts. Os Guinness rightly notes that doubt "is not primarily a Christian problem, but a human problem."[16] The postmodern who rejects absolute truth or the Christian metanarrative will also wrestle with doubt and degrees of uncertainty.

Last, postmoderns are wise to question any meta- or grand narrative that presents a view of reality implicitly or explicitly privileging one group over another. For example, an organizing or grand narrative in America is that idea that a hardworking person will succeed and prosper. America is a level playing field where a "man can pull himself up by his own bootstraps." Julia Wood notes that this narrative is built around the story of Horatio Alger, who was not only successful but white, able-bodied and male.

> Can someone born to homeless parents who doesn't have enough to eat and isn't enrolled in school pull herself up by her bootstraps? Do Hispanics and whites get the same respect and wages for the work they do? Do women and men who have equal skills and experience get equal opportunities for career advancement?[17]

Due to their powerful influence, metanarratives must be carefully examined in terms of power dynamics they establish.

While the concerns postmoderns have toward metanarratives are insightful, their rejection of all metanarratives puts them in a difficult philosophical position.

Area of concern. Is a rejection of metanarratives self-refuting? When considering the validity of a worldview, individuals have an expectation that the worldview in question is logically consistent. If a particular view does not hold together logically, then our skepticism of that view justifiably increases. "Logical incoherence can be more or less fatal depending on whether the contradiction exists among less central beliefs or whether it lies at the very heart of the system."[18] As noted earlier in

---

[16]Guinness, *Doubt*, p. 30.
[17]Julia T. Wood, *Communication Theories in Action: An Introduction*, 3rd ed. (Belmont, Calif.: Wadsworth, 2004), p. 291.
[18]Ronald Nash, *Faith and Reason* (Grand Rapids: Zondervan, 1988), p. 52.

this chapter, Lyotard simplifies postmodern thought to a rejection of metanarratives. Yet, is this foundational tenet of postmodernism logically consistent or self-refuting? Self-refuting statements are "those which fail to satisfy their own criteria of validity or acceptability."[19] If a person walks up to you and in perfect English says, "I cannot speak a complete sentence in English," that statement is self-refuting because the statement itself has been spoken in English. Postmoderns are accused of being self-refuting in their rejection of metanarratives and objective truth.

Critics of postmodernism argue that in asserting a rejection of metanarratives—an overarching or totalizing narrative—they are in fact positing an overarching and totalizing narrative. In reading postmodern thinkers it is apparent that they believe that a postmodern view of language, personhood and truth is superior to opposing views of language, personhood and truth. In reality, they merely swap one metanarrative (modernism) for another (postmodernism). The irony of speaking authoritatively about a loss of authority has not gone unnoticed. Steven Connor writes of fellow postmoderns:

> What is striking is precisely the degree of consensus in postmodernist discourse that there is no longer any possibility of consensus, the authoritative announcements of the disappearance of final authority and the promotion and recirculation of a total and comprehensive narrative of a cultural condition in which totality is no longer thinkable.[20]

Postmoderns respond to these charges by stating that every view of reality, including postmodernism, is fragmented, partial and open to questioning and criticism. Walter Truett Anderson reflects this attitude when he writes that the postmodern worldview is in many ways an arbitrary belief that adherents hold "without knowing how to prove what it presumes."[21] Two responses are in order. First, while denying

---

[19]Norman L. Geisler, *Baker Encyclopedia of Christian Apologetics* (Grand Rapids: Baker, 1999), p. 707.

[20]Steven Connor, *Postmodernist Culture: An Introduction to Theories of the Contemporary*, 2nd ed. (Cambridge, Mass.: Blackwell, 1997), p. 9.

[21]Walter Truett Anderson, *The Truth About the Truth* (New York: Tarcher/Putnam, 1995), p. 268.

claims of truth does rescue the postmodern from being self-refuting, it also strips postmodernism of rhetorical persuasiveness concerning its validity. If postmodernism is merely a fragmented view of reality, then what compels me to consider it? Second, when reading postmodern authors it becomes obvious that they do in fact consider their view superior to other views. While Anderson may believe that postmodernism is an arbitrary belief, he clearly believes it is superior to all other arbitrary beliefs. "A pluralistic civilization can only be built with a great amount of tolerance, and the kind of tolerance that comes from people who believe in the cosmic certainty of their truth (and theirs alone) is both limited and patronizing."[22]

Idea 2: Truth depends on your point of view. Those within our discipline who reject metanarratives often come to embrace some form of personal or cultural relativism. According to relativism, "a claim is true relative to the beliefs or valuations of an individual or group that accepts it."[23] The truths, customs, perspectives, morals or beliefs created by one culture will not necessarily apply to another culture. The mistake individuals make, notes Friedrich Nietzsche, is to forget that the truths and perspectives created by their particular culture are not set in stone, but rather are fluid linguistic constructions. He writes:

> What is truth? A mobile army of metaphors, metonyms, anthropomorphisms, in short, a sum of human relations which were poetically and rhetorically heightened, transferred, and adorned, and after long use seem solid, canonical, and binding to a nation. Truths are illusions about which it has been forgotten that they *are* illusions, worn-out metaphors without sensory impact, coins which have lost their image and now can be used only as metal, and no longer as coins.[24]

All claims to objective truth are useful fictions created by cultures and expressed in laws, customs, taboos and beliefs.[25] In this view, "truth

---

[22]Ibid., p. 267.

[23]J. P. Moreland and William Lane Craig, *Philosophical Foundations for a Christian Worldview* (Downers Grove, Ill.: InterVarsity Press, 2003), p. 133.

[24]Friedrich Nietzsche, "On Truth and Lying in an Extra-moral Sense," in *Friedrich Nietzsche on Rhetoric and Language*, ed. and trans. Sander L. Gilman, Carol Blair and David J. Parent (New York: Oxford University Press, 1989), p. 247.

[25]In contrast to a relativistic view of truth, an objective view maintains that "a claim is made true

is seen as a tool, perpetuated by those in control as a means of oppression and maintaining control of underclasses; the most dangerous creatures are those claiming to know."[26]

Postmoderns are not the first to view truth as being culturally relative. The Sophists Plato debated also viewed truth as being relative to a particular place or culture. In their attempt to sell their particular brand of rhetorical and philosophical skills, Sophists traveled well beyond the confines of Athens. During these travels they observed that in different regions of the world people held different customs, beliefs and values. Observing this diversity caused well-known Sophists like Gorgias and Protagoras to question whether knowledge or value came from the gods or was a mere linguistic invention. If truth was a linguistic creation, then those skilled in logic and rhetoric could force their view of truth and reality on others.[27] The conclusions reached by Sophists prefigured a postmodern understanding of language games, power and the relativity of truth.

Areas of agreement. Surely, postmoderns are correct to argue that time, place and culture greatly influence our perceptions. As you've already read in our discussion of perception (chap. 2) the world and the truths we embrace are greatly influenced by culture and our social position within culture (standpoint theory). Kavosh Dehpanah, the Iranian farmer turned terrorist, believed the West was evil, and blowing up hostages on an airplane was morally acceptable because of the beliefs he received from his particular community.

Not only is our knowledge of the world influenced and conditioned by culture, but our idea of how the world should change is influenced as well. Millard Erickson notes that "the very choice of issues to address is affected by time and place."[28] Not until August 26, 1920, did women have the right to vote in the United States. Before that time many men *and* women did not believe a woman's right to vote was an

---

or false in some way or another by reality itself, totally independent of whether the claim is accepted by anyone" (Moreland and Craig, *Philosophical Foundations*, p. 132).

[26]Graham Johnston, *Preaching to a Postmodern World* (Grand Rapids: Baker, 2001), p. 32.

[27]For an excellent introduction to the strengths and weaknesses of influential Sophists see James A. Herrick, *The History and Theory of Rhetoric*, 3rd ed. (New York: Allyn & Bacon, 2005).

[28]Erickson, *Truth or Consequences*, p. 186.

important social issue. Many believed, due to prevailing views of gender, that women lacked either the intellectual capacity or interest to make informed political choices.

Area of concern. Are there some perspectives and claims to truth that we should not only exclude but vigorously oppose? In critiquing Derrida, Huston Smith asks what should be done when the perspective of the *other* turns out to be skinhead Nazis or the Ku Klux Klan? Should their opinion and claims to truth be respected and moved to the center? "Our hearts invariably go out to the 'others' that deconstructionists name, but do deconstructionist 'skills' include ones for winnowing hard cases?"[29]

By arguing that truth and morality are social constructions, the postmodern struggles to find a moral basis for social activism and challenging the views of others. If a society's ethics are socially constructed and only apply to that culture, then what gives a person the right to judge the ethics and values of another society? Moral relativism implies that moral propositions are not simply true or false. Rather, the truth values of moral principles themselves are relative to the beliefs of a given culture. Postmodern scholars committed to a social justice agenda acknowledge the tenuous nature of their position. Vivien Burr, senior lecturer in psychology at the University of Huddersfield, writes that if "all accounts of the world are equally valid, then we appear deprived of defensible grounds for our moral choices and political allegiances."[30] Steven Connor, while generally favorable to postmodernism, concedes that ethics in a postmodern world easily deteriorates into the "principle that might is right; or to the sunny complacency of pragmatism, in which it is assumed that we can never ground our activities in ethical principles which have more force than just saying 'this is the sort of thing we do, because it suits us.'"[31]

While many individuals holding postmodern beliefs are ardent social activists who would vigorously oppose acts like racism or oppres-

---

[29]Huston Smith, "Postmodernism and the World's Religions," in *The Truth About the Truth*, ed. Walter Truett Anderson (New York: Tarcher/Putnam, 1995), p. 208.

[30]Vivien Burr, *Social Constructionism*, 2nd ed. (New York: Routledge, 2003), p. 23.

[31]Connor, *Postmodernist Culture*, p. 276.

sion, the central issue becomes finding a philosophical or moral principle to ground their activism.

Area of concern. Isn't the assertion that truth is relative to a person's point of view also self-refuting? In the *American Scholar*, biologist Brian Boyd writes that a relative view of truth inherent in postmodernism compromises its own logical consistency.

> The idea that there is no universal truth runs into crippling difficulties straightway, since it claims to be a universal truth. The idea that all is difference, merely local and situated, must apply, if true, to itself, and if this disqualifies its claim to truth, as the implication seems to be, then it contradicts itself.[32]

Boyd notes that scholars outside the postmodern camp resist "the self-contradictory and defeatist claim that all knowledge, except the knowledge of the situatedness of knowledge, is situated and therefore flawed."[33]

The difficulty of embracing a relative view of truth is that, as Peter Berger notes, relativism "bends back upon itself." In the end the "relativizers are relativised, the debunkers are debunked—indeed, relativization itself is liquidated."[34] If all truth claims are relative to a particular place and time, then why should I feel compelled to accept any group's view of truth or reality? Individuals are free to simply pick and choose among competing truth claims motivated by self-interest or attempts to garner personal power.

In *Orthodoxy*, G. K. Chesterton summarizes the position of today's postmodern activist: "Therefore the modern man in revolt becomes practically useless for all purposes of revolt. By rebelling against everything he has lost his right to rebel against anything."[35] By rejecting objective moral values the postmodern forfeits his or her right to label oppression or misogyny wrong for everyone, everywhere. In arguing

---

[32]Brian Boyd, "Getting it All Wrong: Bioculture Critiques Cultural Critique," *American Scholar*, autumn 2006, p. 25.

[33]Ibid., p. 27.

[34]Peter L. Berger, *A Rumor of Angels: Modern Society and the Rediscovery of the Supernatural* (Garden City, N.Y.: Doubleday/Anchor Books, 1970), p. 42.

[35]G. K. Chesterton, *Orthodoxy* (Garden City, N.Y.: Doubleday, 1959), p. 41.

that truth depends on your point of view, the postmodern cripples arguments for his or her worldview being superior to others. In the end the postmodern can only, and often adeptly, identify problems facing us. Unfortunately, the rational and moral beliefs necessary for solving these personal and cultural problems have long since been abandoned.

In chapter ten we'll explore how the two ideas we've just considered influence how postmoderns view what it means to be human, the power of words and how our biases tempt us to twist the truth.

10

POSTMODERN TIMES AND CHRISTIAN COUNTERPUBLICS, PART 2

In a dimly lit room with lightning flashing in the background, Morpheus tells Neo about the Matrix and a false reality that has blinded him since birth. "Have you ever had a dream, Neo, that you were sure was real?" In this chapter we'll consider how postmodern thinkers argue that our belief in a common humanity, an awareness of the world independent of language and personal objectivity are merely dreams we have bought into and perpetuate daily.

POSTMODERN IDEAS

Idea 3: Humans are not as alike as you think. What comforts many people is that despite our many political, ethnic, economic or religious differences, what binds the human race together is that we share a common essence or nature. Postmoderns question this basic assumption. Vivien Burr presents a different point of view about our common humanity: "Since the world, including ourselves as people, is the product of social processes, it follows that there cannot be any given, predetermined nature to the world or people. There are no essences inside things or people that make them what they are."[1] To speak as though all humans have the same essence or nature is to obscure the rich differences between us. To do so, notes Jean-François Lyotard, is to use language to injure the other. Steven Connor summarizes Lyotard's view:

---

[1]Vivien Burr, *An Introduction to Social Constructionism* (New York: Routledge, 1995), p. 5.

This "we," he writes, is a form of grammatical violence, which aims to deny and obliterate the specificity of the "you" and the "she" of other cultures through the false promise of incorporation within a universal humanity. We must therefore wean ourselves away from the "we," that grammatico-political category that can never exist except as a legitimating myth operating in the service of appropriative and oppressive cultures. Instead we must embrace and promote every form of cultural diversity, without recourse to universal principles.[2]

To refer to a common human nature is to obliterate the rich diversity of other cultures for the sake of cultural domination.

Areas of agreement. What concerns Lyotard about arguing for a universal humanity is that it will obliterate the rich differences between cultures. The "we" of a universal humanity will overshadow, obscure and eventually do violence to the diversity of the "she" or "you" of other people groups. In his critique of postmodern cultural studies Brian Boyd argues that a rejection of a common human nature *is* warranted if what postmoderns are objecting to is "Eurocentric hegemony *posing* as universalism."[3] Any attempt to define our common human nature that favors one ethnic group over another amounts to a form of ethnocentrism and must be abandoned.

Christians must heed Lyotard's concerns as we seek to balance both a belief in a universal humanity and the uniqueness of divergent cultures. While we believe that all humans are made in the image of God and share the same essence, we also want to conceptualize the image of God in humanity as being inclusive of the diversity of human life. Theologian John Stott argues that heaven will reflect this rich diversity: "Scripture celebrates the colorful mosaic of human cultures. It even declares that the New Jerusalem will be enriched by them, since the 'kings of the earth will bring their splendor into it,' and 'the glory and honor of the nations will be brought into it' (Rev. 21:24, 26)."[4]

---

[2]Steven Connor, *Postmodernist Culture: An Introduction to Theories of the Contemporary,* 2nd ed. (Cambridge, Mass.: Blackwell, 1997), p. 32.

[3]Brian Boyd, "Getting It All Wrong: Bioculture Critiques Cultural Critique," *American Scholar,* autumn 2006, p. 27.

[4]John Stott, *Involvement: Social and Sexual Relationships in the Modern World* (Old Tappan, N.J.: Fleming H. Revell, 1995), 2:91.

One reason Lyotard wants to avoid obscuring diverse cultures is that he believes there is much to learn from their rich traditions and perspectives. I (Tim) can attest the value of exposing myself to other cultures and how that can challenge entrenched habits and beliefs. My first year out of college I spent a summer in Nairobi, Kenya, helping local churches care for the homeless and poor. I stayed with African families that greatly challenged my Western assumptions about family and connection. In an African context an individual is immersed in a whole series of relationships that include his or her immediate and extended families and even ancestors who have passed on. To a person steeped in Western individualism, I found this context to be very eye-opening and convicting. In a Western context individuals place themselves at the center and often break off relationships when they no longer are convenient. While all of us are share a common humanity, I had much to learn from my African hosts about family, responsibility and God.

Area of concern: If there is no essence to our humanity, what will keep people from treating each other inhumanly? Boyd points out that rejecting a common human nature undermines "the grounds for treating other human beings as equals." He continues, "One of the most extreme advocates of difference was Hitler, with his sense of the special destiny of the Aryan people and the German nation, and of the utter difference between Aryan and Jew. . . . If we reject all claims to commonality, we risk denying a sufficient basis for concern for other humans."[5] The defining essence shared by all men and women is that we equally bear the image of God. Why should a homeless woman living in the streets of New Delhi be treated with dignity and care? Regardless of what her culture or coculture determines her worth to be, she is an image bearer of a God that artfully shaped her in her mother's womb (Ps 139:13), loves her (Jn 3:16) and died for her (1 Jn 2:2). Because we share this common nature—a human nature crafted in God's image—dignity can be bestowed to all.

Idea 4: Reality and meaning are constructed through language. Exis-

---

[5]Boyd, "Getting It All Wrong," p. 27.

tentialists like Jean-Paul Sartre and Martin Heidegger stressed the responsibility alienated individuals had to create personal meaning in a world void of meaning. In contrast, postmoderns argue that identity and meaning are created in social groups through language.[6] It is through language that we come to understand ourselves, others and the world around us. In chapter two we mentioned that as *homo narrans* we impose meaning on our lives through narrative. The stories, narratives and language social groups use determine how members view reality. Postmoderns argue that language does not merely assist individuals' perceptions of themselves and the world. Rather, they argue that without language perception is impossible. It's not that you need language to see the house standing before you as you take a walk. But what the word *house* means to you—in contrast to *home, dwelling, cottage, structure, hut, shack, halfway house* or *crack house*—is dependent on language. The language we use both reflects the values and ideology of a culture and simultaneously reproduces a culture's values and ideology. From this Vivien Burr draws the following conclusion: "This means that the way people think, the very categories and concepts that provide a framework of meaning for them, are provided by language that they use. Language therefore is a necessary pre-condition for thought as we know it."[7]

Postmoderns readily admit the difficulty of ascribing such power to language since language is itself self-referential. Linguists have long noted that there is a distinction between a *signifier* (a particular word) and the *signified* (the meaning a word has to a particular culture). To say that language is self-referential is to acknowledge that a sign "will always lead to another sign. Thus, a language is a chain of signifiers referring to other signifiers, in which each signifier in turn becomes what is signified by another signifier."[8] For example, if your nephew

---

[6]Again, we note that as a whole we find social constructionism to be an extremely productive theoretical lens through which we can explore relationships, gender, language and identity. However, we take issue with social constructionists who advance their theory to include a relativistic view of truth or morality. Peter Berger, for example, is a social constructionist who takes issues with the contradictory claims of relativism.

[7]Burr, *Introduction to Social Constructionism*, p. 5.

[8]Stanley Grenz, *A Primer on Postmodernism* (Grand Rapids: Eerdmans, 1996), p. 144.

asks you what the word *truthful* means, you respond that it means to be "honest" or "sincere." If he's still confused you say that it also means a person is "candid," "factual," "trustworthy" and "veracious." Do you see what you've done? You have used words to explain other words. Yet, what concrete, observable referent can you point to when describing truthfulness? The conclusion for theorists like Jacques Derrida is that meaning is never fixed. The meanings of words are fluid, depending on when, where and to whom they are spoken.

Areas of agreement. The culture and coculture a person belongs to greatly influence his or her perception of the world. Culture provides us with language, concepts and a point of view that colors how we perceive people, objects and ideas. In his classic work on prejudice, Gordon Allport describes an experiment that shows the power of language to shape perception. Thirty photographs of college women were shown to participants who were asked to rate each female on a scale from one to five according to categories of *beauty, intelligence, character, ambition* and *likeability*. Two months later the identical photos were shown to the same group of participants. However, this time names were placed under the photos. Of particular note were photos receiving Jewish surnames such as Cohen and Kantor. When the Jewish names were attached there was a decrease in *liking, character* and *beauty*, and an increased ranking in *intelligence* and *ambition*. The categories created by language shaped the participant's perception of the women.

Area of concern. While a person's culture influences how he or she sees the world and the judgments he or she makes, it goes too far to say that culture determines the judgments a person makes. To argue that language is a precondition for thought and judgment is to minimize what philosophers call *knowledge by acquaintance*, which occurs when we have direct awareness of something. For example, a baby can have direct awareness of the apple without having a concept of an apple or linguistic skills. "Knowledge by acquaintance is sometimes called 'simple seeing,' being directly aware of something."[9] Christian philosophers argue that included in *simple seeing* is our ability to be directly

[9] J. P. Moreland, "Mysticism, Awareness of God, and Postmodern Confusions," *Conversations*, spring-summer 2008, p. 20.

aware of moral values, aesthetic values, numbers, laws of mathematics, laws of logic and God. In light of knowledge by acquaintance "it follows that knowledge does not begin with presuppositions, language, concepts, one's cultural standpoint, worldview, or anything else."[10] For example, while the participants ranking the photos of college women are deeply influenced by cultural stereotypes rooted in a culture's language, each participant could, according to *simple seeing*, still recognize that each woman was valuable as a human being and that harming her would be morally wrong.[11]

Postmoderns deny simple seeing and argue that what stands between us and reality is our worldview. Many communicators—Christian and non-Christian—mistakenly compare a person's worldview to a pair of glasses that an individual looks through to see reality. In other words, a person's worldview stands between the self and reality.

One disturbing implication of this view is that individuals can never correct cultural beliefs, rooted in language, by comparing their beliefs and experiences to reality itself. The result is that we are locked into our culture's particular construction of truth, value and reality. Yet history is replete with examples of individuals who did challenge their culture's view of reality. Sitting in his Birmingham jail cell, Martin Luther King Jr. grew increasingly angry at the thought of his children being excluded from an amusement park and forced to sleep in a car because "whites only" motels refused his family lodging. The angrier he became, the more determined he was to change how his culture treated people of color. In his now famous "Letter from a Birmingham Jail" he explained what gave him confidence to correct his culture's view of blacks. "A just law is a man-made code that squares with the moral law of God. An unjust law is a code that is out of harmony with the moral law."[12] Having an intuitive awareness or knowledge of God's moral law allowed him to challenge his culture's socially constructed view of race.

---

[10]Ibid., p. 21.

[11]While all humans have access to *simple seeing*, there is no doubt that to varying degrees sin has distorted this ability.

[12]Martin Luther King Jr., "Letter from a Birmingham Jail," in *The World Treasury of Modern Religious Thought*, ed. Jaroslav Pelikan (Boston: Little, Brown, 1990), p. 611.

Idea 5: We are all hopelessly biased. Theorists within our discipline who hold to a form of objectivism—believing in a reality independent of human perception and which can be discovered through direct observation—argue that good researchers need to set aside political, intellectual, emotional and spiritual commitments as they seek to discover truth. The goal is to produce knowledge of the *real world* untainted by human subjectivity or bias. As a rule, individuals committed to objectivism want to separate what *is*, from what they think *ought* to be the case.

Postmoderns contend that such goals and rules are naive. A person's passion, upbringing, social location, bias, ideology and emotions powerfully influence a person's perception of reality and the judgments he or she makes about it. "Former surgeon general C. Everett Koop lamented that pro-choice researchers always conclude that abortion does no psychological harm to the mother, whereas pro-life psychologists invariably discover that abortion leaves long-term emotional scars."[13] What can be said about researchers embroiled in the abortion debate can also be said about historians.

Postmodern philosopher and social critic Michel Foucault berated historians for their claims of objectivity. Playing off of Friedrich Nietzsche's "will to power," Foucault claimed that any historical account is a "will to knowledge" that establishes what those in power consider worthwhile history.[14] The values and agenda of a historian determine who is included and excluded in his or her account. Even those who are included are cast in a light determined by the historian. Sometimes the faults of a historical figure are glossed over and sometimes they are highlighted. Take, for example, popular accounts of the Alamo. Five thousand Mexicans surround the Alamo filled with 185 Texas freedom fighters led by James Bowie, William Travis and Davy Crockett. The Texans are surrounded but undaunted. In a series of fierce attacks Travis, Bowie, Crockett and all others die fighting bravely. But is that the

---

[13]Em Griffin, *A First Look at Communication*, 7th ed. (New York: McGraw-Hill, 2009), p. 343.

[14]Michel Foucault, "Nietzsche, Genealogy, History," in *Language, Counter-Memory, and Practice*, trans. Donald Bouchard and Sherry Simon (New York: Cornell University Press, 1977), p. 162.

whole story? Historian Jeff Long argues that making these men larger-than-life legends obscures their humanity.

In his provocative book *A Duel of Eagles*, Long attacks Texans' rosy picture of these heroes and presents William Travis as a playboy with syphilis, Sam Houston as an alcoholic and Jim Bowie as a man running from debtors. Since the book's release Long has received death threats and his books regularly have to be kept under lock and key to keep them from being defaced. Are the men of the Alamo larger-than-life heroes or unseemly characters trying to reclaim their reputations? To a postmodern, it all depends on the perspective of the person telling the story. All historical accounts, concludes Foucault, are byproducts of a historian's perspective, agenda and bias.

Areas of agreement. Unfortunately, today's headlines are filled with politicians, sports figures, financial advisers and religious figures being so caught up in their own agenda that they lie, manipulate or spin facts to serve their purpose. Postmoderns are wise in urging us all to be suspicious of those claiming to be objective, neutral or unbiased. "Without becoming cynical, we will want to ask whether the person making the statement has any vested interest in the matter. If so, we need to scrutinize very carefully both the statement and the supporting evidence."[15] Unfortunately, Christians are not exempt from this postmodern principle of suspicion and bias. In an attempt to present the Christian worldview in the best possible light, Christian communicators often engage in what Christian author Eugene Peterson calls "lying about God."[16] We lie about God, explains Peterson, when we give answers that ignore or minimize certain facts. In describing the goodness of God, we neglect to mention what theologians call the problem of evil. How can God be good when some of his most-loved followers have suffered deeply? We are sure to describe remarkable answers to prayers, yet fail to mention prayers that have remained painfully unanswered. We present sloppy or thin descriptions of other religions as we talk about the strengths of Christianity. We describe Christ as loving, ac-

---

[15]Millard Erickson, *Truth or Consequences* (Downers Grove, Ill.: InterVarsity Press, 2001), p. 200.

[16]Eugene Peterson, *Subversive Spirituality* (Grand Rapids: Eerdmans, 1994), p. 255.

cepting and merciful, yet never talk about his ethical demands and calls for self-sacrifice.

Area of concern. In claiming that we are all hopelessly biased, aren't we minimizing the power of rational objectivity? Postmoderns often confuse two types of objectivity—psychological and rational. Psychological objectivity "is detachment, the absence of bias, and a lack of commitment either way on a topic."[17] We tend to have this type of detachment concerning areas or issues that mean little to us. However, with issues that are important to us we tend to develop strong opinions. For example, the more a follower of Christ studies the Scriptures and comes to believe in its historical accuracy, the more he or she will be psychologically committed and biased toward a Christian worldview. J. P. Moreland notes that "a lack of psychological objectivity does not imply a lack of rational objectivity, and it is the latter that matters most, not the former."[18] If a person has rational objectivity "regarding some topic, then one can discern the difference between genuinely good and bad reasons/evidence for a belief about that topic and one can hold the belief for genuinely good reasons/evidence."[19] A bias may make it more difficult to be rationally objective, but in most cases it does not make it impossible. Consider the case of atheist-turned-theist Antony Flew.

Antony Flew, at age 84, is a legendary British philosopher and champion of atheistic thinkers worldwide. His books, papers and lectures have been an unwavering source of encouragement for unbelievers. With such a psychological commitment and bias toward atheism, how could any arguments toward theism possibly work? Yet through a twenty-year relationship with philosopher and church historian Gary Habermas, Flew began to consider arguments for God. In the summer of 2005 he shocked the philosophical world by stating that he was now a deist. He had come to believe in an Aristotelian God who exhibited, among other characteristics, intelligence and power.

His change of mind has made him the target of attacks from leading atheists who feel slighted and now claim that Flew is in severe mental

---

[17]J. P. Moreland, *The Kingdom Triangle* (Grand Rapids: Zondervan, 2007), p. 79.
[18]Ibid.
[19]Ibid., pp. 79-80.

decline. With every reason not to tamper with his academic legacy (psychological bias), Flew mustered enough rational objectivity to consider compelling arguments challenging his beliefs. He explains, "As a professional philosopher I have changed my mind on disputed topics more than once."[20] Flew's change of mind concerning God was a result of his belief in "following the argument wherever it may lead me."[21] Flew has paid the price, both personally and professionally, for his objectivity.[22]

CONCLUSION

Postmodern author Walter Anderson describes the "postmodern world as a kind of jailbreak from the Grand Hotel, with people charging in all directions."[23] As Christian communicators, our job is to help people understand that some of the directions postmodernism sends them are helpful, while many are not. To serve as guides, we must first understand and wrestle with the probing questions and ideas discussed in chapters nine and ten, and understand how they compliment or contradict a Christian worldview.

Despite our best intentions, sometimes friends and professors respond to the Christian worldview with derision or personal attack. As Christian counterpublics, how should we respond when our views are not merely disagreed with but attacked? The communication strategies offered by Jesus, Paul and Peter found in chapter eleven will be both encouraging and unsettling.

---

[20]Antony Flew and Roy Abraham Varghese, *There Is a God: How the World's Most Notorious Atheist Changed His Mind* (New York: HarperCollins, 2007), p. 56.

[21]Ibid.

[22]The same could be said about C. S. Lewis, who upon conversion described himself as "the most dejected and reluctant convert in all England" (C. S. Lewis, *Surprised by Joy* [New York: Harcourt, 1955], pp. 228-29).

[23]Walter Truett Anderson, *The Truth About Truth* (New York: Putnam Books, 1995), p. 16.

11

ABNORMAL COMMUNICATION

A CHRISTIAN RESPONSE TO THE ARGUMENT CULTURE

In *Letter to a Christian Nation*, Sam Harris says, "Everyone who has eyes to see can see that if the God of Abraham exists, He is an utter psychopath."[1] British scientist Richard Dawkins concurs:

> The God of the Old Testament is arguably the most unpleasant charac-
> ter in all fiction: jealous and proud of it; a petty, unjust, unforgiving
> control freak; a vindictive, blood thirsty ethnic cleanser; a misogynistic,
> homophobic, racist, infanticidal, genocidal, filicidal, pestilential, mega-
> lomaniacal, sadomasochistic, capriciously malevolent bully.[2]

Not to be outdone, Christopher Hitchens says, "As I write these words, and as you read them, people of faith are in different ways planning your and my destruction. . . . Religion poisons everything."[3]

The work of these three atheists is wildly popular with extended stays on the *New York Times* Bestseller List and over one million copies of their books in print. Internet chat rooms, blogs and talk radio have bristled with responses debating the validity *and* tone of their critique of religion, which has been described as militant atheism.[4] While we may never dialogue with public figures such as Harris, Dawkins and

---

[1]Sam Harris, *Letter to a Christian Nation* (New York: Vintage Books, 2008), p. 114.
[2]Richard Dawkins, *The God Delusion* (Boston: Mariner, 2006), p. 51.
[3]Christopher Hitchens, *God Is Not Great* (New York: Hachette, 2007), p. 13.
[4]The purpose of this chapter is to address the tone rather than validity of their arguments. For
a critique of the arguments see Gary H. Habermas, "The Plight of the New Atheism: A Critique," *Journal of the Evangelical Theological Society* 51, no. 4 (2008): 813-27.

Hitchens, we may encounter individuals who have been influenced by the tone and arguments of these thinkers.

People of faith, including Christians, are used to having their religious beliefs attacked and even mocked. Second-century drawings show how many viewed the early Christian's most cherished beliefs. One crude picture lampoons Christians by showing a man nailed to a cross bearing the head of a donkey. To the side stands another man worshiping with outstretched arms. The message is clear: to worship a man who had been crucified is ludicrous. This new wave of atheist writers derides people of faith for a simplistic and dangerous view of God. As Hitchens boldly asserts, religion poisons everything.

How should we as Christian counterpublics respond to such vitriolic accusations? Is there a communication strategy we can employ that would not only answer our critics but do so in a manner that would bring honor to Christ? Specifically, what do we do when encountering people who not only disagree with us but are hostile? In this chapter we consider modern communication scholars' call for abnormal discourse and how the Scriptures offer us advice on how to obtain it. We conclude with a case study of abnormal communication between gays and Christians.

THE ARGUMENT CULTURE

Communication scholars have become increasingly concerned with how individuals approach and talk about their differences. Georgetown linguist Deborah Tannen labels today's communication climate the "argument culture," which she defines as a pervasive warlike atmosphere that makes us approach anything as if it were a verbal fight. "The argument culture urges us to regard the world—and the people in it— in an adversarial frame of mind."[5] In such a negative communication climate individuals adopt a cynical approach to interpersonal communication by adopting an attitude of "hear no good, see no good, speak no good" toward those who hold differing beliefs.[6] James Hunter con-

[5]Deborah Tannen, *The Argument Culture: Moving From Debate to Dialogue* (New York: Random House, 1998), p. 3

[6]Ron Arnett and Patricia Arneson, *Dialogic Civility in a Cynical Age* (New York: State Univer-

trasts debate and argument, and suggests that debate, when properly constructed, assumes that people are at least talking to each other. A more "apt description of Americans engaged in contemporary culture war is that they are only talking *at* or *past* each other. . . . What is heard is rather more like loud bellowing, in the clipped cadences of a shouting match."[7] The two biggest communication casualties of the argument culture, suggests Tannen, are listening and understanding. "When you're having an argument with someone, your goal is not to listen and understand. Instead, you use every tactic you can think of—including distorting what your opponent just said—in order to win the argument."[8]

Regrettably, Christians seem to have adopted this adversarial orientation toward those who disagree with us. Daniel Taylor, a Christian academic, characterizes fellow Christians as the pit bulls of the culture war and suggests that we are often responsible for much of the perceived hostility in our society because of our tenacity, dogmatism and unwillingness to compromise. He writes, "The sad truth is that, in our battle with a hostile culture, we have adopted the culture's tactics. We fight ugliness with ugliness, distortion with distortion, sarcasm with sarcasm."[9] Research conducted by the Barna Group notes that those outside the Christian community overwhelmingly see Christians as being judgmental individuals who feel spiritually superior to others. Those disagreeing with Christians report often feeling "put down, excluded, and marginalized."[10] This sentiment is echoed by Sam Harris, who wrote that the most hostile letters and e-mails he received to his book *Letter to a Christian Nation* came from Christians. "The truth is that many who claim to be transformed by Christ's love are deeply, even murderously, intolerant of

---

sity of New York Press, 1999), p. 21.

[7]James Hunter, *Before the Shooting Starts: Searching for Democracy in American's Culture War* (New York: Free Press, 1994), p. 9.

[8]Tannen, *Argument Culture*, p. 5.

[9]Daniel Taylor, "Deconstructing the Gospel of Tolerance," *Christianity Today*, January 1999, p. 50.

[10]David Kinnaman and Gabe Lyons, *UnChristian: What a New Generation Really Thinks About Christianity . . . and Why It Matters* (Grand Rapids: Baker, 2007), p. 182. The data shows that "nearly nine out of ten young outsiders (87 percent) said that the term *judgmental* accurately describes present-day Christianity" (p. 182).

criticism."[11] This issue—the way we disagree with those who disagree with us—has often been a failure for Christians.

In response to our culture's hostile discursive practices, communication scholars Pearce and Littlejohn ask, "Is it possible to transcend these customary responses to break the pattern, to engage those with whom we disagree on a new level, and to avoid the seemingly unavoidable spiral toward schism, degradation, and violence?"[12] The answer that many communication scholars advocate today is a form of abnormal communication.

NORMAL AND ABNORMAL COMMUNICATION

In our current social climate normal communication often "consists of attempts to persuade, frustrated dialogue, threats, and sometimes violence." A communication tactic far too often utilized between those who disagree is *reciprocated diatribe* in "which participants protect their most precious beliefs by expressing their perceptions of the faults of the other." This fault-finding leads to a "type of dehumanization of the opposition, which can make violence seem like a natural and appropriate response."[13]

Sally Miller Gearhart, educator and ardent environmentalist, illustrates from her own life how reciprocated diatribe results in an escalation of hostility. When seeing a logging truck she would catch the driver's eyes and shoot him an obscene gesture, to which the driver would respond in kind. Next time she saw him she would shout an obscenity, prompting him to put a bumper sticker on his truck: "Earth First! We'll log the other planets later!" About her interactions with loggers Miller writes, "I've marched and rallied and picketed, raged and wept and threatened, crusaded and persuaded and brigaded."[14] Miller realized that her hostility was only making matters worse—she needed to change.

---

[11]Harris, *Letter to a Christian Nation*, p. vii.

[12]W. Barnett Pearce and Stephen Littlejohn, *Moral Conflict: When Social Worlds Collide* (Thousand Oaks, Calif.: Sage, 1997), p. 157.

[13]Ibid.

[14]Sally Miller Gearhart, "Notes from a Recovering Activist," *Sojourner: The Women's Forum* 21, no. 1 (1995). Ultimately, Gearhart eschewed any attempt to persuade others. She, along with accomplished rhetoricians, adopted an invitational form of rhetoric that asks others to consider the context of another person's worldview before making a decision.

This need for change has also been felt by students of communication. "If the participants in a moral conflict only act in ways prefigured by their own social worlds, they cannot transform the situation in which they find themselves; they can only add fuel to the fire by doing 'more of the same,' and nothing changes."[15] The way to avoid doing more of the same is to engage in what philosopher Richard Rorty identifies as *abnormal discourse*. Abnormal discourse occurs when someone enters a discourse that is unaware of established patterns of communication or decides to set them aside. What would constitute abnormal discourse to the argument culture described earlier in this chapter? Scholars suggest that one way to engage in abnormal discourse is to favor a form of communication that values dialogic civility over conquest. The minimum condition for dialogic civility, notes Julia Wood, is "an attitude of respectfulness toward others, topics, different and sometimes inharmonious perspectives" combined with a desire to keep the conversation going.[16]

Christians within our discipline resonate with a call for abnormal discourse and point to the Scriptures for salient examples of abnormal communication in the lives of Jesus, Paul and Peter.

ABNORMAL COMMUNICATION: JESUS, PAUL AND PETER

Jesus. In perhaps Jesus' most famous discourse—what is commonly referred to as the Sermon on the Mount—he shocks his listeners. "You have heard that it was said, 'Eye for eye, and tooth for tooth' " (Mt 5:38). Indeed, Jewish people had grown up hearing this law, found in Exodus 21, Leviticus 24 and Deuteronomy 19. The law was intended for Israel's judges to serve as a guiding principle for judicial proportionality (an eye for an eye, not a life for an eye). The main purpose was "to introduce this element of justice and of righteousness into a chaotic condition and to take from man the tendency to take the law into his own hands and to do anything he likes."[17] However, the people of Jesus'

---

[15]Pearce and Littlejohn, *Moral Conflict*, p. 16.
[16]Julia T. Wood, foreword to Arnett and Arneson, *Dialogic Civility*, p. xii.
[17]D. Martyn Lloyd-Jones, *Studies in the Sermon on the Mount* (Grand Rapids: Eerdmans, 1991), 1:272.

day did the opposite. They took the rule out of the courts and applied it to the settling of personal vendettas. The normal discourse of the day had turned into the idea that if you did some type of injustice to me, I had *the right* to do it back to you. It was a bumper-sticker mentality to interpersonal disputes: "I don't get mad, I get even!"

Jesus shocks his audience by saying, "But I tell you, Do not resist an evil person. If someone strikes you on the right cheek, turn to him the other also" (Mt 5:39). Jesus is most likely describing a sharp slap to the face rather than a forceful blow. "If a right-handed person strikes someone's right cheek, presumably it is a slap by the back of the hand, probably considered more insulting than a slap by the open palm."[18] What Jesus was advocating was painfully clear to his audience—if you are insulted, give up your perceived right to counter with an insult. This principle, though not limited to Christian persecution, is particularly important when the insult is incurred due to a stand for righteousness (Mt 5:10-12). Jesus adds to this three other illustrations. First, if a follower of Christ is sued for his tunic, he or she should willingly include the outer cloak as well. This inclusion is particularly noteworthy since this outer cloak "was recognized by Jewish law to be an inalienable possession (Ex 22:26f.)."[19] Second, if a person—most likely a Roman soldier—forces someone to carry his possessions for a mile, he or she should cheerfully bear the burden for two miles. Last, the follower of Christ should be willing to lend his or her money to those who need it.[20]

D. A. Carson sums up the central point of Jesus' difficult teaching:

> The legalistic mentality which dwells on retaliation and so-called fairness makes much of one's rights. What Jesus is saying in these verses, more than anything else, is that his followers have no rights. They do not have the right to retaliate and wreak their own vengeance (5:39), they do not

---

[18]D. A. Carson, *Matthew*, Expositor's Bible Commentary, ed. Frank E. Gaebelein (Grand Rapids: Zondervan, 1984), p. 156.

[19]D. A. Carson, *The Sermon on the Mount* (Grand Rapids, Baker, 1978), p. 51.

[20]Carson adds an instructive note: "The issue is not the wisdom or foolishness of lending money to everyone who comes along (for which see Prov 11:15; 17:18; 22:26). . . . The burden of the passage is this: Christ will not tolerate a mercenary, tight-fisted, penny-pinching attitude which is the financial counterpart to a legalistic understanding of 'An eye for an eye, and a tooth for a tooth.' . . . Don't be asking yourself all the time, 'What's in it for me? What can I get out of it?' " (ibid., p. 52).

have the right to their possessions (5:40), nor to their time and money (5:41f.). Even their legal rights may sometimes be abandoned (5:40). Hence, it would completely miss the point to interpret 5:41, for example, to mean that the follower of Christ will be prepared to go two miles, but not one inch further! Personal sacrifice displaces personal retaliation.[21]

Paul. Paul writes to believers in Rome, "Bless those who persecute you; bless and do not curse" (Rom 12:14). Paul would have many opportunities to practice this abnormal way of communicating with adversaries. In his letters Paul acknowledges that there are "many who oppose me" (1 Cor 16:9) and even singles out individuals such as Alexander the metal worker who did him "a great deal of harm" (2 Tim 4:14). Yet Paul reiterates that followers of Christ should not "repay anyone evil for evil" (Rom 12:17; see also 1 Thess 5:15; 1 Cor 4:12-13) and should, so far as it depends on them, "live at peace with everyone" (Rom 12:18). Paul is not saying that evil cannot be defeated; he simply and forcefully argues that believers can "overcome evil with good" (Rom 12:21). In what practical sense does blessing those who persecute you overcome or counteract the evil they are inflicting?

Paul responds that believers, by not repaying evil for evil, leave room for God to act (Rom 12:19). In other words, we should respond as Christ did. While insults were being hurled at him, Jesus did "not retaliate" but rather entrusted himself to God (1 Pet 2:23).[22] Paul continues,

On the contrary:
"If your enemy is hungry, feed him;

---

[21]Ibid.

[22]Paul seems to take different rhetorical postures when dealing with religious and nonreligious people. When dealing with Greek Stoics and philosophers on Mars Hill, Paul is respectful and even quotes particular Stoic teachers. However, when he refers to Judaizers—converts who were holding on to the law as the means through which people entered into the covenant community—he calls them "dogs" and "mutilators of the flesh" (Phil 3:2). A key to Paul's differing communication style is found in Acts 20:30 where Paul warns that people from within the Christian community will arise speaking things "to draw away disciples after them." It seems to be important to Paul to identify whether the attack is coming from within or outside the Christian community. In our communication there ought to be a difference between responding to an atheist like Sam Harris or John Shelby Spong, a retired bishop of the Episcopal Church, who denies the deity and resurrection of Christ. The tone of our communication will possibly differ depending on if we are confronting those who attack the gospel (Harris) or those seeking to corrupt it (Spong).

if he is thirsty, give him something to drink.
In doing this, you will heap burning coals upon his head."
(Rom 12:20)

What Paul is advocating is wildly counterintuitive. When your adversaries are hungry and thirsty, they are also vulnerable and weak, and can be exploited. Paul argues that this momentary vulnerability should be ignored, and food and drink should be graciously offered instead. Notice, Paul is not merely advocating that a believer refrain from doing evil; rather, the believer does good by providing food and water. In doing so, the believer "will heap burning coals" on the head of the enemy, perhaps resulting in remorse. Paul is quoting Proverbs 25:21-22 and may be alluding to an Egyptian ritual in "which a man testified publicly to his penitence by carrying a pan of burning charcoal on his head."[23] Regardless of the cultural origin of Paul's metaphor most commentators agree that the burning coals "symbolize the burning pangs of shame and contrition resulting from the unexpected kindness received."[24]

Peter. Persecution is a recurring theme in Peter's first letter to Christians scattered abroad (1 Pet 1:6; 2:12, 19-20; 3:13-17; 4:12, 14; 5:8-10). How should these early followers of Christ respond to the increasing intensity of attacks against their faith?[25] Believers should not "repay evil with evil or insult with insult." Rather, they should respond with a "blessing" (1 Pet 3:9). In classical Greek *blessing (eulogein)* merely meant "speaking well of" another person. New Testament scholar Norman Hillyer argues that Peter is greatly extending the Greek idea of blessing to include spiritual blessings such as praying for adversaries, as Jesus had modeled and commanded (Mt 5:44; Lk 6:28).[26] These spiritual

---

[23]F. F. Bruce, *Romans*, Tyndale New Testament Commentaries 8, ed. Leon Morris (Grand Rapids: Eerdmans, 1990), p. 218.

[24]William Hendriksen, *Romans* (Grand Rapids: Baker, 1981), p. 423.

[25]Guthrie argues for dating 1 Peter just prior to Nero's persecution of Christians around A.D. 64. If Guthrie is correct, then Peter is preparing Christians for one of the bloodiest times in the history of the early church. If these early Christians can respond to insults and persecution with a blessing, then certainly we can respond in a similar manner toward academics who rhetorically attack our faith. See Donald Guthrie, *New Testament Introduction* (Downers Grove, Ill.: InterVarsity Press, 1970), pp. 795-96.

[26]Norman Hillyer, *1 and 2 Peter, Jude*, New International Biblical Commentary, ed. W. Ward

blessings would entail praying for a person's acute awareness of God's love, common grace, impending judgment, offer of salvation and the Spirit's conviction. For Christians to accomplish what Peter is describing they must turn from evil, do good and pursue peace (1 Pet 3:11).[27] He particularly states that a believer must "keep his tongue from evil and his lips from deceitful speech" (v. 10).

No doubt Peter knew how difficult and counterintuitive this response would be for many in the Christian community. It certainly was for him. When Jesus was betrayed by Judas and approached by a detachment of soldiers carrying torches and weapons, Peter drew a sword and wounded the servant of a high priest (Jn 18:10). He is now arguing for a blessing-for-insult approach to those who would do evil.

Peter offers three motivations to a believer seeking to apply the abnormal communication he is advocating. First, a person engaging in this type of communication will "see good days" (1 Pet 3:10). While Peter does not guarantee that a believer will never experience persecution or pain, he or she will experience a qualitatively richer life full of God's blessing and favor. Second, the "eyes of the Lord" will be on the righteous and "his ears . . . attentive to their prayer" (1 Pet 3:12). As a believer seeks to pursue peace and respond to harsh insults with a blessing, he or she can be assured that God is present and attentive in the moment. Third, the "face of the Lord is against those who do evil" (v. 12). Like Paul, Peter is telling his readers that God will, in his time and way, respond to those who do evil to his children.

Before we consider—from a communication perspective—what is gained from the abnormal forms of communication we are advocating, two clarifications need to be considered. First, refusing to pay evil for evil or insult for insult does not mean that Christians cannot intellectually critique or passionately disagree with another person's worldview. In fact, Jesus, Paul and Peter presuppose that the reason a Christian is being insulted is because they are advocating a perspective that is coun-

---

Gasque (Peabody, Mass.: Hendrickson, 1994), p. 105.

[27]Concerning the turn from evil Hillyer notes: "The Greek implies 'not lean toward' evil, not even to give it a passing thought as to whether some advantageous end might result from unworthy means" (ibid., p. 103).

tercultural and possibly offensive. Second, not all people will respond favorably to a blessing-for-insult approach. Peter tells us that even if our actions are done with a clear conscious and presented in a gentle and respectful way, it may still provoke a malicious response (1 Pet 3:16). Sigmund Freud exhibits such a negative response to a Christian's desire to love hostile adversaries. In his book *Civilization and Its Discontents*, Freud ridicules the Scripture's command to "love thy enemies." For Freud, loving a person that does not love us makes no sense. If a person "does not seem to have the least trace of love for me, does not show me the slightest consideration" then he or she will have "no hesitation in injuring me."[28] Freud comments that he would not object if the command read: "Love thy neighbor as thy neighbor loves thee." Only if a person showed Freud love and consideration would he be "willing to treat him similarly."[29]

WHAT ABNORMAL COMMUNICATION ACCOMPLISHES

Students of communication can offer valuable insight into how the abnormal communication method of blessing those who curse you influences the thoughts and actions of others. Abnormal communication has a significant influence on communications spirals and the relational level of communication.

Communication spirals. Communication spirals occur when the actions—both verbal and nonverbal—of one person mirror and accelerate the actions of the other person. Both negative and positive spirals, notes interpersonal-communication scholar William Wilmot, "tend to pick up a momentum that feeds back on itself—closeness and harmony builds more closeness and harmony; misunderstanding and dissatisfaction creates more misunderstanding and dissatisfaction."[30] Spirals contribute to a relationship in either generative or degenerative ways. "Generative spirals promote positive feelings about the relationship and more closeness; degenerative spirals induce negative feelings about the

---

[28]Sigmund Freud, *Civilization and Its Discontents* (New York: Dover Publications, 1994), p. 39.
[29]Ibid.
[30]William W. Wilmot, *Relational Communication* (New York: McGraw-Hill, 1995), p. 65.

relationship and more distance."[31] Generative or degenerative spirals will continue gaining momentum unless individuals stop or slow a spiral through some action. Within generative and degenerative spirals are symmetrical and complementary communication moves. In symmetrical moves each person mirrors the actions of the other such as two people shouting at each other. Complementary moves entail one person doing an action (shouting) and the other person doing the opposite (being silent or disengaging in the conversation).

Wilmot offers a key suggestion for altering degenerative spirals. To check a degenerative spiral you must "alter your usual response—do what comes unnaturally." The key word to keep in mind when in the midst of a negative spiral is *change*. "Change the patterns," notes Wilmot, "and you change the spiral."[32] When a Christian meets evil with evil or an insult with an insult (symmetrical moves), a degenerative spiral with an adversary will continue to pick up momentum. If our response to Dawkins's *God Delusion* is to write a caustic retort titled *The Atheist Delusion*, then we have added fuel to a negative spiral sure to entrench our critics in their opposition.[33] As the proverb states, "An offended brother is more unyielding than a fortified city" (Prov 18:19).

How do we respond to a caustic critic such as Dawkins without adding to a degenerative spiral? We must do what comes unnaturally and apply Wilmot's advice by changing the pattern. Or, to use the language of Peter, "Bless those who curse you." Does that mean that we do not challenge Dawkins's arguments? No, we must. However, challenges to the Christian worldview will require careful answers. Our answers will require study of the Scriptures, reading of Christian thinkers and sensitivity to the Holy Spirit. They will *also* require careful attention to how we communicate and remember that just as a "harsh word stirs up anger," a gentle word has the potential to turn "away wrath" (Prov 15:1).

Relational level of communication. In our communication with others there exist two levels of meaning. The *content* level is the literal

---

[31]Ibid., p. 66.

[32]Ibid., p. 67.

[33]One of the best-selling retorts to Dawkins is David Berlinski's book, unfortunately titled *The Devil's Delusion: Atheism and Its Scientific Pretensions*.

meaning of the words we are using. The *relational* level expresses the affection, respect and power dynamic between people. Both levels can be seen in Peter's admonishment that all believers need to "be prepared to give an answer" for our faith but to do so with "gentleness and respect" (1 Pet 3:15). Our *answer* is the content level, while the *gentleness and respect* we show those who disagree with us establishes the relational level. The same can be seen in Paul's command to speak "the truth [content level] in love [relational level]" (Eph 4:15). Followers of Christ are not called to merely be tolerant of others. We are called to love those who disagree with us. Abnormal communication—blessing those who curse us—establishes the relational level of our communication and demonstrates our concern for others. Because we know that words can wound others like the "thrusts of a sword" (Prov 12:18 NASB) we refuse to harm others with our communication even as others may seek to harm us.

IS ABNORMAL COMMUNICATION PRACTICAL? A TEST CASE

Can the abnormal form of communication advocated by communication scholars and the Scriptures work on an interpersonal level? Some years ago I (Tim) created a study that brought together three self-identified Christians and three self-identified gays to engage in abnormal communication through a four-week, four-phase study conducted at a southern university. Each of the participants of the study was predisposed to degenerative communication spirals due to a series of events that preceded the study. Two months prior to the study, during "National Coming Out Week," angry Christian students wrote caustic letters to the editor of the campus newspaper denouncing the gay lifestyle. These provocative letters in turn produced negative and caustic responses from gay students. The tone of these letters fit Tannen's description of an argument culture in which individuals approach each other in an adversarial frame of mind. In pre-study interviews each participant acknowledged an awareness of the letters sent to the editor and a desire to respond to members of the opposing community face to face.

Some of the highlights of the study were as follows. In the first phase of the study participants were asked to refrain from debating the issues or convictions that separated them. Rather, they would prepare to discuss differences (to occur in the last phase of the study) after first engaging in perspective taking. Each participant was asked to write one page describing the sacred core of their community. "The 'sacred' is that which communities love and revere as nothing else. The 'sacred' expresses that which is non-negotiable and defines the limits of what they will tolerate." Here is a sampling of two narratives:

> What is sacred? As a woman in love with a woman, the sacred I feel I must protect is love. Love. Family. I am tempted to write nothing else, but if this were as self-evident as it seems to me to be, we wouldn't be having this conversation. I want to share my life with the person I love. Walk with our arms entwined, kiss each other good-bye as one of us drops the other off at work, and cling together in the airport after long separation.

*   *   *   *   *

> I do not apologize for the fact that according to the Bible homosexuality is wrong. However, people who condemn homosexuality are wrong as well. The point isn't that homosexuality is any more worse [*sic*] than any other "sin." Christians should view it as any other sin. . . . Christians should not hate the sinner, but only the sin.

After reading their narratives to the group each person exchanged his or her narrative with someone from the opposite community. Phase two involved a commitment to contemplate, ponder and think through each other's sacred cores during the following week. The purpose of thoughtfully reading and rereading these cores was to facilitate what Pulitzer-nominated actress and performance studies professor Anna Deavere Smith calls "walking" in the speech of another. Smith contends that a person learns about another by walking in his or her words. After a week participants came back to present the narrative they had been given in *first person*.

After watching a heterosexual conservative Christian present his narrative, Hank commented, "You did me justice."[34] One Christian was asked to describe how it felt to walk in the words of a gay man. "Up

---

[34]All names have been changed to protect confidentiality.

'til now homosexuality was such a cognitive thing. But now, it's different." The most striking response came from a gay woman named Emily. Before this phase Emily had viewed engaging Barb's words as a type of self-poisoning. Emily wrote she was afraid that her "anger would show through" when presenting what she perceived as Barb's toxic Christian core. In light of these initial comments her journal entry describing what transpired after she watched the Christians perform gay narratives was both surprising and enlightening. She wrote:

> When the group convened, I was amazed and touched by the respect and love with which our Christian counterparts approached our words. Seeing Ann, as a straight woman, perform the narrative of a gay man made me ashamed of my resistance to the process. I think both sides of the project came to understand the beliefs and feelings of the other side more completely through the process; some of us found more empathy with what we came to understand than others.

Participants commented that watching their narratives presented was powerful and confirming. What did the participants mean by "confirming"?

Interpersonal communication scholars Kenneth Cissna and Eric Sieburg argue that acknowledgment is one of the most powerful forms of confirmation. They describe it as the intention to "hear, attend, and take note of the other and to acknowledge the other by responding directly," and is, according to communication scholars, "probably the most valued form of communication—and possibly the most rare."[35] To have an individual acknowledge and attend to your words for days or weeks, as these participants did, was deeply affirming.

The last phase of the study consisted of meeting at my (Tim's) house to discuss differences between the gay and Christian communities. I was anxious to see if the weeks spent engaging in perspective taking would make a difference in how these two groups would treat each other. At times, the discussion was intense, loud and passionate. Each side presented and defended key elements of their worldview. Yet typi-

---

[35]Kenneth Cissna and Eric Sieburg, "Patterns of Interactional Confirmation and Disconfirmation," in *Bridges Not Walls*, ed. James Stewart (New York: Random House, 1986), p. 238.

cal characteristics of the argument culture—stereotypes, reciprocal diatribe, negative persuasion—were avoided. Instead, moments of empathy and understanding could be observed.

After the last phase of the study one participant ended his journal on this powerful note: "Each time something is said about queer folk, whether good or bad, they will see our faces. Just for allowing themselves to do that makes me respect them as fellow humans even more."

His remark made me think of a line from Erich Remarque's classic novel *All Quiet on the Western Front*. Remarque describes the soul-searching that occurs in a young German soldier who contemplates the family photographs of a young French soldier he has just killed.

> Comrade, I did not want to kill you. If you jumped in here again, I would not do it, if you would be sensible too. But you were only an idea to me before, an abstraction that lived in my mind and called forth its appropriate response. It was that abstraction I stabbed. But now, for the first time, I see you are a man like me. I thought of your hand-grenades, of your bayonet, of your rifle; now I see your wife and your face and our fellowship. Forgive me, comrade. We always see it too late.[36]

The goal of abnormal communication is not to remove all disagreements or tensions from a discussion of differences. The goal is to return respect, civility and an acknowledgement of our common humanity back into our conversations.[37]

CONCLUSION

In contrast to the argument culture, the book of Proverbs sets before us a different scenario:

> When a man's ways are pleasing to the LORD,
> he makes even his enemies live at peace with him. (Prov 16:7)

---

[36]Erich Remarque, *All Quiet on the Western Front* (1928; reprint, New York: Fawcett Crest, 1975), p. 174.

[37]If the abnormal form of communication advocated by Jesus, Paul and Peter is an effective way to respond to those hostile to our faith, why then do many Christians resist utilizing it? Taylor offers the following answer: "Turn the other cheek, the first shall be last, lose our life to gain it, love your enemies. Those bold principles of Jesus make for great sermons, but in our bones we appear not to believe they are practical for everyday living in a hostile society" (*Deconstructing the Gospel of Tolerance*, p. 50).

As Christian communicators it is our obligation to communicate with others, even with those hostile to us, in a manner that is both engaging and consistent with spiritual principles that lift us and them up rather than diminishing us all. The abnormal communication modeled by Jesus, Paul and Peter offer a strategy to counteract the argument culture. The end result may not be agreement, but it will at least be respect and civility—a communication goal highly valued by the writers of these ancient proverbs.

Speaking for those who are oppressed, marginalized or abandoned is another communication goal valued in the Scriptures. Being an advocate for those who lack basic resources is at the heart of what communication scholars call social-justice research. Social justice, as described in chapter twelve, mirrors Christ's concern for those regularly ignored by others.

12

SOCIAL JUSTICE

SPEAKING FOR THE MARGINALIZED

The following words come from women in rural India who participated in study conducted by me (Tim) and a Biola research team in the winter of 2007.

> I have no say, no position, and I am valueless. . . . Who am I in this world if I am no one in the sight of culture, society, decision-making?

> Sometimes I wonder whether men will ever understand that women are human beings and have equal rights to decisions, to be part of society.

> In India, it's still male dominated. To make a way for yourself gets very difficult sometimes, because we are not taking a woman as a human being.

These women were struggling to be recognized at a most fundamental level—to be seen as human. Imagine living in a culture where your voice and presence is constantly devalued! Carol Gilligan, a psychologist at Harvard University, notes that to "have a voice is to be human. To have something to say is to be a person."[1] The devaluing of Indian woman begins at birth. In many parts of India a common greeting toward a pregnant woman is, "May you be the mother of a hundred sons." In other words, if you are the mother of son you are blessed; to have a daughter is seen as a burden.

---

[1] Carol Gilligan, *In a Different Voice: Psychological Theory and Women's Development* (Cambridge, Mass.: Harvard University Press, 1982), p. xvi.

"Who am I in this world if I am no one in the sight of culture?" an Indian woman tragically asks. Barbara Myerhoff, in her study of abandoned senior citizens in a secluded Jewish nursing home, concluded that "unless we exist in the eyes of others, we come to doubt our own existence."[2] Communication scholars have long wrestled with how to respond to the narratives of those in our society who feel that they do not exist in the eyes of others. For many communication students being open to the stories of the marginalized means that their narratives and the difficulties they face find a place in our research and activism.

The idea that scholars rooted in the academy should engage in addressing social injustice has been a surprisingly contentious debate. The debate centers on the question, What is the purpose of theory? Most would agree that a good theory describes, explains and predicts particular phenomena. However, should the knowledge gleaned from theories be used to reform society? Should a scholar intentionally pursue positive social change? Is it enough for a scholar to merely understand the historical, political and theoretical forces that marginalize people, or should the scholar seek to change the very social and political structures that produce marginalization?

In this chapter we define social justice and focus on Christianity's rich tradition of pursuing a social justice agenda. We conclude by considering how Christians in the field of communication can participate with those outside the Christian community in social justice research.

SOCIAL JUSTICE RESEARCH

Many within our discipline embrace the need for students and professors to seek positive social change and argue for *social justice research*, which can be defined as "the engagement with and advocacy for those in our society who are economically, socially, politically, and/or culturally under-resourced."[3] Those embracing social justice argue for a "pedagogy of possibility" where professors intentionally help students "de-

---

[2]Barbara Myerhoff, *Number Our Days: Culture and Community Among Elderly Jews in an American Ghetto* (New York: Penguin, 1991), p. 70.
[3]Lawrence Frey et al., "Looking for Justice in All the Wrong Places: On a Communication Approach to Social Justice," *Communication Studies* 47 (1996): 110.

velop a deep and abiding faith in the struggle to overcome social injustices and to change themselves."[4]

Social justice entails four commitments. The first is an active commitment to becoming advocates for the underrepresented in society. As communication researcher Samuel Becker notes, "The major question most of us face in our lives as scholars in not whether our research should be useful; it is rather, what it should be useful for and for whom it should be useful."[5] Second is identifying and challenging social norms, structures and practices that directly or indirectly foster injustice and inequality. Professors interested in social justice are not content to merely change the minds of students in the classroom. They want to influence decision makers who craft policy and set up social hierarchies. "Compassion without justice," argues biblical scholar Marcus Borg, "can mean caring for victims while quietly acquiescing to a system that creates even more victims."[6] Third is making sure that everyone has equal access to intellectual and material resources within a community. Fourth, a social justice orientation entails giving a voice to those in our society whose perspective has been ignored due to lack of social status. This last commitment complements the Latin origins of the word *communication*. Quentin Schultze, a communication scholar who focuses on issues of faith, notes that the word *communication* originates from the Latin word for *community* and *common*. He concludes, "Language, in particular, enables us to *commune* with one another for the sake of defining and addressing our shared interests as citizens."[7] The shared interests of a community cannot be fully explored, and social justice cannot be attained, unless every member has a voice and presence.

A group of scholars, led by Lawrence Frey, sums up the vision of social justice research:

[4]Stanley Aronowitz and Henry A. Giroux, *Education Still Under Siege* (Westport, Conn.: Bergin & Garvey, 1993), p. 46.

[5]Samuel L. Becker, "Response to Conquergood: Don Quixotes in the Academy—Are We Tilting Windmills?" in *Applied Communication in the 21st Century*, ed. Kenneth N. Cissna (Mahwah, N.J.: Lawrence Erlbaum, 1995), p. 102.

[6]Marcus J. Borg, *Reading the Bible for the First Time* (San Francisco: Harper, 2002), p. 301.

[7]Quentin Schultze, *An Essential Guide to Public Speaking: Serving Your Audience with Faith, Skill, and Virtue* (Grand Rapids: Baker Academic, 2006), p. 13.

Social justice is not done when "we" in our largess donate some of our disposable resources to "them"; it is done when we act on our recognition that something is amiss in a society of abundance if some of us are well off while others are destitute. Social justice is not done when "we" give our time and energy to help "them" escape from oppression; it is done when we realize that none of us is truly free while some of us are oppressed.[8]

Communication scholars such as Amardo Rodriquez feel so strongly about social justice that he argues our very definition of *communication* should move away from mainstream definitions and adopt one that embraces social justice. For Rodriquez, communication is "about being vulnerable to the humanity of others." It is through communication "we become human, define our worlds, and help shape the humanity of others."[9] Anything that diminishes the humanity of others—social structures, cultural norms, politics, prejudice, communication—is seen as weakening the humanity of us all. According to Rodriquez this definition has a strong redemptive quality and assumes that "human beings have the potential to heal and that such healing occurs through communication."[10] The writers of the book of Proverbs agree and argue that "reckless words" can pierce another like a sword, yet the words of the wise bring "healing" (Prov 12:18). These ancient writers compared the "tongue that brings healing" to "a tree of life" (Prov 15:4).

Christian students in the field of communication not only embrace social justice research but can point to a rich tradition of social justice concerns in the life of Christ and his church. One of the central beliefs of Christianity is that authentic spirituality shows itself in social action. As John forcefully states, "Dear children, let us not love with words or tongue but with actions and in truth" (1 Jn 3:18). All Christians should be troubled and spurred to action when we encounter individuals who are oppressed, devalued or neglected. Schultze presses the point further

---

[8]Frey et al., "Looking for Justice in All the Wrong Places," pp. 111-12.
[9]Amardo Rodriquez, "Social Justice and the Challenge for Communication Studies," in *Social Justice and Communication Scholarship*, ed. Omar Swartz (Mahwah, N.J.: Lawrence Erlbaum, 2006), p. 26.
[10]Ibid.

and notes that God commands us to speak up about the oppression we have witnessed. "The ancient Hebrews recognized God's calling to speak up for others. Leviticus warned that people would be held responsible for failing to testify publicly about something they knew (5:1). Sometimes silence is a sin."[11] The need to speak up for the marginalized is magnified when we consider the life of activism embodied by Christ and the early church.

SOCIAL JUSTICE AND THE ACTIVISM OF JESUS

In the Gospels we see Christ exhibiting social justice values by reaching out to the most marginalized of his day. In particular, Jesus regularly attends to three groups greatly devalued by the power structures of his time—lepers, women and children.

Lepers. Luke tells us that Jesus is approached by a man "covered with leprosy" (Lk 5:12), a disease carrying the same social stigma often associated with AIDS. The man falls at Jesus' feet and begs to be healed. Rabbis of the day viewed leprosy as one of the major sins of uncleanness. "Not merely actual contact with the leper, but even his entrance defiled a habitation, and everything in it, to the beams of the roof."[12] The burdens of a leper were cruelly exasperated by the reaction of those who came into contact with them.

> No less a distance than four cubits [six feet] must be kept from a leper, or, if the wind came from that direction, a hundred were scarcely sufficient. Rabbi Meir would not eat an egg purchased in a street where there was a leper. Another Rabbi boasted that he always threw stones at them to keep them far off, while others hid themselves or ran away.[13]

Rather than running away, Jesus is moved by the leper cowering at his feet. Christ not only heals him, but to the astonishment of the crowd, *touches* him. This one particular act of charity deeply influenced another Christian advocate of social justice—Francis of Assisi. Upon seeing a leper on the street, his face disfigured and covered with open

---

[11]Schultze, *An Essential Guide to Public Speaking*, p. 16.
[12]Alfred Edersheim, *The Life and Times of Jesus the Messiah* (New York: Longmans, 1912), 1:494.
[13]Ibid, p. 495.

wounds, Francis felt compelled by Christ to kiss him.

> We are told that Francis approached the leper, whose face was one vast
> sore, took his hand, and placed his mouth on the leper's rotting flesh.
> An immense joy swept over the young man, and the kiss of peace was
> immediately returned.[14]

Women. Women in first-century Palestine had no credibility or voice
in a male-dominated culture. Many first-century rabbis taught that it
was better to burn the law than teach it to a woman. One famous saying
stated, "Blessed is he whose children are male, but woe to him whose
children are female." A woman's testimony was viewed as worthless
and only under rare circumstances could be used in a Jewish court of
law. Theologians Glen Stassen and David Gushee note that Jesus shat-
tered the social taboos surrounding male-female interaction and conclude that there "is no evidence that Jesus ever treated women with
anything other than full respect—an extraordinary practice in his
context."[15] Christ not only acknowledges the humanity of women—a
core value of social justice—but elevates their status and importance in
the furthering of his kingdom. The respect described by Stassen and
Gushee is evident in the powerful role Christ gives women in the narrative of his life, death and resurrection.

In his book *Informing the Future: Social Justice in the New Testament*,
professor of religious studies Joseph Grassi notes that in Mark's Gospel
everything depends on the eyewitness accounts of Mary Magdalene
and her female companions. Mary Magdalene's involvement is particularly problematic since Luke 8:2 records that she was once demon-
possessed, thus marginalizing her even further. Mark makes it clear
that women were the primary witnesses of Christ's death and place-
ment in the tomb.

---

[14]Julien Green, *God's Fool: The Life of Francis of Assisi* (San Francisco: Harper, 1987), p. 20.

[15]Glen H. Stassen and David P. Gushee, *Kingdom Ethics: Following Jesus in Contemporary Context* (Downers Grove, Ill.: InterVarsity Press, 2003), p. 319. The authors offer as examples:
"He did not hesitate to touch or be touched by women in order to heal them (Mt 9:18-26;
Lk 13:10-16). He spoke at length to the Samaritan woman at the well (Jn 4), and to a lowly
Canaanite woman (Mt 15:21-28). He affirmed Mary in her desire to sit at his feet and receive
his teachings along with his male followers (Lk 10:38-42) and treated both Mary and Martha
as close friends" (pp. 318-19).

To emphasize this witness, the author keeps repeating the verb *see*. They [the women] saw him dying on the cross (15:40); they saw where he was laid (15:47); They saw the stone rolled back (16:4); they saw the young man dressed in white garments, who directed them to *see* the place where Jesus had lain (16:5, 6).[16]

To a culture that devalued and dismissed the testimony of women, the Gospels elevate their perspective and place their testimony at the *center* of the resurrection narrative. In doing so the social norms of the day that sought to silence women are challenged and turned on their head. A woman's testimony, so devalued and marginalized, becomes the foundation for the veracity of Christ's resurrection.

Christ also elevates the status of women by singling out the actions of one woman and commands that what she has done for him should be told wherever the gospel is proclaimed. What actions are worth such an enduring tribute?

While in Bethany Christ stays in the home of Simon the leper. He reclines at a table as a woman comes into the room with a vial of extremely expensive perfume. She shocks everyone by breaking the vial and pouring it over Jesus' head. Those watching, led by Judas, are indignant. They are of the opinion that the perfume has been wasted, when it should have been sold to assist the poor. Jesus disagrees. What the disciples call wasteful, he describes as beautiful. McKenna notes: "Mark translates the Greek word *kalos* as 'good work' (vs. 6), but in its larger meaning, it conveys a sense of beauty that gives goodness and artistic glow beyond its instrumental value."[17] At the heart of social justice is the idea that everyone's words, actions and perspectives are worthy of our attention and acknowledgement. Christ acknowledges the actions of this woman and commands that "wherever the gospel is preached throughout the world, what she has done will also be told, in memory of her" (Mk 14:9). Today, her testimony lives.

Children. Grassi notes that children were "in the lowest household rung of hierarchy, just above slaves. They had no one to whom they

---

[16]Joseph Grassi, *Informing the Future: Social Justice in the New Testament* (New York: Paulist, 2003), p. 128.

[17]David McKenna, *Mark*, Communicator's Commentary (Dallas: Word, 1982), p. 280.

could go for defense of their rights."[18] Because of their low status, children trying to gain an audience with Christ are chased away by the disciples. On one occasion Christ becomes angry and forcefully says to his disciples, "Let the little children come to me, and do not hinder them, for the kingdom of God belongs to such as these" (Mk 10:14-15). Grassi asserts that in this one act "Jesus completely reverses the position of children from the lowest to the highest rank."[19] Jesus also bestows a blessing on children that is not extended to any other people group in Scripture. After taking a child in his arms Jesus turns to the crowd and says, "Whoever welcomes one of these little children in my name welcomes me" (Mk 9:37). Jesus makes it clear that in a culture utterly devoid of child services, he is now the personal advocate of children and links God's future blessings to treating them well.

New Testament writers such as Paul continue this advocacy when Paul addresses parent-child relations in his letter to the church at Ephesus. Social justice scholars note that parent-child relationships are critical for advancing social justice. "When a parent physically, verbally, sexually, or emotionally abuses a child," notes Linda Potter Crumley, "the parent not only practices social injustice at the moment of abuse, but he or she also teaches the child that such behavior is a prerogative of the powerful."[20]

In New Testament times there were none more powerful than a father. By Roman law—*patria potestas*—a father had the power of life and death over his entire household. He could cast members out of the house, sell them as slaves or even kill them, and be accountable to no one. A father's fair, consistent love for his children would have been hard to imagine. With this abuse of power in mind, Paul writes, "Fathers, do not exasperate your children" (Eph 6:4). The New American Standard Bible puts it even more forcefully and states that fathers are not to "provoke your children to anger." Exasperating or provoking a child to anger, notes one theologian, entails "a repeated, ongoing pattern of treatment that gradually builds up a deep-seated anger

---

[18]Grassi, *Informing the Future*, p. 117.

[19]Ibid.

[20]Linda Potter Crumley, "Social Justice in Interpersonal and Family Relationships," in *Social Justice and Communication Scholarship*, ed. Omar Swartz (Mahwah, N.J.: Lawrence Erlbaum, 2006), p. 180.

and resentment that boils over in outward hostility."[21] In contrast, Paul commands fathers to bring up their children in the "instruction of the Lord" (Eph 6:4) with all of God's gracious disposition toward children of God.

THE EARLY CHURCH

The Christian church, since its infancy, has supported a social justice orientation. In *The Rise of Christianity* sociologist Rodney Stark asks a provocative question: How did an obscure, marginal Jesus movement become the dominant religious force in the Western world within a few centuries? Stark concludes that two factors significantly accelerated the growth of the early church—the treatment of women and compassion toward outcasts.

Treatment of women. The status of women in Roman times was extremely low. Stark describes the treatment of Athenian women:

> Girls received little or no education. Typically, Athenian females were married at puberty and often before. Under Athenian law a woman was classified as a child, regardless of age, and therefore was the legal property of some man at all stages of her life. Males could divorce by simply ordering a wife out of the household. Moreover, if a woman was seduced or raped, her husband was legally compelled to divorce her.[22]

Infanticide and abortion were rampant in Greco-Roman culture.[23] While only healthy, well-formed babies were allowed to live, female babies were especially at risk. Stark quotes from the letter of a husband writing to his pregnant wife that reflects the cultural attitude of the Greco-Roman world:

> I ask and beg you to take good care of our baby son, and as soon as I receive payment I shall send it up to you. If you are delivered of a child [before I come home], if it is a boy keep it, if a girl discard it. You have sent me word, "Don't forget me." How can I forget you. I beg you not to worry.[24]

---

[21]John MacArthur, *Ephesians* (Chicago: Moody Press, 1986), p. 317.
[22]Rodney Stark, *The Rise of Christianity* (Princeton, N.J.: Princeton University Press, 1996), p. 102.
[23]Stark notes that abortion in the Greco-Roman world often consisted of women—many times teenage women—drinking herbal drinks that often proved poisonous to the mother.
[24]Stark, *Rise of Christianity*, pp. 97-98.

Unwanted infants, typically female, were placed outside, where the elements took their toll or birds and animals would attack. Such actions had the full support of Rome's most noted statesman. Seneca writes: "We slaughter a fierce ox; we strangle a mad dog; we plunge a knife into a sick cow. Children born weak or deformed we drown."[25]

Adult married women seldom existed on equal footing with husbands. While virginity and fidelity were demanded of brides, "men tended to be quite promiscuous and female prostitution abounded in the Greco-Roman cities—from the two penny *diobolariae* who worked the streets to high-priced, well-bred courtesans."[26] From a social justice perspective these women were socially, politically and culturally under-resourced. They had no voice to protest or power to change their status in a Greco-Roman world.

In contrast, women found life in the Christian community to be qualitatively different. First, from earliest Christian writings emerged an unwavering opposition to abortion and infanticide. In the *Didache*, a first-century collection of Christian teachings and practices, we read: "Thou shalt not murder a child by abortion nor kill them when born."[27] This prohibition continued through the writings of Justin Martyr, Athenagoras, Minucius Felix and others. Because abortion and infanticide was banned, birth rates—especially among females—soared within the Christian community.

Second, women were not merely tolerated within the Christian community, but they assumed positions of leadership. In Romans 16:2 Paul specifically highlights the contributions of "our sister Phoebe," who played a vital role in the church at Cenchrea. Clement of Alexandria wrote of women deacons, and the Council of Chalcedon in 451 laid out qualifications for a deaconess. "Deacons were of considerable importance in the early church," notes Stark. "They assisted at liturgical functions and administered the benevolent and charitable activities."[28]

Last, the church expected *both* husbands and wives to embrace mar-

---

[25]Seneca, quoted in MacArthur, *Ephesians*, p. 316.
[26]Stark, *Rise of Christianity*, p. 117.
[27]Ibid., p. 108.
[28]Ibid.

ital fidelity and to love and respect each other. Paul specifically exhorts husbands to "love your wives, just as Christ loved the church and gave himself up for her" (Eph 5:25). Similarly, husbands are to "love their wives as their own bodies" (Eph 5:28). Just as ridiculous as it would be for a man to hate and abuse his physical body, Paul argues that it equally absurd to hate and harm a wife who has become one flesh with him (Gen 2:23 24). Peter tells husbands that they are obligated to be considerate and respectful to wives and mindful that as a physically "weaker partner" they are vulnerable to physical abuse (1 Pet 3:7). Peter warns husbands that if they fail to treat their wives in an honorable way, their prayers will be hindered and their relationship with God marred. Considering the imbalanced and often abusive power relationship between husbands and wives in the Greco-Roman world, Paul and Peter's admonishment to husbands to be faithful, sacrificial, respectful and nonabusive toward wives can be seen as a powerful call to social justice in a culture where women were physically and emotionally at risk.

Compassion toward the outcast. In an ancient world lacking social services Christians often spent their time and resources helping those abandoned by culture. Stark describes a plague that ravaged the Roman Empire in A.D. 165, in which mortality rates climbed higher than 30 percent. The sick were often left to die in the gutters. The Christian community nursed the sick, buried the dead and cared for orphaned girls and boys regardless of social status. Christians viewed such actions not as a burden but a calling. Michael Green argues that the early Christian community had qualities—most of which underscore social justice concerns—that were unparalleled in the ancient world.

> Nowhere else would you find slaves and masters, Jews and Gentiles, rich and poor, engaging in table fellowship and showing a real love for each other. That overflowed to outsiders, and in times of plague and disaster the Christians shone by means of their service to the communities in which they lived.[29]

Welcoming all to the fellowship table—regardless of social status, ethnicity or sex—was a natural outpouring of a theological belief that

---

[29]Michael Green, *Evangelism in the Early Church* (Grand Rapids: Eerdmans, 2003), p. 20.

there is "neither Jew nor Greek, slave nor free, male nor female, for you are all one in Christ Jesus" (Gal 3:28). I (Tim) will never forget kneeling at a Communion table in New Delhi, India, with fellow believers of diverse social and ethnic backgrounds. We knelt in silence, shoulder to shoulder, as the Communion cup was passed. The cup moved from the hands of a homeless woman to a sharply dressed businessman to an American professor to a street child who daily begs for scraps of food. Being part of that service was a powerful confirmation that the foot of the cross is beautifully level and completely indifferent to education, gender, wealth or social status.

This rich tradition of caring for the oppressed and marginalized continues today in modern movements such as Jim Wallace's Sojourners and Ron Sider's Evangelicals for Social Action. More and more Christians, inside and outside the university, are realizing that the Scriptures do not merely speak about personal morality but social action aimed at addressing social injustice.[30]

Social Justice and Open Doors

All followers of Christ should feel a pang of conscience when we observe anyone made in God's image being marginalized. What is surprising to many Christians is that we are often not the first to notice or respond to oppression or neglect. Through the outpouring of God's common grace upon humanity, many outside the Christian community also experience an acute pain of conscience concerning the needs of others.[31] Today, more and more students and scholars within the field

---

[30]For an excellent discussion of social justice themes emerging from the Scriptures, see Stassen and Gushee's *Kingdom Ethics*. For example, the authors write that a scriptural view of justice "has four dimensions: (1) deliverance of the poor and powerless from the injustice that they regularly experience; (2) lifting the foot of domineering power off the neck of the dominated and oppressed; (3) stopping the violence and establishing peace; and (4) restoring the outcasts, the excluded, the Gentiles, the exiles, and the refugees to community" (p. 349).

[31]For an insightful discussion of common grace, see Wayne Grudem, *Systematic Theology* (Grand Rapids: Zondervan, 1994). Grudem defines common grace as "the grace of God by which he gives people innumerable blessings that are not part of salvation" (p. 657). Grudem notes that common grace when applied to the intellectual realm means that all people have the ability "grasp truth and distinguish it from error" and "experience growth in knowledge that can be used in the investigation of the universe and in the task of subduing the earth" (p. 659). In the moral realm a person's God-given conscience convicts people when they do wrong and affirms them for doing good. Grudem makes an interesting point in arguing that "unbelievers

of communication are embracing social justice values and describe a "helper's high" when helping the marginalized.

Communication scholar Phillip Tompkins at the University of Colorado at Boulder has taken on the concerns of the homeless in Denver. In order to bring attention to homeless people Tompkins organized a forum called "Faces of Homelessness" and invited policy makers, clergy, academics, elected officials and the homeless to address the audience. Along with students Tony Palmeri, a communication professor from the University of Wisconsin Oshkosh, cocreated an alternative campus newspaper called *Praxis*. The mission statement of the paper declared that it would be a place of expression for historically marginalized voices and would focus on social justice issues. Julia Wood, Lineberger Professor of Humanities and professor of communication studies at the University of North Carolina at Chapel Hill, edited a theme issue for the *Journal of Applied Communication* that presented first-person narratives of women within the communication discipline who had experienced sexual harassment. The issue gave women a powerful voice, allowing victims to speak for themselves and receive the attention of communication scholars.

Each one of these projects is rooted in social justice values. As fellow students of communication these are individuals and projects we can support and collaborate on. The problem is that Christians and non-Christians often respond to the needs of others independently. Instead of dismantling our private sanctuaries we fortify them. The issue for believers within the field of communication is not whether we should respond to the physical and spiritual needs of those around us. If our goal is to imitate Christ, then we must act. We must ask, Will we meet the needs of the marginalized by ourselves or by linking arms with those outside the walls of Christian universities or our churches?

Collaborating with others on social-issue projects allows us to not only work at eliminating specific acts of injustice but also to begin a

---

often receive more common grace than believers—they may be more skillful, harder working, more intelligent, more creative, or have more material benefits of this life to enjoy" (p. 663). Consequentially, it is entirely possible for us to meet unbelieving students and faculty more committed and involved in social justice than self-identified followers of Christ.

conversation with our colaborers about the very notion of justice.

Linda Potter Crumely asserts that justice "implies a moral impera-
tive, a definite sense of right and wrong. . . . It implies a certain level of
stability in assessing what is right-living, right-relating, perhaps even
right-communicating."[32] However, who gets to decide what constitutes
right-living or right-relating? What standard can be used to distinguish
right from wrong? In fact, Julia Wood takes issue with the definition
and vision of social justice offered by Frey earlier in this chapter. Wood
notes that "the nature of social justice and injustice are deeply contested
matters" and notions of social justice are "discursively crafted and le-
gitimized" by individuals or groups with often dramatically different
conceptualizations of social justice and injustice.[33] Semantic precision,
notes Wood, will be needed by scholars as they define social justice.

Everyone interested in social justice, Christian and non-Christian
alike, must wrestle with some disturbing questions: If ethical principles
are not grounded in God, then does one culture's set of ethics apply to
a different culture? What if two cultures disagree over what is just or
unjust? Even within a particular culture, those who benefit from an
unjust power structure may not notice or care about inequities. "Social
justice is, to a large extent, a judgment. Who makes the judgment?
Who decides that social justice has or has not occurred? One may see
the relationship as being perfectly just while the other views the relationship as fundamentally flawed."[34]

Christians believe that social justice must be anchored in the moral
character of God. For example, denying Indian women their humanity
is wrong because God has decreed that *every* person bears the *imago
Dei* (Gen 1:26).[35] To not acknowledge a person's humanity, or—to use

---

[32]Crumley, "Social Justice in Interpersonal and Family Relationships," p. 176.

[33]Julia T. Wood, "Social Justice Research: Alive and Well in the Field of Communication,"
Communication Studies 47 (1996): 128. Wood also takes issue with Frey's assertion that communication scholars have been slow to research issues of social justice and offers a rich history
of social justice research and activism within our field.

[34]Crumley, "Social Justice in Interpersonal and Family Relationships," p. 183.

[35]Grudem comments: "The Latin phrase *imago Dei* means 'image of God.' The word *image
(tselem)* means an object similar to something else and often representative of it. The word is
used to speak of statues or replicas of tumors and mice (1 Sam. 6:5, 11), of paintings of soldiers
on the wall (Ezek. 23:14), and of pagan idols or statues representing deities (Num. 33:42;
2 Kings 11:18; Ezek. 7:20; 16:17; et al.)" (*Systematic Theology*, p. 442).

Martin Buber's language—to relate to a person as an *it* and not a *thou* is unjust. However, these are questions to be worked out *as* we work to address social injustice with both Christian and non-Christian students and faculty. We do not have to completely agree with a person's motivation or worldview to work together in opposing social injustice.

CONCLUSION

The call for social justice research resonates deeply with Christians in the field of communication. In the earliest New Testament book written, James states that "religion that God our Father accepts as pure and faultless" is coming to the aid of "orphans and widows in their distress" (Jas 1:27). Orphans and widows were the most oppressed and marginalized people in Jewish society. Their distress, literally translated *pressure*, came from their desperate need for food, shelter and the constant search for an advocate. The Christian Scriptures teach that the marginalized and underresourced in society should have an advocate—the follower of Christ. To follow the teachings of Christ necessarily entails adopting his concern for the marginalized and oppressed.

Final Thoughts

Two horses pull a plywood casket draped with a wreath of black roses. The funeral procession moves through downtown Detroit led by Detroit mayor Kwame Kilpatrick, Michigan governor Jennifer Granholm, local clergy, civil rights workers and leaders of the NAACP. The crowd stops in front of the capitol building where NAACP chairman Julian Bond addresses the crowd: "This is the first funeral I've been to where people are happy to be here. The entity in this casket deserves to be dead."[1] His words are met with a raucous cheer. This odd funeral, held on a humid July afternoon in 2007, received national exposure because of what, not who, was buried. Hundreds met that day not to bury a person but a word. "Today, we're not just burying the n-word, we're taking it out of our spirits," stated Detroit's mayor.[2]

Think of it. The people of Detroit had determined that a word—not a gun, hanging noose or terrorist bomb—was so hurtful to people of color that it must be symbolically buried and discarded forever. What was buried was not a person or object but a symbol. Rhetoric scholar Judith Butler writes concerning our vulnerability to words: "When we claim to have been injured by language, what kind of claim do we make? We ascribe an agency to language, a power to injure, and position ourselves as the objects of its injurious trajectory."[3] In *Authentic Communication* we have discussed both the necessity of communication and the power of our words. We are, notes Butler, "linguistic beings"

---

[1]Kevin Krolicki, "U.S. Civil Rights Group Holds Funeral for 'N-Word,'" *Reuters*, July 9, 2007 <www.reuters.com/article/domesticNews/idUSN0929653620070709>.
[2]Ibid.
[3]Judith Butler, *Excitable Speech: A Politics of the Performative* (New York: Routledge, 1977), p. 1.

that have been "formed in language."[4] To be formed in language means that our sense of self—the ability to reflect on ourselves through the perspective of others—has been shaped by our conversations with others. As we interact with parents, siblings, friends, coworkers, fellow students, professors, employers, lovers and God, we allow their collective views of us shape how we see ourselves. Just as we have been molded by our interaction with others, as Christian communicators we must seek to be life affirming in our communication with those we encounter. Even when others use language to hurt us, we must respond in a way that pleases God.

The importance the Scriptures place on words and communication has also been a focal point of this book. The emphasis Christ places on our communication is evident when he tells us that we all will be held accountable for every word uttered. At the end of our lives each of us will have to give an account of the millions of words we have spoken (Mt 12:36). Why are our words so important? Christ explains: "The mouth speaks out of that which fills the heart" (Mt 12:34 NASB). In New Testament thinking, the heart represents the center of a person's personality, emotions, intellect and volition. Through our communication with others we glean a robust picture of a person. Our righteousness, Paul states, consists of both words and deeds (Col 3:17).

While all of communication exposes our inner person, Christ particularly isolates "careless" words that are spoken with little forethought (Mt 12:36).[5] Communication scholar Irving Goffman helps us understand why careless or offhand remarks can be powerful indicators of who we are. The focus of Goffman's research was *impression management*, which he defined as the attempt to manage our words, nonverbal communication, dress and situation to present a particular image of ourselves. Occasionally, despite our best efforts, we communicate in a

---

[4]Ibid., pp. 1-2.

[5]In contrast to careless words are carefully scripted statements that strategically help present a particular image to another person. While not all scripted statements are inherently disingenuous, they can easily feed into what theologian Alfred Plummer labels "calculated hypocrisy." This type of hypocrisy is evidenced by carefully crafted statements that present an image that does not match personal convictions or behavior. See Alfred Plummer, *An Exegetical Commentary on the Gospel According to Saint Matthew*, 5th ed. (London: E. Stock, 1920), p. 181.

way that works against the impression we are trying to give. Our actions, words or even inflections work against us. As one humorist notes, a person who is nice to you but not to the waiter is not a nice person. Interesting observation! During dinner, I do my best to present an image of a nice, kind person, but then I snap at the waiter. In doing so, my reaction—what Goffman calls speaking out of character—perhaps reveals a side of me I desire to keep hidden. As students of communication, we must become attentive to all our words, even the seemingly careless ones.

Understanding and being attentive to communication are necessary not only for students who want to flourish in the field of communication, but for any follower of Christ who wants to pursue God's priorities.

> The point of our lives is not to get smart or get rich or even to get happy. The point is to discover God's purposes for us and to make them our own. The point is to learn ways of loving God above all and our neighbor as ourselves and then to use these loves the way a golfer uses certain checkpoints to set up a drive. The point is to be lined up right, to seek first the kingdom of God, to try above all to increase the net amount of shalom in the world.[6]

Loving God and neighbors, and increasing shalom and authenticity in our often-troubled world, requires a rich understanding of the Scriptures, reliance on God's power and a fresh understanding of the intricacies of human communication. As evidenced by the mock funeral in Detroit, just as one word can destroy shalom, words can also restore it.

---

[6]Cornelius Plantinga Jr., *Not the Way It's Supposed to Be: A Breviary of Sin* (Grand Rapids: Eerdmans, 1995), p. 37.

Index